The Ideology of Work

Historical Materialism Book Series

The Historical Materialism Book Series is a major publishing initiative of the radical left. The capitalist crisis of the twenty-first century has been met by a resurgence of interest in critical Marxist theory. At the same time, the publishing institutions committed to Marxism have contracted markedly since the high point of the 1970s. The Historical Materialism Book Series is dedicated to addressing this situation by making available important works of Marxist theory. The aim of the series is to publish important theoretical contributions as the basis for vigorous intellectual debate and exchange on the left.

The peer-reviewed series publishes original monographs, translated texts, and reprints of classics across the bounds of academic disciplinary agendas and across the divisions of the left. The series is particularly concerned to encourage the internationalization of Marxist debate and aims to translate significant studies from beyond the English-speaking world.

For a full list of titles in the Historical Materialism Book Series available in paperback from Haymarket Books, visit: www.haymarketbooks.org/series_collections/1-historical-materialism.

The Ideology of Work

Theoretical Humanism, Work and Labour

Samuel J. R. Mercer

Haymarket Books
Chicago, IL

First published in 2024 by Brill Academic Publishers, The Netherlands
© 2024 Koninklijke Brill NV, Leiden, The Netherlands

Published in paperback in 2025 by
Haymarket Books
P.O. Box 180165
Chicago, IL 60618
773-583-7884
www.haymarketbooks.org

ISBN: 979-8-88890-358-2

Distributed to the trade in the US through Consortium Book Sales and Distribution (www.cbsd.com) and internationally through Ingram Publisher Services International (www.ingramcontent.com).

This book was published with the generous support of Lannan Foundation, Wallace Action Fund, and the Marguerite Casey Foundation.

Special discounts are available for bulk purchases by organizations and institutions. Please call 773-583-7884 or email info@haymarketbooks.org for more information.

Cover art and design by David Mabb. Cover art is a detail from *Construct 26, Morris, Chrysanthemum / Rodchenko, Boots*. Paper mounted on canvas (2006).

Printed in the United States.

Library of Congress Cataloging-in-Publication data is available.

Contents

Acknowledgements VII

Introduction: The Ideology of Work 1
 1 A Crisis of Marxism   2
 2 Structure of the Book   5

1 The Humanist Controversy 9
 1 Humanism as a Theoretical Problem   10
 2 Humanism as a Political Problem   16
 3 Anti-humanism after Althusser: The Spinozist Detour   23
 4 Anti-humanism after Althusser: The Hegelian/Lacanian Detour   29
 5 A Sociological Detour: Anti-humanism and Work   37
 6 Conclusion   43

2 The Concept of 'Labour' in Marx's Critique of Political Economy 44
 1 Marx Explodes the Concept of 'Labour'   45
 2 A 'Politics of Labour'   58
 3 Labour and Ideology   65
 4 Conclusion   73

3 'Social Labour' and the Critique of Work in Marxist Theory 75
 1 'Social Labour'   76
 2 Theory, Politics and 'Social Labour' in the Marxist Critique of Work   82
  2.1 *'Experience', Labour and Class*   83
  2.2 *De-skilling and the Labour Process*   86
  2.3 *The Sociology of Immaterial Labour*   90
  2.4 *The Crisis of Work*   93
 3 Conclusion   97

4 Theoretical Humanism and the Post-work Imaginary 99
 1 A Brave New World of (Post-)work   100
 2 The Problem with Post-work   109
 3 The Theoretical Humanism of Post-work Thought   116
  3.1 *The Theoretical Problem*   116
  3.2 *The Political Problem*   120
 4 Conclusion   126

5 Social Reproduction and Theoretical Anti-humanism   128
    1   A 'Crisis' of Feminism?   130
    2   Emotion, Alienation and Reproductive Labour   135
    3   Towards an Anti-humanist Theoretical Feminism: Social Reproduction Theory   147
    4   Conclusion   158

6 'Making' History: The Concept of Labour and the Anthropocene Discourse   160
    1   Labour and the Theoretical Humanism of the Anthropocene   161
    2   Alienation, Modernity and the Anthropocene   170
    3   Humanism, Historicism, Marxism: Labour Between 'Fossil Capital' and the 'Capitalocene'   181
    4   Conclusion   192

Conclusion: Marxism in Sociology   194

References   199
Index   207

Acknowledgements

This book is based on my doctoral studies and my thesis entitled *Humanism and the Ideology of Work*. I completed this thesis under the supervision of Joe Rigby, Katherine Harrison, Cassie Ogden and Peter Cox. I thank them for their ongoing wisdom and guidance and for encouraging me with this research from the beginning.

I would like to give special thanks also to Dhruv Jain, who organised and encouraged the publication of this manuscript. Dhruv has been a mentor and has invited me into a circle of intellectuals, many listed below, of which I had no business being a part. I thank him for this and for his continued friendship.

There are a number of people without whose input, across the completion of the initial PhD research and in the completion of this book, has been essential. Claudio Aguayo, Alya Ansari, Taylor Backman, Étienne Balibar, Bori, Fabio Bruschi, Roberto Catello, Emma Dowling, G.M. Goshgarian, Lea Idinopulos, David Isserman, Rafael Khachaturian, Thomas A. Laughlin, Jonathon Louth, David Maruzzella, Thomas McGlone Jr., Andrew McWhinney, Dave Mesing, Warren Montag, Lara Rettondini, Charles Umney, ben wallis and Imogen Woods.

Chapter 3 of this book is adapted from an article published in *Décalages*, titled '"Social Labor" and the Marxist Critique of Work'. Chapter 4 of this book is adapted from an article published in *Economy and Society*, titled 'Humanism and the Sociology of Post-Work'. I am grateful to the editorial boards of these two journals for their permission to re-print this material here.

I would like to thank Danny Hayward, Tegan Jaye-Luzhin, Sebastian Budgen and the anonymous reviewers of this manuscript with *Historical Materialism* for publishing this manuscript.

INTRODUCTION

The Ideology of Work

In his text *On the Reproduction of Capitalism*, Louis Althusser cited an appendix to the text which, it seems, remains lost or was never completed. This appendix was titled 'the Ideology of Work'.[1] This book in no way claims to fill the gap left in Althusser's oeuvre by this appendix. Rather, it takes inspiration from this appendix in order to think about what is at stake for both Marxism and sociology in analysing work from an Althusserian perspective today.

The book argues that the foremost problem for Marxism within the sociology of work today is *ideology* and of one ideology in particular: that of *theoretical humanism*. 'They never stop singing this old song to us in one variant or another',[2] so Althusser said of the ideology of theoretical humanism. Theoretical humanism – the refraction of the knowledge of social phenomena through an ideological apparatus constructed around the image of the human subject, its consciousness, essence and psychology – is a persistent problem for Marxism, repeatedly obscuring important social relations from view, rendering class struggle and the inequalities reflected within it incomprehensible. Some of the most enthusiastic verses in this old song are sung today by those thinking about the problem of work and society. The argument forwarded in this book is that the persistence of theoretical humanism throughout contemporary analyses of work undermines both their explanatory and political potential.

A cursory glance across contemporary studies of work and employment reveals the continued presence of the human subject and vague notions of humanity, human behaviour and human essence in pronouncing the harms produced by work today. The ritual of work 'is one that signifies a stressful waste of potential. Beautiful human faculties totally unused but still observable in the shadow form they take of acute anxiety, high blood pressure and an early death'.[3] Work is a problem insofar as it alienates the worker from their 'cultural, intellectual and physical sensibilities',[4] from 'being able to relax, spend time with loved ones, pursue self-directed activity and have freedom from a boss' which 'are all essential parts of what it means to be human'.[5] Today, 'work does

---

1 Althusser 2014a, p.139.
2 Althusser 2020a, p.81.
3 Fleming 2017, p.140.
4 Srnicek and Williams 2015, p.80.
5 Stronge and Lewis 2021, p.3.

not represent a source of joy or self-expression, but that blank part of the day which must be endured until five p.m.: the coveted hour when work releases its grip and we can finally be ourselves again'.[6] More than a semantic decision, the argument forwarded in this book is that the framing of work in this way is illustrative of a deeper theoretical problem: a problem of theoretical humanism, where work as a set of complex social relations is obscured behind moralistic theses on human behaviour, human alienation and human freedom.

The book tracks and exposes the persistence of this theoretical humanism through a number of important discourses within the sociology of work today. The book argues that this persistent theoretical humanism obscures the complexity of the social relations reflected in the contemporary appearance of work, in particular through the bracketing of class struggle within its formulations. Humanist ideology produces an impoverished analysis of the nature of the problem with work today, where this problem is interpreted as a problem of human subjectivity, of human alienation from particular thoughts or acts and of harm empirically observed upon concrete individuals. In so doing, the book argues that this produces an equally impoverished political sociology. Social change finds itself forwarded as a project of the amelioration of individual circumstances, of re-constructing the relationship between the human subject and that from which they have been alienated by work, as opposed to a strategy organised around class struggle and the political intervention this struggle can make.

1   A Crisis of Marxism

To what extent can this resurgence of theoretical humanism be linked to what Althusser called a 'crisis of Marxism?' Althusser used this notion of a crisis of Marxism in order to pronounce the relationship between theory and practice, demonstrating the political stakes of the theoretical impasse that haunted the Communist movement at the time. As Althusser argued, reflected in the theory adopted by the European Communist parties in the twentieth century was 'the extreme difficulty ... and perhaps even, in the present state of our theoretical knowledge, almost the impossibility of providing a really satisfactory Marxist explanation of a history which was, after all, made in the name of Marxism!'[7] Here, Althusser identifies a *décalage* or disjuncture between the theory and

---

6   Frayne 2015, p.18.
7   Althusser 1979, p.227.

practice of the Communist movement, where its inability to think the problem is reflected in the impotence of its political intervention to fix it.

Theoretical humanism, as it emerges within Marxism, is precisely a product of this crisis of Marxism. Faced with the inability to explain the horrors of Stalinism, Althusser described how a humanist ideology began to take root in the theory of the European Communist parties, to the detriment and erasure of any historical analysis of these failings. As Althusser wrote, 'the critique of Stalinist "dogmatism" was generally lived by Communist intellectuals as a "liberation." This "liberation" gave birth to a profound ideological reaction, "liberal" and "ethical" in tendency, which spontaneously rediscovered the old philosophical themes of "freedom", "man", the "human person" and "alienation"'.[8] In other words, theoretical humanism emerges and functions ideologically where it fills a gap left *in theory*, a gap created by a lack or impossibility of materialist analysis. However, this problem is not simply theoretical but, as alluded to in his lecture on the crisis of Marxism, simultaneously political. As Althusser continued, this ideological reaction found itself reflected in a 'disappearance of the class struggle' from the policy of the Communist Party of the Soviet Union, and a spirit of political reformism among the Communist Parties of Europe, 'guided by certain slogans of related resonance, in which the accent is put on the "peaceful transition to socialism", on "Marxist" or "socialist humanism", on "dialogue", etc'.[9]

To what extent does this crisis of Marxism today describe the current predicament within Marxist theory? Panagiotis Sotiris has recognised that the crisis of Marxism that faced Althusser is emblematic of the crisis which faces the communist movement today. As Sotiris writes, 'this is the challenge we still face today. Not just as intellectuals, but as part of a broader movement to rethink in practice the possibility of social transformation, the actuality of communism'.[10] Nick Nesbitt situates his re-visitation of Althusser's work within the same context of theoretical crisis, asking:

> Whether, ultimately, it is possible and even essential today, after what Badiou has called the 'obscure disasters' of the twentieth century, as postsocialist, neoliberal capital lunges in ever greater exhaustion from one crisis to the next, finally to read Marx's *Capital* ... as the systematic, conceptual, and, yes, scientific exposition and critique of the capitalist mode of production.[11]

---

8   Althusser 1996, p.10.
9   Althusser 1996, p.11.
10 Sotiris 2021, p.533.
11 Nesbitt 2017, p.13.

For Natalia Romé, 'the topic of "the crisis of Marxism" appears to be the current starting point for any productive approach to Marxism'.[12] For Romé, the precipice of this crisis is at the meeting-point between economism and humanism, 'the menace of a joint venture between technocratic ideology and the worse kind of political spontaneism, the sort of *right-wing leftism* embodied in desperate or paranoid masses'.[13] This insight is instructive for this book, as the technological determinism of the celebration of automation so often finds itself in a joint venture with the problematisation of the desperation of the worker's alienated condition at work today.

In relation to the critique of work specifically, it was perhaps André Gorz who first recognised the existence of this crisis of Marxism. 'There is no crisis in the workers' movement, but there is a crisis in the theory of the workers' movement',[14] argues Gorz in his text *A Strategy for Labour*. Though it would be incorrect to characterise Gorz's project as an anti-humanist one, Gorz argues that moralistic theses on poverty and deprivation are stifling the theory of the workers' movement and becoming increasingly reliant on automatic, determinist theories of human alienation: 'Like the theory of the inevitability of catastrophic crises which was current in the Stalinist era, it bases itself on the *growing discontent of the masses* as if that were an absolute impasse toward which capitalism were headed'.[15] For Gorz, the reformulation of the critique of work is the necessary solution to this crisis, a reformulation which 'links the condition of the workers at the place of work with their condition in society, thus shifting the struggle away from the purely economic level ... toward the level of class struggle'.[16]

It is Kathi Weeks who has most forcefully taken up re-thinking work in the context of this crisis of Marxism, observing its presence within a 'failed political imagination'[17] that finds its expression, *par excellence*, in the limited politics that has emerged from the contemporary critique of work. Echoing Romé, Weeks problematises the various techno-utopian and humanist developments within the critique of work today, arguing that 'although they may appear to be categories of nonwork, they fail to escape the imaginary of productivity or the models of the subject that would deliver it'.[18] Theoretical assumptions about

12 Romé 2021, p.153.
13 Romé 2021, p.154.
14 Gorz 1968, p.20.
15 Gorz 1968, p.23.
16 Gorz 1968, p.32.
17 Weeks 2016, p.258.
18 Weeks 2016, pp.257–258.

human subjectivity are an important element of this crisis, for Weeks. It is for this reason that Weeks looks to a return to Marxist-Feminist critiques of subjectivity, particularly anchored in the gendering of these subjects. This critical displacement of human subjectivity is vital for solving this crisis and for thinking the future, as 'we are not the targets of this change, not the subjects of this future, even if we might be among its agents'.[19]

This book argues that the contemporary critique of work ought to be observed as a symptom of today's crisis of Marxism. For Althusser, this crisis – and the humanist ideology symptomatic of its eruption – took hold at the intersection between theory and practice: that is, at the border between the theoretical analysis of capitalist social formations and the practical and political interventions that would ultimately lead to their overthrow. Today, this book argues that sociologists of work are increasingly represented at this border, with the critique of work repeatedly mobilised as the vehicle within which theory and practice are thought together.

2   Structure of the Book

The first chapter will ground the book and its argument within Althusser's Marxism more generally and in his critique of theoretical humanism in particular. The chapter will begin with an exposition of Althusser's critique, arguing that, despite ongoing debate around the continuities and breaks within Althusser's work, the critique of theoretical humanism has persisted as a crucial element of his Marxism. The chapter engages with those interlocutors within the so-called 'post-Althusserian' moment who have continued to develop theoretical anti-humanism in their thinking, focusing in particular on the work of Étienne Balibar, Slavoj Žižek and the respective schools of thought that have emerged from their engagement with Althusser's thought here. The chapter will also look specifically at the ways in which this theoretical anti-humanism has been developed with a specific view to analysing work as a social and political phenomenon, centralising the contribution of Frédéric Lordon in order to demonstrate this relationship in its most contemporary form.

Chapter two of the book engages in a reading of Marx's writings, in order to situate the concept of 'labour' within the anti-humanist theoretical operation at the heart of Marx's critique of political economy. The chapter focuses on a number of important contributions within Marx's works that are frequently

---

[19]   Weeks 2016, p.265.

cited within the contemporary sociology of work: in particular, chapter 10 on 'The Working Day' in *Capital Volume I*; the section on the division of labour in *The German Ideology*, home of the 'hunter, fisherman, shepherd [and] critic';[20] and chapter 48 on 'The Trinity Formula' in *Capital Volume III*, in which Marx makes reference to the 'realm of freedom'[21] and its relation to the shortening of the working day. The argument forwarded in this chapter is that the operationality of the concept of labour across these examples relies, in different ways, on its conceptual transformation and explosion through a theoretically anti-humanist operation, destroying the simple concept of labour deployed by the classical political economists and replacing it with new, developed concepts revealing of the social relations of work under capitalism. The chapter argues that it is this operation which facilitates the development, in Marx, of a materialist theory of sociology, politics and ideology across these important contributions.

Chapter three argues that despite Marx's own writings and the power of Althusser's intervention, Marxist theory has always struggled to think about work without a reliance on humanist ideology. The chapter demonstrates this through a reading of some important contributions to the Marxist critique of work throughout the twentieth and early twenty-first centuries, including E.P. Thompson, Harry Braverman, Michael Hardt and Antonio Negri and André Gorz, focusing particularly on their mobilisation of the concept of 'social labour'. Though Marx cannot be accused of a theoretical humanism in his development of the concept of social labour in the first pages of the *Grundrisse*, it is evident that Marx's evacuation of certain semantic devices characteristic of his early works had not been successful in the pronouncement of this concept. The chapter argues that this failure by Marx has been reproduced in contemporary Marxist thought on the topic of work under capitalism, particularly where this concept of social labour is deployed. As with Marx's own writing, this chapter does not argue that these contemporary accounts ought to be ignored due to this: rather, the chapter seeks only to highlight a persistent difficulty that runs throughout Marxist thought on work under capitalism and demonstrate its theoretically humanist character.

The legacy of this problem within Marxist theories of work is demonstrated in chapter four, which analyses the continuation of humanist ideology within contemporary post-work thought. What I have elsewhere called the 'sociology of post-work' is an important and influential discourse within the contempor-

---

20   Marx and Engels 1976, p.47.
21   Marx 1991, p.958.

ary sociology of work, which has developed a critique of work under capitalism in the context of automation, the growing precariousness of work and the swelling of the ranks of the global unemployed. Alongside this critique, the sociology of post-work offers a solution to these problems, based on the reduction or abolition of wage-labour from society. As the foremost political sociology of work today, this chapter argues that it remains haunted by a persistent humanist ideology which repeatedly undermines the strength of its formulations. The chapter argues that many of the criticisms levelled at this discourse – its technological determinism, its reliance on the state or its lack of appreciation for the nuances of value, labour-power and money within capitalist production – can all be located in the gaps subsequently filled by humanist ideology. The post-work imaginary offers a post-work vision grounded in an analysis of the alienation of the human subject, with the success of its vision dependent on a political project that seeks to reunite this subject with its autonomy and self-reliance, ultimately offering more of a moral project as opposed to a political intervention.

Chapter five analyses the persistence of humanist ideology within contemporary feminist critiques of work and reproduction. The chapter situates its critique within the context of a 'crisis of feminism', reconstructed through the works of Marxist feminists such as Lise Vogel, Natalia Romé, Kathi Weeks and Susan Ferguson. According to these interlocutors, feminist theory stands on the precipice of a crisis, increasingly reliant on theoretically humanist concepts and problematics, which are powerless in interpreting the present conjuncture. Evidence of this is presented in the chapter through an analysis of contemporary feminist sociological critiques of gender, work and reproduction, particularly in emerging critiques of domestic service, sex work, surrogacy and tissue donation. The chapter argues that humanist ideology is re-deployed throughout these sociological critiques, often through the concept of 'emotional labour.' Through this concept, this discourse relies on the observation of the alienation of particular subjects from essential emotional capacities such as love, care and compassion, which it then uses to critique contemporary capitalism and the contemporary forms of reproductive labour that it exploits. The resolution to this problem is located in a reconstruction of social reproduction theory. Echoing the Marxist feminists cited above, the chapter argues that social reproduction theory contains a necessary theoretical anti-humanism by virtue of its contact with Marxism, which can be developed and deployed within feminist sociologies of work today in order to deconstruct these ideological obstacles and reveal the material realities of capitalist reproduction today.

Chapter six tracks the continuation of this humanist ideological problem in contemporary ecological theory and the way it thinks the relationship between labour and planetary history. The main story represented in this discourse is that of the 'Anthropocene': the notion that human activity has indelibly marked planetary history to the point of constituting a distinct geological epoch. This chapter will argue that contained within this story is a theory of human alienation, represented in the notion that human beings have unknowingly and unwittingly – as a result of contemporary capitalism – laboured themselves into a geological catastrophe. Proponents of this discourse argue that this alienated condition ought to be overcome by re-uniting human and planetary histories, in order to raise the historical consciousness of the human subject endowed with the power to 'make' history in this way. Despite the problematic nature of this Anthropocene discourse – which brackets or completely removes capitalism and class struggle from its analysis – this chapter argues that this theoretical humanism finds itself reproduced in certain Marxist approaches to the problem of climate change and ecological crisis. By mobilising an encounter between Andreas Malm and Jason W. Moore, this chapter demonstrates the relationship between the concept of 'labour' within these two accounts and the extent to which this concept emerges as a site of continued difficulty in thinking about ecological crisis without reliance on theoretical humanism. The chapter reaches the conclusion that Moore's account of capitalist 'world-ecology' is more successful in handling this difficulty than Malm's history of 'fossil capital'.

The book concludes with a call to re-visit Althusser's critique of theoretical humanism for the reconstruction of a Marxism *in* sociology today. If sociology is to truly act as an arbiter between theory and practice, and offer a theory of capitalism capable of producing a meaningful political intervention against it, then it must critically reflect on the mechanisms it relies upon to produce this knowledge. Until now, the sociology of work has been too heavily dependent upon humanist ideology, productive of an impoverished critique of capitalism and a toothless political strategy. Any political sociology must obviously not lose interest in questions of human emancipation and the goal of eventual liberation of human beings from wage-labour. However, if it is to seriously engage in such a task, it must remember the principal discovery of Marxist theory: that 'it is impossible to *know* anything about men except on the absolute precondition that the philosophical (theoretical) myth of man is reduced to ashes'.[22]

---

22 Althusser 1996, p.229.

CHAPTER 1

The Humanist Controversy

This opening chapter sets the pace for the remainder of the book, establishing its position within the anti-humanist tradition of Marxist thought. The master of this tradition is, of course, Louis Althusser, who demonstrates that the power of Marx's theoretical operation resides in a philosophical practice that can be described (among other things) as theoretically anti-humanist.

Althusser's theoretical anti-humanism is not confined only to his readings of Marx. In 1946, Althusser penned his critique of what he called the *International of Decent Feelings*, in which he identifies how humanist and moralistic appeals to 'fear' as the dominant social relation between human subjects risks masking a material analysis of the conditions in Europe after the end of the Second World War. Unlike the proletariat, 'defined by sociological, economic, and historical conditions', the so-called *'proletariat of terror'* summoned by this humanist international 'would seem to be defined by a psychological state: intimidation and fear'.[1] In his analysis of Montesquieu's political science, Althusser isolates its theoretical anti-humanism as an important component of its operationality: Montesquieu's scientific method resides in 'the refusal to take the motives of human action for its dynamic, the ends and arguments men consciously propose to themselves for the real, most often unconscious cases which make them act'.[2] And it is evident also in his reading of Jacques Lacan's separation of psychology and psychoanalysis, which turns on Lacan's acknowledgement that 'what precedes the becoming-human of the little human being isn't psychology, it's not the psychological subject, but what he calls "the order of the symbolic"'.[3]

This commitment to theoretical anti-humanism has been a recurring feature of Althusser's work, from his earliest writings through to those of his maturity. But it is always when it is developed in contact with Marx's political economy that it finds its most interesting and convincing expression. This chapter will set out the parameters of this position by re-tracing Althusser's theoretical anti-humanism as it pertains to Marxist thought. In order to do this, the chapter will analyse humanism as both a theoretical and a political problem for Marxism through Althusser's work. Alongside the work of Althusser, the chapter will

---

1 Althusser 2014b, p.3.
2 Althusser 2007, p.36.
3 Althusser 2016, p.60.

also look at the work of those who have developed Althusser's critique of theoretical humanism in various directions. The chapter focuses on two schools of thought in particular: the Spinozist school, led largely by the work of Étienne Balibar; and the Hegelian/Lacanian school, led largely by Slavoj Žižek. These are by no means the only examples of this development, but the encounter between these two schools has set the parameters for the development of anti-humanist thought within the Marxist canon today.

The chapter will also begin to think about the ways in which this debate has influenced contemporary Marxist thought in relation to the problem of work today. For this, the chapter turns largely to the work of Frédéric Lordon. In his contribution to theoretical anti-humanism, the problem of subjectivity and of the humanist assumptions often attached to this problem, lie at the heart of the present (in)ability to think about the problem of work adequately or completely from a Marxist perspective.

1   Humanism as a Theoretical Problem

Firstly, it is important to establish humanism as a theoretical problem, what Althusser called the problem of *theoretical humanism*. 'Innocent is the last thing philosophy is',[4] so Althusser famously declared, arguing instead that philosophy is itself a battlefield upon which 'every philosophy is in a state of war, at the limit, with the other philosophical tendency, materialist or idealist'.[5] In this philosophical struggle between idealism and materialism, concepts and words emerge, which provide the site of this battle: 'Words are also either weapons and explosives or tranquilizers and poisons ... Certain words fight like enemies. Others offer the opportunity for vacillation: they are the location of a decisive but as yet undecided battle'.[6] Theoretical humanism and its persistence throughout theoretical discourse is best interpreted as a symptom of this ongoing battle. The theoretical struggle over the human subject and its origin, its capacities and its destiny have been so many concepts, ideas and words which have been occupied by both materialist and idealist philosophies, in a bid to 'take preventive action against the enemy in order to get the better of him'.[7]

---

4   Althusser 2017, p.34.
5   Althusser 2017, p.59.
6   Althusser, cited in Macciocchi 1973, p.16.
7   Althusser 2017, p.59.

For Althusser, as both a Marxist and a materialist in philosophy, theoretical humanism is a strategic foothold for idealism within this ongoing struggle, one that must necessarily be dismantled if Marxism and materialism are to make ground. Althusser describes humanism in terms of an 'epistemological obstacle'[8] that lies on the theoretical path struck out by materialist philosophy. Humanism represents such an obstacle insofar as 'the theory comes up against an obstacle that prevents it from advancing' and that 'this obstacle blocks a path and hides objects *that are in some sense behind it*'.[9] It is in this sense that humanism can therefore be described as a *theoretical* problem: it is a problem insofar as, as a set of theoretical assumptions, it *blocks* the advancement of materialist theory and obstructs the attainment of its *object*, of that which it attempts to produce knowledge. As a theoretical problem, theoretical humanism can therefore only be dismantled through 'a real labour of theoretical production'.[10]

In his critique of theoretical humanism, Althusser targets these theoretical representations of concrete human subjectivity and their reflection through several different conceptual devices. Althusser here points towards the various ways in which these concepts manifest themselves theoretically:

> The notion of Man (the essence or Nature of Man); The notion of the human species or Human Genus (Man's generic essence, defined by consciousness, the heart, inter-subjectivity, etc.); The notion of the 'concrete,' 'real', etc., individual; The notion of the subject ('concrete' subjectivity, the subject constitutive of the speculary relation, the process of alienation, History, etc.); The notion of consciousness (for example, as the essential defining feature of the human species, or as the essence of the ideological); The notion of labour (as the essence of man); The notion of alienation (as the externalization of a Subject); The notion of dialectic (so far as it implies teleology).[11]

Across numerous contributions, Althusser tracks and exposes the persistence of these theoretical concepts through various discourses of knowledge. In modern political theory, Althusser demonstrated how modern conceptualisations of law upon which these political theories were based were 'steeped in exi-

---

8   Althusser 2003, p.271.
9   Ibid.
10 Ibid.
11 Althusser 2003, p.273.

gencies arising from human relations. Law thus presupposed human beings, or beings in the image of man, even if they surpassed it'.[12] In philosophy – particularly German idealism – this humanism emerges again, in the consideration of history as the expression of the struggle of the human subject against alienated reason: 'At the end of history, this man, having become inhuman objectivity, has merely to re-grasp as subject his own essence alienated in property, religion and the State to become total man, true man'.[13] Althusser also observes this humanism in theories of political economy too, arguing that 'Political Economy relates economic facts to their origin in the *needs* (or 'utility') of human *subjects*',[14] where 'it is the need (of the human subject) that defines the *economic* in economics'.[15]

The problem with theoretical humanism in all these examples is that it provides idealism a facade of materialism, by claiming to ground its analysis in that which *exists*: the concrete individual, the psychological human subject and the *relations* that exist between them. The history of human societies can be explained as the culmination of a set of relations that emerge quite 'naturally' from the interactions between human beings that they *enter into* themselves. The fact that this narrative of human societies is grounded in the human being itself gives this narrative the guise of a materialist thesis. However, as Althusser argues, 'in theory, no-one has yet, to my knowledge, met a flesh-and-blood man, only the *notion* of man'.[16] The same can be said for the 'natural' relations that therefore emerge between these flesh-and-blood men: 'What gives you the right to consider it natural to do what you are doing?'.[17] The concepts of 'nature' and of 'the human' are ideological 'bedfellows'[18] in the narrative of human societies that they construct together, where:

> Nature produces everything, the producer who produces to satisfy his natural needs, including the natural needs of the woman whom he has taken to wife to satisfy his natural needs, and those of the children whom she has borne him, that is, whom he has begotten upon her to satisfy the human race's natural need to reproduce itself.[19]

---

12 Althusser 2007, p.31.
13 Althusser 1996, p.226.
14 Althusser 2015, p.314.
15 Althusser 2015, p.315.
16 Althusser 2003, p.264.
17 Althusser 2020a, p.28.
18 Althusser 2020a, p.85.
19 Althusser 2020a, p.86.

Missing in this narrative of course are the gendered material realities that govern this arrangement of concrete individuals: that is, the *social relations* between them. Contrary to the narrative offered here, social relations are 'neither relations between men nor relations between certain men' but are in fact 'relations between men with respect to things, the things called means of production'.[20] It is these relations, rather than the men who 'enter into' them that provide the material reality of human society. In this way, the focus on human subjects is not the materialist thesis, but merely an idealist one 'cloaking itself in its adversary's arguments'.[21]

For Althusser, one of the most important theoretical characteristics of Marxism is its ability to deconstruct this humanist ideology and reveal beneath it the trespass of idealist concepts in order to subject them to materialist critique. The theoretical functioning of Marx's critique of political economy turns on a displacement of the human subject from the epistemological centre, in favour of social relations and of the class struggles reflected in those relations. The pronouncement that 'the history of all hitherto existing society is the history of class struggles'[22] can exist only to the extent that human subjects are removed from the centre-stage of history itself, replaced with a material analysis of the social relations that arrange these subjects: in this sense, Marx produces a theory of history as a 'process without a subject',[23] in which 'there is, in the last instance, no history but the history of modes of production'.[24] This is the culmination of an important theoretical operation that exists at the basis of Marxist theory, the mechanics of which are visible and evident in the development of Marx's critique of political economy. As Althusser argues, 'it is against the general background of this history that we can bring out our carefully considered reasons for defending the thesis of *Marx's theoretical anti-humanism*'.[25]

In order to demonstrate the ideological qualities of humanism in this way, Althusser developed his most influential – and indeed, most controversial – theory: that of the *epistemological break* between the works of 'Young' and 'Mature' Marx. Althusser developed the distinction between the early works of the 'Young Marx' and the more sophisticated political economy of the 'Mature Marx' in order to highlight how the ability to theorise class struggle and society was possible only with the *critique of humanist ideology* as an absolute pre-

---

20 Althusser 2020a, p.71.
21 Althusser 2017, p.59.
22 Marx and Engels 2002, p.322.
23 Althusser 2008, p.83.
24 Althusser 2020a, p.134.
25 Althusser 2003, p.232.

condition. Althusser argues that whilst the mature political economy of Marx critiqued capitalism through concepts which allowed him to think about the primacy of class struggle in the capitalist mode of production, the works of the 'Young Marx' were much less sophisticated, relying on humanist ideology in order to construct this critique of capitalism. Therefore, Althusser argues that the sophistication of Marx's mature political economy (and the development of the concepts that defined it) was anchored fundamentally in the deconstruction of humanism as a theoretical obstacle in the move between the 'Young' and 'Mature' Marx, with the disappearance of humanism in his works the *sine qua non* of Marx's theoretical operation. The concepts of Marx's mature political economy and the theory of society driven by historical class struggle there developed, emerged 'because of his ferocious insistence on freeing himself from the myths which presented themselves to him as the *truth*'[26] in the form of the humanist ideology of his youth.

According to Althusser, the early works of the 'Young Marx' (those texts written before 1845 such as *The Holy Family* and *The Economic and Philosophic Manuscripts of 1844*) critiqued capitalism based on a fundamentally humanist problematic, which Marx 'borrowed'[27] from the German idealism of Ludwig Feuerbach. In his critique of religion, Feuerbach argued that religion was the manifestation of an alienated human reason, obstructing the human subject's full attainment and enjoyment of its human capacities. Althusser argues that this central humanist problematic was traced by the Young Marx into his critique of capitalism. The Young Marx argued that capitalism was but the manifestation of alienated human reason, reflected in the alienation of human labour in private property. Communism, for the Young Marx, was therefore no more than the human overcoming of this alienated condition, as the process through which 'the proletariat will negate its own negation and take possession of itself'.[28] In analysing these early works, Althusser argues that the central theoretical problematic of the Young Marx was not society, but Man. Althusser charges the Young Marx with 'merely applying the theory of alienation, that is, Feuerbach's theory of "human nature"'[29] to political economy, in which he does not espouse his own original theory of society but 'literally espoused Feuerbach's problematic'[30] of human nature and its alienation in society. Crucially, the theoretical consequences of this predominant humanist ideology in

---

26   Althusser 1996, p.84.
27   Althusser 1996, p.46.
28   Althusser 1996, p.226.
29   Althusser 1996, p.46.
30   Ibid.

the work of the Young Marx were that it acted as a theoretical obstacle in Marx's political economy, mystifying the role of class struggle and its reflection in the relations of society. In these early works, the critique of capitalism through the lens of class struggle and social structure is silenced by the persistence of humanist ideology throughout his analysis:

> Marx could not state what he was trying to say – not only because he did not yet *know* how to say it, but also because he prevented himself from saying it by dint of the simple fact that he began his first sentence with the phrase 'the *essence of Man*'.[31]

The developed concepts of class struggle and its reflection in the social relations of capitalism for which Marx's political economy would be become well-known remain silent in the works of the 'Young Marx' because they are hidden behind the theoretical obstacle of humanist ideology. Althusser here demonstrates how the Feuerbachian ideological problematic of human nature and the Marxist problematic of class struggle cannot coexist and instead struggle against one another in these early works, with the former decisively silencing the latter to the detriment of the sophistication of Marx's political economy.

The sophisticated critique of capitalism that Marx developed in his mature political economy – where the capitalist mode of production is shown by Marx to be the reflection of historically determined class struggle in both the forces and relations of production – emerged with the abandonment of humanist ideology and the replacement of the humanist problematic by one of class struggle and social relations. The analytic method of the mature Marx 'does not proceed from *man* but from a given economic period of society',[32] critiquing capitalism not as the alienation of human reason but as the product of an historically determinant class struggle. For Althusser this fundamental break with humanist ideology is specifically responsible for the emergence of class struggle at the forefront of Marx's political economy and thus responsible for all the concepts Marx provided to his readers in order to understand it. As Althusser writes, 'Marx established a new problematic, a new systematic way of asking questions of the world, new principles and a new method'.[33] In replacing humanist ideology with this new set of theoretical postulates organised around class and society, 'Marx did not only propose a new theory of the history of societies, but at the same time implicitly, but necessarily, a new "philosophy",

---

31 Althusser 2003, p.254.
32 Marx 1989b, p.547.
33 Althusser 1996, p.229.

infinite in its implications'.[34] This epistemological break in Marx's work was a formative development in his critique of capitalism and of political economy. As Althusser goes on to demonstrate in *Reading Capital*, not only did Marx recognise the role of humanist ideology in his own work, but he also recognised it as the foundational ideology of classical political economy as well. By pulling at the thread of humanist ideology in the works of Adam Smith and David Ricardo, Marx 'rejected the very structure of the object of Political Economy',[35] exposing the inaccuracies of classical political economy by showing how 'the social relations of production do not bring *men alone* onto the stage, but the *agents* of the production process and the *material conditions* of the production process, in specific "combinations"'.[36] Althusser positioned the critique of humanism to demonstrate not only the originality of Marx's individual contribution, but also to demonstrate the origins of the explanatory power of Marxism itself, which would be taken up by many long after Marx.

Taken together, this forms the analysis by Althusser of humanism as a theoretical problem. The grounding of any social scientific analysis in an observation of the human subject or of the relations between human individuals is not a materialist thesis but merely the imposture of an idealist theory draped in the facade of an ideology made to *appear* as materialism. The truly materialist analysis of human societies, as Marxism shows more forcefully than any other theoretical system, is in the displacement of the human subject in favour of an analysis of the history of the social relations that position these subjects, and the historical class struggle that is always reflected in these relations. The very workability of Marxism as a theoretical system is dependent upon this displacement and it is only on the condition of this displacement that any knowledge of capitalism and capitalist social formations can be produced at all.

2   Humanism as a Political Problem

Relatedly, humanism represents an important political problem for Althusser, not simply as an epistemological obstacle, but also as an obstacle to effective political intervention within a particular conjuncture. It is not accurate to say that the theoretical and the political problem of humanism are separate: on the contrary, the relationship they share is much more immanent, with each

---

34   Ibid.
35   Althusser 2015, p.319.
36   Althusser 2015, p.328.

informing and co-constituting the other. The immanence of the link between theory and politics in this way is captured in Lenin's thesis, that 'without a revolutionary theory, there can be no revolutionary movement'.[37] Taken in this way, the theoretical work of deconstructing humanist ideology necessitates the political work of struggling against its material expression in class struggle itself.

Althusser's introduction of theoretical humanism as a problem took place within a very specific political conjuncture in the late 1950s and early 1960s. A member of the French Communist Party (PCF) at the time of the Twentieth Congress of the Communist Party of the Soviet Union (CPSU) and the beginning of the process of de-Stalinisation, Althusser sees the problem of theoretical humanism as one that is inextricable from the political crisis underway within the Communist movement at the time. Althusser argues that the theoretical problem of humanism is reflected in an immanent political shift in the policy of the Soviet Union, away from a Leninist conception of 'class humanism' (in which 'the end of exploitation meant the end of *class* exploitation'[38]) towards a 'socialist humanism of the person'.[39] The effect of this political humanism, much the same as its expression in theory, is the erasure of social relations and of class struggle from view, creating a field of political intervention targeted at the level of the concrete individual as opposed to the material relations responsible for the social arrangement of these individuals. Regarding the politics of this socialist humanism:

> The Soviets say, in our country antagonistic classes have disappeared, the dictatorship of the proletariat has fulfilled its function, the State is no longer a class State but the State of the whole people (of everyone). In the USSR men are indeed now treated without any class distinction, that is, *as persons*.[40]

Althusser shows that the source of humanism as a political problem relates, in this specific case, to the attempt by the CPSU to reckon with the problems and the horrors inherited from Stalin. As Althusser writes, 'the themes of socialist humanism designate the existence of real problems: *new* historical, economic, political and ideological problems that the Stalinist period kept in

---

37 Lenin 1973, p.28.
38 Althusser 1996, p.221.
39 Althusser 1996, p.222.
40 Ibid.

the shade, but still produced while producing socialism'.⁴¹ Althusser continues, demonstrating that 'the themes of socialist humanism (free development of the individual, respect for socialist legality, dignity of the person, etc.) are the way the Soviets and other socialists are *living* the relation between themselves and these problems, that is, the *conditions* in which they are posed'.⁴²

Given the gravity of these political problems, the question remains: 'Why then all this stress so deliberately laid on *man*?'.⁴³ In much the same way that theoretical humanism appears in the works of the Young Marx out of a theoretical impossibility of posing particular questions about the class struggle and its reflection in history and political economy (an impossibility caused by the dominant ideological arrangement *in theory*), the problem of humanism appears in politics as a symptom of the political impossibility of particular interventions (an impossibility caused by the dominant arrangement of particular social conditions). In other words, the recourse to socialist humanism within the CPSU is not, as they would have it, the product of a material critique of the errors of Stalinism: rather, it is symptomatic of an idealist attempt to correct these errors whilst leaving intact the very material conditions responsible for these errors in the first instance. In politics, humanism is symptomatic of an erasure of historical social relations in favour of a fetishism of the human person: a convenient political manoeuvre that provides space for an ideological denouncement of Stalin alongside the maintenance of the social conditions inherited from him. It is for this reason that Althusser would denounce the Khrushchevite reforms as nothing more than 'Stalinism with a human face'.⁴⁴

This line of thinking is continued outside of this particular political conjuncture and is evident in other political reflections made by Althusser, such as those made of the strikes and occupations among Italy's automotive factory workers in the 1960s and 70s. In order to analyse the political stakes of these struggles and assess the appropriate intervention to make into them as communists, Althusser argues that the 'workers' as concrete, empirical individuals must be removed from the centre of enquiry. As Althusser writes:

> Some people believe that it is enough to address an appeal to those involved, to ask them about their lives, their jobs, how they are exploited, and the like ... Well and good. The workers are writing, they are saying a

---

41 Althusser 1996, p.238.
42 Althusser 1996, pp.238–239.
43 Althusser 1996, p.238.
44 Elliott 2009, p.25.

great many interesting, incredible, overwhelming things. This can provide *some* material for concrete analysis. It is not a concrete analysis.[45]

In contrast to humanist empirical sociologies that begin with the experience of the individual, Althusser argues that enquiry must instead prioritise the 'primacy of contradiction over the contraries, primacy of the class struggle over the classes', in order to 'go into the field, in the "concrete", to see, *in detail*, what forms this antagonism historically takes, and what historical forms it confers on the classes it constitutes'.[46]

Humanism emerges as a problem insofar as it fetishizes the experience of the worker as an empirical individual, neglecting the material social relations responsible for the arrangement not only of this worker within the factory itself, but also the factory within the broader system of global capitalism. Speaking of the factory workers in Italy, Althusser demonstrates that though these workers no doubt had knowledge of the conditions of their own work, what they do not know (because they *could not* know) is the way that these conditions fit with broader patterns of industrial production across the Italian conjuncture:

> While they knew what was going on in their plant and trust, they had *absolutely no idea* of what was really going on in Fiat, that is, in the same branch of production; and they had *absolutely no idea* of what was going on in the other branches of production in Italy: metalworking, textiles, the petrochemical industry, mining, agriculture, transport, the financial trusts and the trusts that control commercial distribution, and so on.[47]

Moreover, whilst these workers undoubtedly had specialist knowledge of how to construct the various components of an automobile and fit them together in its creation, what they did not know (because they *could not* know) was how the very production of automobiles fit within patterns and strategies of capital accumulation on a broader scale. As Althusser explains, the automobile 'was conceived of as an indispensable means of enabling workers ... to transport themselves from their homes to the factory gates and present themselves there about as fresh as they would have been had they lived in the immediate vicinity'.[48] In other words, the work of these workers was part of a much broader historical narrative that included consumption, geography and space

---

45 Althusser 2020b, p.3.
46 Althusser 2020b, p.2.
47 Althusser 2020b, p.5.
48 Althusser 2020b, p.9.

and the primitive accumulation and reproduction of labour-power: a reality 'that not even the most conscious workers at Alfa Romeo could know'.[49] Politically speaking, therefore, to focus only on the experiences, knowledge or personal testimonies of individual workers severely limits the *knowledge* of the militant as to the concrete reality of the situation, and therefore limits the political scope of intervention within it. Instead, 'it is a question of *theoretical* and *political* preparation'[50] by the militant for their encounter with this individual worker, which must begin with the concrete historical social relations that arrange their work in the first place.

It is not satisfactory to leave things here. Althusser's argument was not simply one of prioritising the higher knowledge of the individual militant or the philosopher over that of individual workers. Such a thesis would be its own kind of vulgar humanism. Rather, the act of theoretically and politically preparing for an encounter with individual workers is acknowledgement of the fact that within the testimonies of individual workers there might be things that the militant themselves does not know (because they *could not* know). It is for this reason that Althusser argues that the militant must not simply listen to workers, but learn to 'listen *correctly*' to what they say:

> To be able to listen to them, those listening must know which questions to ask and which not to; they must know how to put what the workers say into relation with what the workers themselves do not know about the effects that the general process has on their own condition; finally, and above all, they must be open to learning, by way of this relation, what they do not know and the workers do, but without knowing that they know it, and yet say after all – albeit obliquely, indirectly, and even in their omissions and silences.[51]

In this way, humanism is even a problem when it comes to the interpretation of the direct testimonies of human workers. To take these testimonies at face value, rather than positioning them within the context of historical social relations, is to risk overlooking the very thing which the workers *know* but the militant does not. This thing may pass in the silences, or even the things unsaid by individual workers, illuminated only by their positioning against the background of broader historical social relations. Putting this into practice in his

---

49 Althusser 2020b, p.10.
50 Althusser 2020b, p.3.
51 Althusser 2020b, p.12.

correspondence with Maria Macciocchi during her election campaign in Italy, he writes that the militant:

> Must raise pertinent questions of his own in order to break down these silences and make the speaker discover things that he knows, but that he is not aware of knowing because they are disguised – clouded over, repressed – covered over by causes that go to the very heart of the conditions in which these people live.[52]

What Althusser develops here is an anti-humanist approach to political interaction with individual workers, reinforcing the principle that if one *really* wants to alter the conditions of life for individual people, then one's political intervention must begin with the social relations responsible for the positionality of this individual. Fetishizing the human individual does a disservice to the political project of improving the lives of human beings and worse still, misses the important knowledge contained within the very experiences and testimonies of these individuals by neglecting the social conditions in which these experiences are articulated.

This political problem of humanism is expressed in Althusser's search for a theory of political action based on a rejection and displacement of anthropological assumptions: a theory he locates in his analysis of political thinkers like Machiavelli and Spinoza. In Machiavelli, for example, Althusser finds a theory of political action that displaces traditional political anthropologies based on the subject of the law, towards a theory of political action organised around a concept of the *masses* as the subject of an encounter between multiple historical social relations. In reading *The Prince*, Althusser argues against the traditional humanist reading of Machiavelli's political theory, as a narrative of a charismatic, strategic and powerful individual: 'It is not a matter of such and such an individual's opinion. His purpose is not to elaborate an anthropology or psychology of individual passions and opinions'.[53] Rather:

> The Prince belongs to a different realm of existence. It is not satisfaction of his needs that motivates him, or assuagement of his passions that should guide him ... he pursues a completely distinct goal: a historical goal – founding, consolidating and expanding a state that endures.[54]

---

52 Althusser cited in Macciocchi 1973, p.52.
53 Althusser 2000, p.89.
54 Althusser 2000, p.92.

In founding a theory of political action of the Prince, as a non-anthropological figure, Althusser argues that Machiavelli establishes a theory of political action that prioritises the encounter between historical social relations. 'The Prince' is not a charismatic individual but precisely the moment in which these historical relations encounter one another in a way that takes hold or 'lasts', producing a new conjuncture.

Althusser's reading of Machiavelli is an allegory for his reading of the political problem of humanism within the communist movement at the time. What Althusser sees in Machiavelli's displacement of traditional political anthropologies, and the move away from the human subject of the law to the aleatory encounter of social relations, is precisely the formula for the theoretical and political preparation required of the communist movement and its militants amid their current political crisis. For Althusser, contained in Machiavelli's departure from political humanism are the elements of political *strategy*, from which the communist movement must learn:

> Machiavelli thinks as a politician and as a materialist, and that he knows, as someone who thinks under the domination of 'humanism', but in radical opposition to it, that politics is a matter not of individuals, but of strategy, time, and the right means for realizing this strategy.[55]

By displacing the human subject from the centre of political practice and focusing instead on the encounter between historical social relations, a political strategy can be developed that seeks an appropriate intervention into this encounter that looks to make a favourable encounter *last* and, with it, the political subjectivity it brings into existence. It is only by this act of displacement, this anti-humanism within politics itself, that a 'concrete analysis of the concrete situation'[56] can be completed, with this analysis being the absolute prerequisite for any emancipatory politics and the achievement of any human liberation whatsoever. It is the acknowledgement of this fact that gives meaning to Althusser's insistence that 'only theoretical anti-humanism justifie[s] genuine, practical humanism'.[57]

In what follows, the chapter will look more closely at the development of this theoretical and political problem of humanism within the context of Marxism specifically, by focusing on two prominent *detours* in which Althusser's

---

55 Althusser 2020b, p.64.
56 Althusser 2020b, p.77.
57 Althusser 1993, pp.185–186.

insights were elaborated. The chapter will focus on a 'Spinozist' and a 'Hegelian/Lacanian' detour to this end. These are certainly not the only examples of such detours in which this theoretical anti-humanism was developed: those articulated in the works of Jacques Derrida, Michel Foucault and Gilles Deleuze are examples of other important ways in which Althusser's problematic could be said to have been developed. However, it is in these two detours that the problem of theoretical humanism as a problem of and for Marxism specifically maintains its place at the centre, and it is for this reason that the chapter places particular focus on their development.

3   Anti-humanism after Althusser: The Spinozist Detour

Within the Althusserian tradition itself, Étienne Balibar has continued to develop the critique of humanism, in order to think about the consequences of theoretical humanism upon the construction and development of effective political theory. This comes to the fore in Balibar's development of the political philosophy of Spinoza, who is seen as an interlocutor with whom Althusser – often silently – maintained a dialogue throughout his works. Balibar reads Spinoza and Althusser together in order to think about the possibility of a political anthropology that can be constructed based on an initial displacement of the human subject from the centre of theoretical production.

The starting point for such a project is, of course, not Spinoza, but Marx. Balibar reads a break between the 'Young' and mature Marx in the constitution of the problem of political subjectivity, visible in the movement by Marx from the Feuerbachian concept of 'alienation' to the concept of 'commodity fetishism' developed in the first volume of *Capital*. The nature of this break is anti-humanist in nature, observed in the displacement of the idea of consciousness as residing *within* the subject, in favour of the notion that consciousness is something *produced* by social relations. In other words:

> Marx did not produce a theory of 'class consciousness' here, in the sense of a system of ideas which might be said, consciously or otherwise, to express the 'aims' of a particular class. He produced, rather, a theory of the class character of consciousness, i.e., of the limits of its intellectual horizon which reflect or reproduce the limits to communication imposed by the division of society into classes.[58]

---

58   Balibar 2017, p.48.

The theoretical turning point of this operation is what Balibar calls the notion of 'intellectual difference' introduced by Marx, or the exposition of 'the division between manual and mental labour'.[59] For Balibar, this concept of intellectual difference is a theoretically anti-humanist one, as it 'changes the theory of consciousness, wresting it away from any kind of psychology ... and making it a question of political anthropology'.[60]

The consequences of this move are read by Balibar in the concept of commodity fetishism. In trying to capture the phenomenon in which complex social relations are reflected in the appearance of particular commodities – such as money or labour-power – Balibar argues that, in opposition to the more Feuerbachian notion of alienation, 'fetishism is not a subjective phenomenon or a false perception of reality, as an optical illusion or a superstitious belief would be. It constitutes, rather, the way in which reality (a certain form or social structure) cannot but appear'.[61] The theoretical anti-humanism inherent in this conceptual shift therefore contributes towards the collapse of the distinction between intellectual and manual labour: that is, between the representation of the world in the 'consciousness' of the subject and its representation in objective reality. 'Fetishism' in this way does not describe the 'false class consciousness' of the working class within a capitalist social formation (which they must only 'see through' in order to make revolution), but rather indicates what Althusser calls 'ideology', that is, 'individuals' imaginary relation to their real conditions of existence'.[62]

The philosophical importance of this theoretically anti-humanist concept within Marx's political economy is precisely its collapse of the distinction between subjectivity and objectivity. As Balibar writes, 'by rethinking the constitution of social objectivity, Marx at the same time virtually revolutionized the concept of the "subject."'[63] The concept of fetishism demonstrates the immanent nature of the relationship between the subjective and the objective, as it 'does not depend on the prior givenness of a subject, a consciousness or a reason' but shows that subjects are 'a part of objectivity itself or which are, in other words, given in experience alongside "*things*," alongside commodities, and *in a relation to them*'.[64] In this way, Marx demonstrates that 'the constitution of the world is not, for him, the work of a subject, but a genesis of subjectiv-

---

59   Balibar 2017, p.49.
60   Ibid.
61   Balibar 2017, p.60.
62   Althusser 2014a, p.181.
63   Balibar 2017, p.65.
64   Balibar 2017, p.67.

ity (*a* form of determinate historical subjectivity) as part (and counterpart) of the social world of objectivity'.[65]

In order to think through the consequences of this theoretically antihumanist shift in Marx's political economy, Balibar takes a detour through Spinoza. Balibar reads in Spinoza the consequences of a political anthropology located in the shift away from the psychological individual and its existence *a priori*, towards a notion of political subjectivity that is co-constituted and produced within the limits of a social conjuncture. Balibar reads the theory of ideology and intellectual difference contained in Marx's concept of fetishism in Spinoza's conceptualisation of 'socialisation' and his collapse of the traditional political scientific distinction between the individual and the state. As Balibar indicates:

> Our 'fellow man' … does not exist as such naturally, in the sense of a being who is simply there, who is given. Rather, he is constituted by a process of imaginary identification, which Spinoza calls the 'imitation of the affects'. This process is at work both in mutual recognition between individuals and in the formation of the 'multitude' as an unstable aggregate of individual passions.[66]

According to Spinoza, such a situation cannot exist without social institutions capable of its maintenance and reproduction. Just as Althusser demonstrated how the existence of ideology necessarily suggested the existence of the state, in Balibar's reading of Spinoza, 'there must be an authority which can polarise the affects of individuals and direct their movements of love and hatred by defining once and for all the common meaning of good and evil, right and wrong'.[67] This authority is, of course, the state. However, Balibar argues that Spinoza's conception of the state is not realised in its separation from individuals: rather, just as the worker and the fetishized representation of its relation to society are absolutely immanent to one another, so too is the individual and the representation of its relation to society within the state itself. In this way, 'we cannot say that the State is "against nature" … Society and State constitute a single relationship, at once imaginary and rational, through which the natural singularity of human individuals is expressed'.[68]

---

65   Ibid.
66   Balibar 2008, p.87.
67   Balibar 2008, p.88.
68   Ibid.

In much of the post-Althusserian literature, it is through this Spinozist detour that the legacy of Althusser's critique of theoretical humanism has continued. Warren Montag argues that Spinoza's 'refusal to set the human apart from nature, mind from body, thought from action thus makes him perhaps the most thoroughgoing anti-humanist in the history of philosophy'.[69] Montag reads in Spinoza's political philosophy the elements of a materialist politics, founded in a break with existing political anthropologies. 'Freedom' and 'liberty' do not stem from the mastery of the human individual over the property of their own body; rather, freedom can only be understood as something conferred upon the body in its relation to other bodies, both human and non-human, with the *social relation* between these bodies the material basis for freedom itself. As Montag writes,

> Spinoza demands the liberation not simply of minds ... not simply the liberation of an individual who is the owner of himself and his rights, but the liberation of the collectivity outside of which the individual has no existence and apart from which the freedom of the individual is inconceivable.[70]

For Montag, this represents 'an extraordinary example of Spinoza's philosophical anti-humanism'.[71] Spinoza here troubles and decentralises the human subject from the centre of political theory as the subject of the law, replacing it instead with 'the multitude' as the assemblage of social relations between subjects and each other, but also between subjects and the objective world around them, collapsing again the distinction between the subjective and objective integral to Marx's own philosophical method. In this way, a materialist theory of politics is produced in Spinoza, in which 'right, far from belonging to a human world of freedom, outside of and beyond the necessity that governs the natural world, becomes coextensive with that very necessity, outside of which nothing exists'.[72]

Pierre Macherey follows Spinoza's anti-humanism philosophically, observing it in the break with Hegel and the Hegelian conception of the 'absolute as subject'. 'What is an individual?' asks Macherey, in his reading of Spinoza: 'A "union of bodies," that is, a certain assemblage of elements of the same nature

---

69 Montag 1999, p.xvii.
70 Montag 1999, p.63.
71 Montag 1999, p.64.
72 Ibid.

that agree among themselves, not only in terms of their essence ... but in terms of their existence'.[73] Here, Spinoza exposes and dispenses with the 'astonishing collusion with classical reason'[74] at the heart of the idealist Hegelian dialectic of subjectivity, instead forwarding the material thesis that 'the unity that constitutes an individual is nothing eternal, but it depends upon the conditions that make and unmake it'.[75] Macherey continues:

> The individual, or the subject, thus does not exist by himself in the irreducible simplicity of a unique and eternal being, but it is composed in the encounter of singular beings, who agree conjuncturally within him in terms of their existence, that is, who coexist there but without this agreement presupposing a privileged relationship, the unity of an internal order at the level of their essences, which subsist identically, as they were themselves before being thus assembled and without in so being in any way affected.[76]

Here, the human subject as a singular essence, disappears, and is replaced instead by a notion of the individual that is irreducible to subjects whose encounter reflects the very appearance of this individual. On the contrary, the individual 'explains itself relatively through a mechanical and transitive sequence, in a series of interminable constraints'.[77]

Jason Read has updated this Spinozist anti-humanism in thinking through the concept of 'transindividuality' as the anchor of Balibar's political anthropology, produced through Balibar's own Spinozist detour. Read finds the concept of transindividuality located in Spinoza's anti-humanist critique of God, in the:

> Critique of the idea of an anthropomorphic god, a god that acts as humans do, towards particular ends, demonstrating how ultimately it stems from an inadequate anthropocentric understanding of the universe, the assumption that whatever exists does so for our needs.[78]

Read demonstrates here the foundations of a critique of humanist ideology in Spinoza's thought where, much as ideas of human 'consciousness' or 'reason'

---

73   Macherey 2011, p.175.
74   Macherey 2011, p.169.
75   Macherey 2011, p.176.
76   Ibid.
77   Macherey 2011, p.183.
78   Read 2016, p.20.

have already been shown to do, the idea of God steps in to represent to the individual a mystification of the real conditions of their existence. As Read writes:

> The entirety of the world is viewed in terms of its relation to final causes, to human purposes. The individual who believes him or herself to be free constitutes a world, a world seen as made up of objects that advance or hinder our desires, and are seen as intrinsically good or bad. This judgement comes prior to our understanding. God enters the picture as a supplement to this limited grasp of the world: when nature helps or limits my intentions, it appears as if I am the beneficiary or intention of some other intention, some divine intervention.[79]

Spinoza's innovation is to rethink the nature of the individual within this narrative, not as a subject that exists independently of the relations that make the world what it is (between which God enters as the mediator), but rather as a *produced* (or as Althusser would say, *interpellated*) subject called forth by these very relations. In order to think this through, Spinoza relies on the concept of 'desire' as the interpellating force of subjectivity. As demonstrated by Read, the focus on desire by Spinoza displaces the human subject in favour of an analysis of the ever-transforming relations that constitute the desiring-subject: 'Desire is by definition intransitive, without a specified object that its objects are formed by history'.[80] Spinoza thinks this through with the help of another concept, that of 'affects', which describes the various modalities in which desire manifests itself as it interpellates the subject into being. As Read continues, 'the ideas of love and hate begin to constitute objects, objects that are defined not by any of their intrinsic qualities (they are good or bad), but by their relations'.[81] The importance of these relations give rise to the fact that 'there is thus an irreducible historical dimension to the affects',[82] meaning that the source of the desiring-subject is not any essential characteristic, but rather these historically determined relations. In this way, Spinoza critiques 'the idea of a subject, understood as a universal capacity for will and knowledge', de-centralising the subject and replacing it with 'the conatus which does not exist outside of its particular determinations, its particular striving. There is no will in general, just specific acts of willing'.[83]

---

79 Read 2016, p.21.
80 Read 2016, p.28.
81 Ibid.
82 Ibid.
83 Read 2016, p.29.

For Read this forms the basis of transindividuality as a theoretically antihumanist concept. Through this demonstration of the relation of the affects and the interpellation of subjectivity that is produced by this relation, Spinoza demonstrates that the individual can no longer be interpreted as an isolated, independent entity, but must instead be viewed only as the product of an encounter between historical relations. Spinoza shows that 'it is through the affects that we can see that the individual, both the individual person and object, cannot be separated from relations with others, nor can the collective, nation, or class, be thought of as anything other than a particular relation of strivings'.[84]

In these ways, Althusser's critique of theoretical humanism has been reconstructed in the detour through Spinoza. This detour answers the critique often levelled at Althusser, that in making subjectivity the product of an interpellation of social relations, there is no space to account for why the subject acts in the ways that it does, a gap that poses a threat to the ability to formulate an understanding of revolution. Through Spinoza and through the antihumanism offered by his political thought, it is possible to reconstruct this Althusserian theory whilst at the same time creating the space to think about subjectivity and how it acts with greater clarity, without essentialising or centralising that subject in a way that displaces the importance of material social relations.

4   Anti-humanism after Althusser: The Hegelian/Lacanian Detour

Though he cannot be said to belong exclusively to this tradition in complete opposition to that of those in the Spinozist school, Michel Pêcheux introduces the question of psychoanalysis to the Althusserian theory of ideology, through Freud, Lacan and the problem of the unconscious. The question posed by Pêcheux, in response to Althusser's theory of interpellation, is the following one:

> If it is true that ideology 'recruits' subjects from amongst individuals (in the way soldiers are recruited from amongst civilians) and that it recruits them *all*, we need to know how 'volunteers' are designated in this recruitment, i.e., in what concerns us, how all individuals *accept as evident* the meaning of what they hear and say, read and write (of what they *intend* to say and of what it is *intended* be said to them) as 'speaking subjects'.[85]

---

84   Read 2016, p.31.
85   Pêcheux 1982, pp.108–9.

For Pêcheux, Althusser's theory of ideology and of interpellation is important because it offers a theoretically anti-humanist answer to this question. It is clear for Pêcheux that the answer to this question is not to be found in human psychology, or in 'a certain notion of "man" as anti-nature, transcendence, subject of history, negation of the negation'.[86] Rather, the theory of interpellation allows for the observation of what Pêcheux calls the 'theatre of consciousness', providing a vantage point from which to observe this theatre 'from behind the scenes, from the place where one can grasp the fact that the subject is spoken *of*, the subject is spoken *to*, before the subject can say: "I speak"'.[87] What can be observed behind the scenes, of course, is what Marx called the 'social relation', the relations of production in capitalist society.

However, for Pêcheux the Althusserian theory of interpellation is incomplete and to some extent dilutes the complexity of this relationship between the social relation and the ideological interpellation of the subject as an individual. For whilst it offers some clarity on how subjective behaviour is structured socially, it does not shed light on what Pêcheux calls the 'strange familiarity' of ideology recognised by the subject: in other words, the compulsion of the subject to act as if those social relations, so represented to their consciousness in ideology, are in fact 'natural' or 'correct'. Pêcheux finds the explanation that 'the reproduction of the relations of production needs no explanation because they "go of their own accord" *so long as they are left alone*'[88] to be limited, but also not adequately addressed in Althusser's theory of interpellation. For Pêcheux, a theoretical paradox is created here between the notion of interpellation as producing a subject, with its motor the simple determinism of the relations of production: a theoretical paradox he describes in terms of the *Münchhausen Effect*, 'in memory of the immortal baron who *lifted himself into the air by pulling on his own hair*.'[89] In other words, though the theoretical anti-humanism of the theory of interpellation certainly removes the human subject from the centre of enquiry, without producing specific knowledge of the social relation and how it is reproduced, all that remains is a paradoxical situation in which subjects with no historical point of origin nonetheless appear to make themselves 'go'. The answer to this paradox, for Pêcheux, lies in the introduction of psychoanalysis.

In order to draw this out, Pêcheux operationalises psychoanalytic concepts in order to bring forward a contradiction within the process of ideological

---

86   Pêcheux 1982, p.103.
87   Pêcheux 1982, p.106.
88   Pêcheux 1982, p.101.
89   Pêcheux 1982, p.109.

interpellation between, on the one hand, the position of the subject as always-already interpellated (because there are no subjects without ideology, nor ideology without subjects), but on the other, the existence of an 'identifiable, responsible subject, answerable for his actions',[90] the 'volunteer' of the analogy posed by Pêcheux at the beginning of this section. Pêcheux proposes a theoretically anti-humanist analysis of this contradiction, through the Freudian concept of the 'unconscious', and its Lacanian reading through the concepts of the 'signifier' and the 'signified'. In doing so, Pêcheux dispenses with a humanist thesis which argues that the power of ideology should simply be sought in the power or persuasiveness of *language* (liberation requires only that revolutionaries choose the correct *words* to convince the workers of their subjugation and therefore make them *conscious* of their condition), instead arguing that the problem which is at the core of this contradiction is that described by Lacan as the signifier, that which '*represents the subject for another signifier*'.[91] Privileging this Lacanian problematic:

> Treats of *the subject as process (of representation) inside the non-subject constituted by the network of signifiers, in Lacan's sense: the subject is 'caught' in this network* – 'common nouns' and 'proper names', 'shifting' effects, syntactic constructions, etc. – *such that he results as 'cause of himself'*, in Spinoza's sense of the phrase.[92]

More so than any original or essential ability to consent that exists within the concrete individual, the ability of the subject to 'volunteer' in the face of ideologies that appear already familiar resides in this problem of the shifting network of signifiers, underpinned by the social relations of production, but not necessarily reducible to them in a simple determinism.

In Pêcheux's reading of Althusser, Natalia Romé finds an important moment for an Althusserian politics, 'as that contradictory place that exceeds the symbolic alienation of the subject'.[93] In order to explain the problem of the 'volunteer' which Pêcheux poses, Romé places this problematic in conversation with the theory of *action* at the heart of Althusser's understanding of reproduction and ideology. As Romé writes, 'Pêcheux's reading of interpellation shows that Althusserian theory thinks of the problem of the Real as a mismatch – that

---

90   Pêcheux 1982, p.107.
91   Pêcheux 1982, p.108.
92   Ibid.
93   Romé 2021, p.34.

is, as an affective "remainder" that is not "substance" but *activity*.[94] For Romé, this insight emerges from Pêcheux's holding-together of this Lacanian problem of the unconscious and the network of signifiers, with Althusser's Spinozist structuralism at the heart of his theory of ideology. Pêcheux privileges Spinoza insofar as:

> His practical method of reading allows us to think of the historical condition of discursive transformation (that is, the material existence of an ideology) in the form of a unity in division, a unity that is only realized as a struggle of opposites that sustains the claim to the true in the form of the contradictory.[95]

In other words, this contradiction between the always-already interpellated subject and the subject who is answerable for their actions, is the motor of what Romé describes as a 'materiality of the imaginary', which is theoretically antihumanist insofar as it privileges the network of signifiers over language, but also the active social relations of class struggle over the action of the concrete individual, 'the primacy of unconsciousness over conscience and the primacy of contradiction over contraries'.[96]

Slavoj Žižek, has followed this psychoanalytic detour most fully in reconstructing (though eventually displacing) the Althusserian problematic. However, whilst Pêcheux attempts to hold Lacan and Spinoza together, Žižek's work replaces Spinoza with Hegel. Echoing Pêcheux's original problematic (that of producing a more specific knowledge of what is the 'social relation'), Žižek finds the essence of this problem within the Spinozist tradition itself. In a critique of the idea of 'transindividuality' central to the Spinozist thinkers discussed above, Žižek finds fault with the formulation which describes the social relation as one in which 'I am bound to this other who is bound to me, and that my life is bound up with the other's life'.[97] For Žižek, this misses the essential point: 'Yes, I am bound to the other who is bound to me, but it is only *through* destroying/dominating that mutual recognition emerges: we arrive at mutual solidarity only through acting as solitary and suffering consequences'.[98] For Žižek, there is something missing in the simple displacement of the human subject in favour of the centralisation of social relations, something which fails

---

94   Ibid.
95   Romé 2021, p.41.
96   Romé 2021, p.45.
97   Žižek 2022, p.23.
98   Ibid.

to demonstrate that which theoretical anti-humanism sought to bring to light: namely, why the subject acts *as if* it were a solitary individual, even (and often) with the knowledge that this solitary condition is not true or real. In this way, as Žižek argues:

> Lacanian psychoanalysis goes a decisive step further than the usual 'post-Marxist' anti-essentialism affirming the irreducible plurality of particular struggles – in other words, demonstrating how their articulation into a series of equivalences depends always on the radical contingency of the social-historical process: it enables us to grasp this plurality itself as a multitude of responses to the same impossible-real kernel.[99]

The dialectic of subjectivity introduced by Hegel is important to Žižek, but in order to maintain the materialism granted by a theoretically anti-humanist critique, Žižek argues that this dialectic must be held together with the conceptual repertoire offered by Lacanian psychoanalysis: 'To reactualize Hegelian dialectics by giving it a new reading on the basis of Lacanian psychoanalysis'.[100]

Žižek works through this problematic most fervently – and in close dialogue with Althusser – in his text *The Sublime Object of Ideology*. Much like Balibar, Žižek's critique of ideology begins with Marx's concept of commodity fetishism. In contrast to Balibar, Žižek stresses the importance of *form* and argues that what must take priority in this investigation is not necessarily the character of social relations themselves, but the particular form in which they are represented to the subjects of those relations. According to Žižek, the true anti-humanist manoeuvre contained within Marx's notion of commodity fetishism is not the simple displacement of the human subject from the centre of enquiry and the exposure of its position in relation to a world of objective things, but rather the revelation of a particular form of subjective 'work' which takes place independently of the 'reason' or 'consciousness' of this subject, which gives this commodity its very form. As Žižek explains,

> During the act of exchange, individuals proceed *as if* the commodity is not submitted to physical, material exchanges; *as if* it is excluded from the natural cycle of generation and corruption; although on the level of their 'consciousness' they 'know very well' that this is not the case.[101]

---

99 Žižek 2008, p.xxvii.
100 Žižek 2008, p.xxx.
101 Žižek 2008, p.12.

The material reality of social relations, and the effects of the ideology that is produced by these relations, is therefore, for Žižek, located in this gap between what the subject knows and how the subject behaves. What Marx demonstrates, according to Žižek, is that the social relations that are reflected in the form of money as a fetishized commodity, are observable *precisely* in this gap, in this subjective 'misrecognition', where 'individuals proceed as "practical solipsists", they misrecognize the socio-synthetic function of exchange: that is, the level of the "real abstraction" as the form of socialization of private production through the medium of the market'.[102] Here, what the subject overlooks is not the 'reality' of the situation (the humanist theory of 'false consciousness') but, necessarily, the illusion itself, the very form of the fetish:

> Individuals know very well that there are relations between people behind the relations between things. The problem is that in their social activity itself, in what they are *doing*, they are *acting* as if money, in its material reality, is the immediate embodiment of wealth as such.[103]

According to Žižek, it is in this illusion, in this symbolic order itself, that the material reality of social relations and the way that these relations arrange individual subjects, are truly visible.

For Žižek, this is the truth brought to light by Althusser's theoretical anti-humanism and his theory of ideology. The essence of this operation is not to remove the subject from the scene entirely in favour of a simple replacement of this subject with social relations, but to centralise the symbolic order which interpellates this subject into being, acknowledging the primacy of the relations that reflect this symbolic order but nonetheless acknowledging that this interpellation is not seamless, with the gap producing its own subjective effects. In this way, 'this "internalization", by structural necessity, never fully succeeds, that there is always a residue, a leftover, a stain of traumatic irrationality and senselessness sticking to it'.[104] This gap, and the acknowledgement of this gap, is the true theoretically anti-humanist operation, as it denies the notion that ideology is 'a dreamlike illusion that we build to escape insupportable reality', but instead is 'an "illusion" which structures our effective, real social relations and therefore masks some insupportable, real, impossible kernel'.[105]

---

102   Žižek 2008, p.14.
103   Žižek 2008, p.28.
104   Žižek 2008, p.43.
105   Žižek 2008, p.45.

Psychoanalysis is the theoretical ingredient that facilitates this reading of Marx and brings out the reality of ideology in this way. Lacanian psychoanalysis, according to Žižek affords the theoretical opportunity to acknowledge the importance of social relations without forfeiting the analysis of the subject, revealing how 'the most intimate beliefs, even the most intimate emotions such as compassion, crying, sorrow, laughter, can be transferred, delegated to others without losing their sincerity'.[106] The innovation of Althusser's theory of ideology and the true theoretical implications of its anti-humanism, are grasped best when read in conjunction not with Marx, but with Freud. The Marxian reading alone tends towards the production of a vulgar materialism, according to Žižek, where social relations are afforded a positive theoretical value without the very material force that gives these relations their reality – that is, the way in which they are symbolically represented and 'acted out' by the interpellated subject – goes unthought. As Žižek argues, 'in Marxism, a fetish conceals the positive network of social relations, whereas in Freud a fetish conceals the lack around which the symbolic network is articulated'.[107]

Whilst Pêcheux attempts to remain loyal to the Althusserian problematic, Žižek looks to break with it in some way due to its inadequacy. However, Romé, in her discussion of the encounter between Pêcheux and Žižek argues that this break is mistaken. 'The level at which the fundamental disagreement between Althusser and Žižek is produced is not that which Žižek assumes',[108] argues Romé. Whilst Žižek offers Lacan as a replacement for Althusser in the construction of his theory of ideology, Romé argues that the true point of divergence lies not here (a difference 'which seems to be minor in the context of the remarkable closeness of the developments of Žižek to those of Althusser'[109]), but rather 'is rooted in a considerable ontological divergence, which could be synthesized in the Hegel/Spinoza controversy'.[110]

With respect to Althusser's theoretical anti-humanism, Agon Hamza has suggested that this ontological divergence is not as severe as it is often made out to be. Hamza forwards a thesis which recognises the anti-Hegelian intent of Althusser's anti-humanism but argues that there is a particular fidelity to Hegel's philosophy that remains at the core of this operation. Hamza focuses specifically on Althusser's anti-humanist theory of history, as a 'process without a subject', arguing that 'his thesis on the process without a subject, which is

---

106   Žižek 2008, p.32.
107   Žižek 2008, p.50.
108   Romé 2021, p.34.
109   Ibid.
110   Romé 2021, pp.34–5.

intended to elaborate an anti-Hegelian position, comes as close as possible to the Hegelian conception of the subject *qua* substance'.[111] For Hamza, what Althusser elaborates with his theory of history as a process without a subject is, essentially, the Hegelian Subject, which exists in a necessarily dialectical relationship with Substance. The Hegelian Subject is, according to Hamza, not a subject which controls or directs historical progress: rather, the Substance of history is 'only a retroactive presupposition of the Subject', where the Subject 'presupposes the Substance ... as a split, a cut'.[112] Contrary to the Spinozist interpretation, Hamza argues that this Hegelian notion of the Subject offers Althusser that which Spinoza never could: namely an ontology, 'a theory of subjectivity' which 'allows us to ask, like Hegel before – "but what are the conditions of possibility for ideological interpellation?"'[113]

For Hamza, this is most evident in Althusser's thinking about revolution. As Hamza explains, 'for Althusser there is no revolutionary subject, but only agents of the revolution' which means that 'the proletariat can be read from the perspective of the Hegelian thesis'.[114] This is because the proletariat is not a historical subject which brings the revolution into being or 'realises' revolution at the end of its own historical development. Rather, revolution, as historical substance, occurs retroactively in the proletariat's very becoming-as-Subject. Contrary to the humanist reading (Hamza cites Lukács here), the revolution does not emerge from the proletariat as an existing subject: rather, both the revolution as historical Substance and the proletariat as Subject emerge immanent to one another, in a dialectical relationship. The condition for this dialectical becoming is, according to Hamza, the very *non-being* of the proletariat as Subject to begin with: 'We need to bear in mind that the very fact that the proletariat *lacks being* (there is no subject) is what makes it capable of *being the agent of its own coming to be*'.[115] Hamza's argument here is that it is precisely the fact that the proletariat does not exist as a subject *a priori* which gives it the character of a Subject in the Hegelian sense, as a force or a process which retroactively gives Substance to the historical situation: 'The passage from non-being to being, through a historical process, is indeed very much Hegel's subject'.[116] Finally, for Hamza, it is this idea of Subject as a process which remains in Althusser's thinking here, particularly in his anti-humanist view of his-

---

111 Hamza 2016, p.50.
112 Ibid.
113 Hamza 2016, p.51.
114 Ibid.
115 Ibid.
116 Ibid.

tory, and survives the declared Spinozism and anti-Hegelianism that Althusser claimed to offer: '"Process without a subject", as an anti-Hegelian/teleological thesis/conception of history ... gains its complete meaning *only* if it is posited, and read, from the Hegelian Substance-Subject'.[117]

Whilst distinct, both the Spinozist and the Hegelian/Lacanian detour have attempted to think about why subjects do the things that they do in the context of Althusser's theoretically anti-humanist intervention. In recent years, this question has become increasingly pertinent for the analysis of work within advanced capitalist societies. Theoretical anti-humanism has been developed with increasing frequency alongside questions of work and employment, as these interlocutors and their contemporaries attempt to grapple with the question of why workers continue to work in the face of its myriad sociological, economic and political problems.

5   A Sociological Detour: Anti-humanism and Work

There are a number of examples within the writings of Althusser where work and labour present themselves as specific problems for theory. The most compelling and well-developed of these examples is the critique of the concept of labour and of 'social labour' undertaken by Althusser in his text *The Humanist Controversy*. Here, Althusser problematises the concept of 'labour' and the assumption of its centrality within Marx's critique of political economy, arguing that this critique depended absolutely on an explosion of this concept into several different concepts: 'concrete' and 'abstract labour', 'labour-power', the 'labour-process', among others. Althusser argues that the theoretical operationality of this explosion is set in motion by Marx's theoretical anti-humanism and in the movement away from a simple concept of 'labour' presumed by the classical political economists as the simple interchange between human beings and nature, in favour of a number of alternative concepts that seek to describe labour as a complex articulation of different social relations. The book will develop and apply this critique in much greater detail across the next two chapters.

The space here will be used to look closer at another dealing with work as a problem, which adopts a slightly more sociological register within Althusser's writings. Through the example of work, Althusser demonstrates the extent to which humanism is an ideological weapon wielded by the dominant class to

---

117   Hamza 2016, p.52.

facilitate the exploitation of workers. In the opening chapters of *On the Reproduction of Capitalism*, Althusser describes the landscape of work with which he is faced at the time: one emblematic of the post-Fordist shift to 'white-collar' work, expressed in a peculiar and more detailed division of labour of 'workers and diversely qualified technicians on the one hand and, on the other, the whole hierarchy of managers, administrators, engineers, upper-level technicians, supervisors, and so on'.[118] Signified by this contemporary landscape of work is, for Althusser, a very peculiar set of *class relations*: the division of labour inherent to the post-Fordist workplace signified a *social division of labour*, stratified along class lines. As Althusser wrote, 'the division [of society] into social classes is thus present in the division, organization and management of the process of production, *by virtue of the distribution of posts on the basis of the class affiliation* of the individuals who hold them'.[119] In this instance, work is a useful area of study precisely because it holds clues as to the composition of class antagonism in wider society: and it is precisely, therefore, through the primacy of class struggle (and the social relations of work that are reflected this struggle) that work itself is to be understood at all.

Crucially, Althusser identifies humanism as a vital ideological tool in the maintenance and mystification of this class division at work. Humanism emerges as an ideological tool of class domination at work because it presents this division of labour to the consciousness of the worker, not as the result of a socially reproduced class antagonism, but as the 'natural' outcome of specific differences between individuals. Althusser exposes the existence of an 'economistic-humanist'[120] ideology of work – reproduced by 'an "ultramodern" staff trained in the pseudo-scientific techniques of "human-resources" [and] "social psychology"'[121] – which mystifies the class character of this division of labour by asserting that it is a division of labour stratified not along lines of class, but along lines of education, technical know-how, skill and work-ethic. Humanism is not used to invisibilise the division of labour (for this division is in no way denied), but humanism allows for this division to be *represented* in a mythical form, expressed not as the direct result of class positioning in capitalist society, but as an expression of the differing capabilities and personalities of individual workers, that *anyone* can traverse providing they have the right attitude. As Althusser writes:

---

118 Althusser 2014a, p.35.
119 Althusser 2014a, p.37.
120 Althusser 2014a, p.36.
121 Althusser 2014a, p.39.

> As for the worker who becomes an engineer or even a manager, he is, in our society, a museum piece exhibited to encourage belief in the 'possibility' of the impossible and the idea that there are no social classes or that someone born a worker can 'rise above his class'. Plain, unvarnished reality cries out against these disgraceful exhibitions.[122]

According to Althusser, this ideological operation, rooted firmly in humanism, is an integral part of the social mechanics of capitalist exploitation that exists in the workplace at the point of production. The mystification in this way of the social relations of work and of the class character of these relations is an important ideological precondition for the justification of exploitation and all its related exercises: the interpellation, motivation, reward and repression of workers on the production line. Exploitation at work does not, for Althusser, *simply* operate through the ownership of the means of production, or the appropriation of surplus-value, but 'also "works" thanks to *the bourgeois ideology of work*. The workers are the first to be subjected to its effects because it is an ideology of the capitalist class struggle'.[123]

Frédéric Lordon has developed this sociological detour most forcefully and specifically in relation to the problem of work. Belonging to the Spinozist tradition of anti-humanism outlined above, Lordon opens a space for sociology to act as the vehicle through which to develop a Spinozist anthropology that does not centre the human subject simply as a concrete individual, nor social relations as the simple interaction between these individuals. As Lordon writes:

> Sociology, however, takes a very different view of 'society'. On the one hand, it asserts that the cohesive principle underpinning societies is to be understood independently of the external influence of the state, but, above all, it asserts that there is much more to human collectivities than the effects of voluntary associations and that bonds arise elsewhere than from carefully-thought-through 'engagements'.[124]

There is a surplus to society that is the object of sociological study, with the introduction of Spinoza demonstrating the fact that this surplus is not simply the sum of the parts of that society (the addition of human individuals together) but something more complex. As Lordon continues,

---

122 Althusser 2014a, p.37.
123 Althusser 2014a, p.42.
124 Lordon 2022, p.36.

> The group affects itself, and in a way that exceeds the actions of each of its members, giving rise *from* them but also *above* them to something that transcends all of them. To this production of the social, Spinoza gives a name: the power of the multitude.[125]

The central question, for Lordon, is then that which asks how this surplus figures within structures of domination and interpellation, how it is that subjects can either be *made* to do certain things, or *act as if* certain conditions were natural or rational. For this, Lordon turns to the topic of work.

For Lordon, the sociology of work is useful insofar as it has attempted to provide an insight into these questions of domination and interpellation, even if its attempts to do so have been flawed in many ways. As Lordon writes, 'the sociology of work did set out to peek behind the gleaming façade of the idea of consent and expose its shortcomings, but without always asking what should be the first question: what exactly does consent mean?'[126] From an anti-humanist position, the answer to this question cannot be one rooted in a moment of human alienation, in which the human subject is in some way detached from their ability to make the decision to consent to authority. This would assume that the decision to work is a decision already made in some way and that human beings, removed of this alienating force, would 'naturally' choose not to work. Lordon troubles this picture, demonstrating that some 'employees go to work to avoid starving ... some spend all their waking hours working, and appear satisfied; others enthusiastically join in the running of the company; then, one day, they rebel (or throw themselves out of a window)'.[127] In other words, the system of relations that is observable in the phenomenon of work is too complex to be reduced down to a question of human psychology or the decision-making of the concrete individual. It is therefore necessary to develop an approach to the sociology of work that can adequately account for this.

For Lordon, the starting-point is 'desire': not as a simple individual psychological phenomenon, but in its Spinozist definition, as the particular configuration of passions and affects within a given social structure. This starting-point allows Lordon to overturn longstanding approaches within popular sociologies of work regarding the 'enjoyment' of work, arguing that the essence of 'consent' cannot be sought in a humanist notion of whether the subject 'enjoys' the work

---

125 Lordon 2022, p.40.
126 Lordon 2014, p.xii.
127 Lordon 2014, p.xi.

that they do, but rather that enjoyment ought to be observed from a theoretically anti-humanist perspective, as a structure of affects which act upon the subject. As Lordon explains:

> Once the idea of joy is purged of all connotations of effervescence and enthusiasm, it is perfectly correct to say that securing the money that allows the satisfaction of the basal desire causes joy – but in the same way that escaping death by becoming a slave causes joy.[128]

For Lordon, this anti-humanist notion of desire, grounded in Spinoza, is the very thing which facilitates the Marxist critique of work. By observing enjoyment (and the 'consent' of the subject which is derived from this enjoyment) as the outcome of a structure of affects in this way then permits the question as to what, precisely, informs this structure. From here, the question of *social relations*, as posed by Marx, becomes available, as 'it is the social structures, in this case of employment, those of the capitalist relations of production, that configure desires and predetermine the strategies for attaining them'.[129]

It's from this theoretical point that important concepts within the Marxist critique of work become available for use. For example, the concept of alienation. Reformulated from here, the question of alienation and desire can no longer stand as one describing some form of essential human separation but must be informed by the relationship between ideology and the social relations of production: 'No doubt our force of desire, our power of acting, fully belongs to us. But it owes everything to the interpellations of things, namely, to external encounters, when the issue is knowing the path and the direction it takes'.[130] More than this, Lordon finds in the etymology of the word 'alienation' the key to an important connection between Spinoza and Marx:

> To the real etymology of alienation, which declares the presence of something other than the self (*alien, alius*) within self-direction, we can add an imaginary etymology, one which would rather hear in 'alienate' the word 'lien', tie, thus rediscovering in it the infinite chain of the production of effects within which we are both caused and causing. If, understood to be thus, to be alienated is to be chained, then far from applying only to exceptional attachments – and such that we are unable to say what is

---

128 Lordon 2014, p.29.
129 Lordon 2014, p.14.
130 Lordon 2014, p.57.

exceptional about them (apart from not wishing it for ourselves) – alienation is our most ordinary condition, and our most inexorable one.[131]

By reformulating the concept of alienation through Spinoza and Marx, it is possible to observe the point of domination at work in what Spinoza identified as the multitude and the necessarily transindividual nature of its structure, or what Marx more definitely called the social relation. It is these relations, not reducible to the relations between concrete individuals, that provide the appropriate window through which to observe work as a sociological phenomenon and how it is experienced by subjects under capitalism.

Theoretical anti-humanism is the crucial operation that secures the workability of these concepts and of the Marxist critique of work more generally. As Lordon concludes,

> Contemporary readings of the young Marx, keen on reviving his concept of alienation, while not necessarily falling into subjectivist apologetics almost inevitably return to schemas of loss and separation, and thus to imagining emancipation in the form of a *reunion*.[132]

This is a problem, because it misrecognises the location and character of power within a given social formation. 'There is nothing to regain that is not there already, for how could individuals lose or be separated from their power when that power is their very being?'[133] In this way, by reproducing a theoretical humanism, through schemas of enjoyment, alienation, loss and separation – narrowly defined – the sociology of work fails to overcome both the theoretical and political problems presented by humanism. Lordon, more so than other inheritors of this tradition, has appreciated the importance of this sociological detour, and in particular its focus on the topic of work, for the continuation of theoretical anti-humanism. More than this, Lordon demonstrates its workability and the power of this theoretical operation in opening up the very space for sociology to observe its object when it comes to the phenomenon of work: that surplus of the social formation, contained in the *social relation*.

---

131   Lordon 2014, p.58.
132   Lordon 2014, pp.142–3.
133   Lordon 2014, p.144.

6   Conclusion

This chapter has therefore set out several principles that will inform the direction of the enquiry made in the remainder of this book. Firstly, that the problem of humanism is both a theoretical and a political problem for Marxism, producing an obstacle to the knowledge of the social relations of capitalist social formations and, therefore, to the political strategies dedicated to overthrowing them. Secondly, the problem of the knowledge of the 'social relation' within Marxism ought to be reconstructed through theoretical detours, in which concepts from outside of the Marxist tradition are utilised in order to develop with greater clarity and precision that which Marx discovered in his use of this concept. Spinoza, Hegel, Freud and Lacan are just some of the guides along these necessary detours. Thirdly, sociology itself can be the site of such a detour. In particular, the sociology of work provides potentially useful theoretical ground on which the Marxist problematic of the 'social relation' can be reconstructed through the deployment of theoretical anti-humanism. At the same time as clarifying Marxist theory, the object of the sociology of work itself becomes clarified in this operation, as the social relations of work come to the forefront of enquiry as the productive consequence of this anti-humanism.

In the next chapter, the book begins to reconstruct the Marxist problem of the knowledge of the 'social relation', by examining Marx's interaction with the concept of 'labour' within his critique of political economy. In so doing, the chapter reveals how knowledge of social relations is produced by Marx through a theoretically anti-humanist transformation of the simple concept of labour, producing instead a complex picture of social relations and the ways in which they are (re)produced at the point of production within capitalist social formations. Work and labour under capitalism cannot be reduced simply to the relationship between bosses and workers as concrete individuals alone. Marx's anti-humanism reveals the ways in which these concrete subjects act only as *bearers* of a complex network of relations that cannot be reduced to the individual level, necessitating a theoretical system capable of making sense of this network, and a politics appropriate for its change.

CHAPTER 2

The Concept of 'Labour' in Marx's Critique of Political Economy

As a concept, 'labour' does not hold a consistent nor straightforward place within Marx's writings. Across the development of Marx's critique, the concept of labour changes position, at one time indicating the existence of an interchange between human beings and the natural world, and at another a complex social relation whose observation is contingent on its attachment to other relations. This chapter undertakes a reading of the critique of political economy constructed by Marx and Engels, in order to track the development of the concept of labour across these works and, crucially, *isolate and analyse the theoretically anti-humanist nature of this development*. The reading completed here will focus its attention on a number of key texts and passages from these works, often quoted (though, perhaps, misunderstood) within contemporary political sociologies of work: in part one, chapters 6 through 11 of *Capital Volume I*; in part two, the discussion of the division of labour in *The German Ideology* and passages from *The Communist Manifesto*; and in part three, the *Critique of the Gotha Programme* and chapter 48 of *Capital Volume III*. Through a reading of these sections together, this chapter will demonstrate how the concept of labour – and the theoretically anti-humanist transformation of this concept – allows for the production of a theory of work, politics and ideology in Marx's critique of political economy.

The concept of labour has always presented a particular problem when forwarding a reading of Marx's theoretical anti-humanism. 'Labour', as a concept, is one that carries a significant amount of ideological baggage, described even by Michel Foucault as one of the vital 'empricities'[1] of modern knowledge and as the source of political economy's anthropological dimension. It is for this reason that Althusser argues that 'the concept of *labour*, in the ambiguity that constantly tempts one to establish it as a basic concept of the theory of historical materialism, *is not a Marxist concept*'.[2] For Althusser, there is no theory of labour in Marx *per se*; what is important is the way in which Marx constructs a critique of this concept and lays the theoretical groundwork for a persistent

---

[1] Foucault 1970, p.250.
[2] Althusser 2003, p.289.

departure from this concept in its dominant understanding, with this departure producing, precisely, knowledge of the material reality which this concept was attempting to grasp. Given the anthropological nature of the concept of labour, this theoretical departure always (but not only) takes an anti-humanist form, and it is in isolating this theoretical process that this chapter is interested.

The reading here completed will take place in three parts. Firstly, the reading will construct a juxtaposition between the *Economic and Philosophic Manuscripts of 1844* and *Capital Volume I*, particularly those chapters which deal with the working-day, in order to demonstrate what Althusser calls an 'explosion'[3] of the concept of labour in Marx's writings. In so doing, this section analyses the theoretically anti-humanist nature of the explosion and multiplication of the concept of labour and its importance in producing Marx's analysis of work under capitalism. Secondly, the reading will focus on the development of the concept of labour within *The German Ideology* and through into *The Communist Manifesto*, demonstrating the production of what Étienne Balibar calls a 'politics of labour'[4] as part of a materialist theory of politics. Thirdly, the reading looks to the beginning of the *Critique of the Gotha Programme* where Marx produces a theory of ideology through the critique of the concept of labour, with this reading tracking the continuation of this theory *Capital Volume III*, in the chapter on 'The Trinity Formula' in which Marx introduces the notion of the 'realm of freedom'. Taking these readings together, this chapter evidences the relationship between the concept of labour, its theoretically anti-humanist transformation, and the development of theories of work, politics and ideology within Marx's critique of political economy.

1   **Marx Explodes the Concept of 'Labour'**

This reading of Marx's writings aims to demonstrate how, in the movement from his early works to those of his maturity, Marx explodes the simple concept of 'labour' into several other concepts. As Althusser writes, 'we cannot but admit that Marx's whole critique of classical Political Economy consisted in exploding the concept of *labour* accepted by the Economists, in order to suppress and replace it with new concepts'.[5] The explosion of the concept of labour takes the form of a break with an ideological system, which defines labour as a distinctly human process, evident in the interchange between the human sub-

---

3   Ibid.
4   Balibar 1994, p.141.
5   Althusser 2003, p.289.

ject and the objective world. It will be shown here that Marx explicitly breaks with this ideological system, and in so doing produces a whole new set of concepts, 'in which the *word* "labour" figures, to be sure, but always in conjunction with other words that confer a distinctive meaning upon the new concept'.[6]

The ideological baggage of the concept of 'labour' is evident in some of the earlier dealings with the concept found in the works of the Young Marx, in particular in the *Economic and Philosophic Manuscripts of 1844*. Labour was descriptive of the 'continuous interchange'[7] between Man and Nature, in which the human individual must necessarily engage in order that they could survive. Labour, this interchange, defined what Marx called the 'species-being'[8] of the human animal, that is the very quality that marked them as human from other animals. As Marx wrote:

> In creating a *world of objects* by his practical activity, in his *work upon* inorganic nature, man proves himself a conscious species-being, i.e., as a being that treats the species as its own essential being, or that treats itself as a species-being.[9]

Crucially, Marx argued that it was the ability to consciously engage in this labour that separated human beings from animals. Whereas animals only interacted with nature in order to secure the means of their immediate subsistence and reproduction, human labour differed because it could be engaged in spontaneously and *freely*: the animal 'produces only under the dominion of immediate physical need, whilst man produces even when he is free from physical need and only truly produces in freedom therefrom'.[10] Human society was therefore viewed by Marx as a product of this conscious activity, as the very objectification of this species-being.

Marx used this concept of labour as the pivot for his critique of capitalism. For Marx, capitalism was a process of production that depended inherently upon an interruption of this continuous interchange between humans and nature. Capitalism, so Marx argued, *alienated* the human worker from both the product and process of this activity, transforming its nature from one of universal human production into an activity productive of private wealth alone. Marx argued that capitalism depended fundamentally upon both an

---

6 Ibid.
7 Marx 1981, p.67.
8 Marx 1981, p.68.
9 Ibid.
10 Ibid.

interruption and, crucially, an alienation of labour as the continuous interchange between Man and nature, a fact that was mystified by discourses of political economy: 'Political economy conceals the estrangement inherent in the nature of labour by not considering the direct relationship between the worker (labour) and production'.[11] For Marx, this alienation of labour explained the inherent inequalities of production under capitalism:

> It is true that labour produces wonderful things for the rich – but for the worker it produces privation. It produces palaces – but for the worker, hovels. It produces beauty – but for the worker, deformity. It replaces labour by machines, but it throws one section of the workers back to a barbarous type of labour, and it turns the other section into a machine. It produces intelligence – but for the worker, stupidity, cretinism.[12]

For Marx all the elements of capitalist society – private property, the price of wages, profits and class divisions – stemmed from this initial alienation of the human species-being from the activity that defined its being: that is, its labour. Under capitalism, 'labour is *external* to the worker, i.e., it does not belong to his intrinsic nature; that in his work, therefore, he does not affirm himself but denies himself'.[13]

For Marx, the crime of capitalism was that in order to direct the labour of human beings towards the ends of accumulation, it must transform this process from one of social praxis, to one of alienated production. The problem of alienation under capitalism was thus twofold in relation to the human subject: firstly, the worker was alienated from labour as their essential species-activity (as that which allowed them to transcend nature); secondly, the social relations that were produced out of the process of labour under capitalism were thereby relations of alienation themselves (workers under capitalism *reproduced* their own alienation). For example, the primacy of alienated labour was used by Marx to explain the origins of private property as a social institution. If labour was a distinctively human process that was conducted both collectively and universally, then the establishment of private property required an interruption and enclosure of this process. Private property relied upon the alienation and enclosure of the products of what was, essentially, a universal process. Private property, that is, the privatisation of the products of labour, thus confronted the worker as an *external* or *alienated* product. Rather than intelligible

---

11   Marx 1981, p.65.
12   Ibid.
13   Ibid.

as products of the human world, generated through the dialectical process of labour with the natural world, private property was totally unintelligible as something belonging to the worker: 'Private property is thus the product, the result, the necessary consequence, of *alienated labour*, of the external relation of the worker to nature and to himself'.[14]

Alienated labour was also reflected in the proletarian's experience of work under capitalism. That which the worker came to understand as 'work' was essentially the systematic organisation of their alienation into a labour-process that produced wealth for the capitalist and misery for the worker. Marx pronounced exploitation through this discourse of alienation, locating its roots in the separation of the human subject from the object of their labour. For example, in describing work under capitalism, Marx wrote:

> This relation is the relation of the worker to his own activity as an alien activity not belonging to him; it is activity as suffering, strength as weakness, begetting as emasculating, the workers *own* physical and mental energy, his personal life – for what is life but activity? – as an activity which is turned against him, independent of him and not belonging to him.[15]

This tendency is reproduced right throughout this early set of manuscripts produced by Marx. Marx recognised that *something* was occurring under capitalism that was producing such profound inequalities. There was *something* which produced the appearance of the labouring masses in such beleaguered and beaten form. But precisely *what* produced this was still missing: that is, the precise social relations and the class struggle reflected in these relations, responsible for this mass exploitation. Every time Marx was faced with this *something*, he expressed it through this humanist prose, in discourses of alienation, problematising capitalism in the only way available to him: as a problem of the alienation of the human subject.

This 'something' would not be discovered by Marx until the critique of political economy that takes shape in his mature works. However, in looking at those mature works, it is evident how Marx's deliberations on the topic of work and labour have continued to be a vehicle for the persistence of theoretically humanist readings of Marx's critique. In *Capital Volume 1*, difficulties in this regard are encountered in chapter 7 on 'the Labour-Process and the Process of

---

14   Marx 1981, p.72.
15   Marx 1981, pp.66–7.

Producing Surplus-Value'. This chapter begins with a description of 'labour' that echoes its description in the *1844 Manuscripts*. Marx for example argues that 'labour is, in the first place, a process in which both man and Nature participate, and in which man *of his own accord* starts, regulates, and controls the material re-actions between himself and Nature'.[16] Marx continues, arguing that 'we presuppose labour in a form that stamps it as exclusively human ... what distinguishes the worst architect from the best of bees is this, that the architect raises his structure in imagination before he erects it in reality'.[17] Marx here sets up the concept of labour as turning in some way on the conscious and deliberate nature of this activity by human beings, as something of which they are intellectually aware and into which they enter of their own will. There are two conditions of labour as it is found under capitalism, described by Marx: 'First, the labourer works under the control of the capitalist to whom his labour belongs', and 'secondly, the product is the property of the capitalist and not that of the labourer, its immediate producer'.[18] So far, a similar explanation to that found in the *Manuscripts*.

However, a number of concepts begin to emerge which are not present in the *Manuscripts*, and which begin to trouble the centrality of this humanist concept of labour in Marx's analysis of the capitalist labour-process. The first are those of 'surplus-value', and 'labour-time'. With the story just told in mind, Marx explains to his reader that 'up to this point, we have only considered one aspect of the process' and that in order to move forward in the analysis of capitalism, the frame of this analysis must shift from the production of use-values alone: 'Let us now examine production as a creation of value'.[19] According to Marx, in order to explain how the labour-process under capitalism produces surplus-value, it is necessary to break with this humanist understanding of labour as the conscious and deliberate activity of human beings, towards a different concept, 'labour-time'. 'We have now to consider this labour under a very different aspect from that which it had during the labour-process' writes Marx, in which 'we viewed it solely as that particular kind of human activity which changes cotton into yarn'.[20] However, when examining how value is created, 'where we consider the labour of the spinner only so far as it is value-creating, i.e., a source of value, his labour differs in no respect from the labour of the man who bores cannon or ... from the labour of the cotton-planter and spindle-

---

16 Marx 2013, p.120, emphasis added.
17 Marx 2013, pp.120–1.
18 Marx 2013, p.126.
19 Marx 2013, p.127.
20 Marx 2013, p.129.

maker'.[21] In the analysis of value creation, 'we have nothing more to do with the quality, the nature and the specific character of the labour, but merely with its quantity',[22] that is, the quantity of labour-time embodied in a particular commodity.

Another concept here emerges, in order to further the analysis of the capitalist labour-process as one productive of value: 'labour-power'. In chapter 6, Marx describes labour-power as 'the aggregate of those mental and physical capabilities existing in a human being, which he exercises whenever he produces a use-value of any description'.[23] However, labour-power under capitalism cannot be fully analysed where it remains the simple expression of human faculties: it is, rather, the appearance of these faculties on the market to be bought and sold in definite quantities as a commodity. A crucial and theoretically anti-humanist move takes place here in order to describe this concept. The appearance of labour-power as a commodity to be bought and sold does not emanate from an alienation or separation of the human subject from its essential activity; nor is it the selling of human life itself on the marketplace. Rather, it is the sale of a definite quantity of labour-power, expressed in a definite quantity of labour-time:

> The continuance of this relation demands that the owner of the labour power should sell it only for a definite period, for if he were to sell it rump and stump, once for all, he would be selling himself, converting himself from a free man to a slave, from an owner of a commodity to a commodity.[24]

In order to describe work under capitalism, Marx demonstrates that it is inappropriate to think in moralistic or humanist terms, of work as being the 'selling of oneself' or one's 'life-activity' on the market. Labour-power is, quite simply, the sale of a definite quantity of labour-time in the form of a commodity.

Returning to chapter 7 on the labour-process, these two new concepts of labour-power and labour-time come together to help explain how value is produced within the labour-process. The products which emerge from this labour-process are not simple use-values, but commodities with a value which is reflective of the labour-power and labour-time embodied within the production of these commodities. As Marx explains, 'at the end of one hour's spinning,

---

21   Ibid.
22   Marx 2013, p.130.
23   Marx 2013, p.113.
24   Ibid.

that act is represented by a definite quantity of yarn; in other words, a definite quantity of labour, namely that of one hour, has become embodied in the cotton'.[25] Here, Marx further reminds his reader of the (theoretically antihumanist) nature of the shift in perspective here, away from a concept of labour as 'the labourer working' towards the reflection of labour-power and labour-time in 'the thing produced': in this way 'the special work of spinning counts here, only so far as it is the expenditure of labour power in general, and not in so far as it is the specific work of the spinner'.[26]

With this, 'not only the labour, but also the raw material and the product now appear in quite a new light, very different from that in which we viewed them in the labour-process pure and simple'.[27] Marx here makes a definite and theoretically anti-humanist movement in his analysis of the labour-process under capitalism. Marx argues that it is no longer appropriate to describe labour as the simple and observable act in which human beings engage, but that labour must instead be appreciated in its commodity-form, as labour-power, as the expression of a definite quantity of labour-time, if the production of value (and, as will be demonstrated, surplus-value) is to be in any way appreciated. As Marx explains, 'we are here no more concerned about the facts, that the labour is the specific work of spinning, that its subject is cotton and its product yarn, than we are about the fact that the subject itself is already a product and therefore raw material'.[28] Whether the specialist act of spinning, or that of mining coal, the product there produced would at all times 'represent a definite quantity of absorbed labour'.[29]

There is further to go here. In explaining how labour-power is productive of value, Marx argues that it is important to consider what he calls the 'two-fold character of labour'.[30] The two-fold nature of labour-power exists in the fact that it is, on the one hand, a concrete act crystallised in a particular activity (the act of spinning, coal-mining and so on, taken part in by human beings and productive of use-value) and on the other a general expenditure of labour-time (which, when reflected in a commodity, adds new value to this commodity). Other aspects of the labour-process – for example, the means of production, such as machines or tools used to do particular types of work – do not share this double-character. In the course of its lifetime, a machine will transfer the

---

25   Marx 2013, p.130.
26   Ibid.
27   Ibid.
28   Marx 2013, pp.130–1.
29   Marx 2013, p.131.
30   Marx 2013, p.139.

full amount of its value into the commodities it produces, without adding any additional value: 'Suppose a machine to be worth £1,000, and to wear out in 1,000 days. Then one thousandth of the value of the machine is daily transferred to the day's product'.[31] For this reason, Marx describes these means of production as 'fixed capital', because 'the means of production can never add more value to the product than they themselves possess independently of the process in which they assist'.[32] For labour-power, this is not the case:

> While the labourer, by virtue of his labour being of a specialised kind that has a special object, preserves and transfers to the product the value of the means of production, he at the same time, by the mere act of working, creates each instant an additional or new value.[33]

Unlike the means of production, labour-power has the ability to add more than the value that is embodied in its expenditure. A machine of £1,000 can transfer only £1,000 worth of value into a set of commodities across its lifetime; however, three shillings of labour-power, the value of which may correspond to six hours of labour-time, can be carried on for twelve hours and therefore add an additional three shillings of value into the commodity produced. 'This value is the surplus, of the total value of the product, over the proportion of its value, that is due to the means of production'.[34] It is by virtue of this special characteristic, to add a variable amount of additional value to the commodity, that Marx describes labour-power as 'variable capital'.

How is this additional value added, and where does it come from? To explain this, nowhere does the concept of 'alienation' appear as it did in the *1844 Manuscripts*. Rather, Marx here introduces a further three concepts on which we must rely in order to answer these questions: 'necessary labour', 'surplus labour' and 'the working-day'. First, 'the labourer, during one portion of the labour-process, produces only the value of his labour power, that is, the value of his means of subsistence'.[35] It is this portion of the labour-process where labour-power most closely corresponds in character to that of other means of production, transferring the total of its value following expenditure into the commodity it produces. Much as after a £1000 machine stops working, the £1000 transferred into the commodities it has produced, once sold, may then

---

31 Marx 2013, p.142.
32 Marx 2013, pp.142–3.
33 Marx 2013, pp.143–4.
34 Marx 2013, p.144.
35 Marx 2013, p.150.

be used to replace this machine, so too can three shillings of labour-power, once the commodity they have produced has been sold, be bought again the next day (often from the same supplier, which means that the price paid for this is necessarily equal to the cost of reproducing this supplier as a human labourer each day). It is for this reason that Marx describes this part of the labour-process as constituted by '*"necessary"* labour-time, and the labour expended during that time ... "*necessary*" labour'.[36] Second, and unlike fixed capital, the variable capital advanced in the form of labour-power has the ability to add additional value to a commodity over and above the value of its own reproduction. Here, 'the workman, it is true, labours, expends labour-power; but his labour, being no longer necessary labour, he creates no value for himself. He creates surplus-value'.[37] In order to distinguish this, Marx describes this using the concept 'surplus labour-time, and to the labour expended during that time ... the name of surplus-labour'.[38] Taken together, this combination of necessary and surplus labour constitutes the length of the 'working day' under capitalism.

In order to explain why this is the case, Marx must necessarily introduce a new element into this discussion: not simply the forces of production, collected together in the labour-process, but the *relations of production* which govern the appearance and adaptation of this labour-process. In order to explain how the variable levels of necessary and surplus labour appear as they do, and therefore how surplus-value is both produced and captured by the capitalist, Marx makes necessary the introduction and analysis of *social relations*. It is for this reason that following chapter 9 in which these concepts are first introduced, is perhaps the most famous of *Capital Volume I* for the sociologist of work: chapter 10 on 'The Working Day'.

Chapter 10 is often defended as a remnant of Marx's humanism within his mature political economic work, equal in character and tone to Friedrich Engels' *Condition of the Working Class*.[39] In this chapter, Marx describes the working conditions experienced by the working classes during Britain's industrial revolution, describing in turn the effects that it has had upon men, women and particularly children. Citing the reports of factory inspectors and numerous commissions into the industrial working conditions of Victorian England, Marx describes the widespread poverty, hunger, exploitation and overwork characteristic of the period, a manufacture in which 'Dante would have found

---

36 Ibid.
37 Ibid.
38 Marx 2013, p.151.
39 See Hobsbawm 2011.

the worst horrors of his *Inferno* surpassed'.[40] However, it would be reckless to interpret this chapter as a simple continuation of the theoretical humanism first developed in the *Manuscripts*, with the preceding chapters a mere justification of this continuation. Rather, the theoretically anti-humanist move made by Marx in these preceding chapters is continued here and allows Marx to explain *why* this sociological condition of the working classes appears as it does.

From the outset, Marx can be seen to resist the interpretation of the working-day as something whose length is determined by the greedy nature of the individual capitalist. On the contrary, Marx reassures the reader as to the continuity of his analysis as to why the working-day is as long as it is:

> The capitalist has his own view of this *ultima Thule*, the necessary limit of the working-day. As capitalist, he is only capital personified. His soul is the soul of capital. But capital has one single life impulse, the tendency to create value and surplus-value, to make its constant factor, the means of production, absorb the greatest possible amount of surplus-labour.[41]

As Marx will reaffirm later in the chapter, the length of the working-day 'does not, indeed, depend on the good or ill will of the individual capitalist' but instead brings into relief 'the inherent laws of capitalist production, in the shape of external coercive laws having power over every individual capitalist'.[42] In analysing the working-day, Marx insists that we must move away from an analysis of human subjects alone, towards an analysis of the social relations, of the 'inherent laws' of production, responsible for the arrangement of these subjects within the capitalist labour-process. Thus, in the same way that Marx argues that labour-power cannot be explained through simple recourse to the essential characteristics of the human labourer, its exploitation cannot be explained through simple recourse to the essential characteristics of the capitalist. Focus on the human characteristics of either of these actors alone, mystifies the social causes of their respective positions. This is because workers and capitalists, bourgeois and proletarians, are not individuals but *classes*.

An important social relation now emerges on the scene: that of *class struggle*. Classes are not reducible to individuals. Facing the capitalist, Marx says 'you may be the model citizen, perhaps a member of the Society for the Prevention of Cruelty to Animals ... but *the thing that you represent face to face*

---

40   Marx 2013, p.171.
41   Marx 2013, pp.161–2.
42   Marx 2013, p.186.

with me has no heart in its breast'.[43] That which the capitalist class represents is not the capitalist as human subject: it is, what Marx describes as 'collective capital', the laws of capital accumulation themselves. Therefore, in describing the length of the working-day, Marx writes, 'in the history of capitalist production, the determination of what is a working-day, presents itself as the result of a struggle, a struggle between collective capital, i.e., the class of capitalists, and collective labour, i.e., the working-class'.[44]

In order to understand this, another concept emerges, that of 'mode of production'. The struggle over the working-day appears as the dominant site of class struggle under capitalism because it is here that the struggle over surplus-labour and its appropriation takes place. However, as Marx indicates, 'capital has not invented surplus labour' and that

> Wherever a part of society possesses the monopoly of the means of production, the labourer, free or not free, must add to the working-time necessary for his own maintenance an extra working-time in order to produce the means of subsistence for the owners of the means of production.[45]

With modes of production that are not capitalist in nature, such as the *corvée*-labour of the Danubian Principalities, the main site of struggle in terms of surplus-labour did not take place over the length of the working day. This is because, 'their original mode of production was based on community of the soil' where 'part of the land was cultivated in severalty as freehold by the members of the community [and] another part ... was cultivated by them in common'.[46] When applying the categories of surplus and necessary labour to such a mode of production, what becomes clear is that 'the necessary labour which the Wallachian peasant does for his own maintenance is distinctly marked off from his surplus-labour on behalf of the Boyard. The one he does on his own field, the other on the seignorial estate'.[47] Under a capitalist mode of production, this separation of necessary and surplus labour does not take place, as 'they glide into one another' and it is for this reason that 'the capitalist greed for surplus-labour appears in the straining after an unlimited extension of the

---

43 Marx 2013, p.163, emphasis added.
44 Ibid.
45 Ibid.
46 Marx 2013, p.165.
47 Marx 2013, p.164.

working-day'.[48] In this way, the class struggle that commences over the length of the working-day cannot be said to emanate from the worker and capitalist as human subjects: rather, it is the struggle between collective labour and collective capital, so positioned in relation to the capitalist mode of production that produces the appearance and character of this struggle. Class struggle as a social relation is irreducible to a relationship between human individuals.

What follows is the famous exposition of the history of this struggle between proletariat and bourgeoisie over the length of the working-day, observed in agitations, protests, strikes and legislations. Social policies introduced to regulate the working-day and the attempts by capital to frustrate their implementation, reveal the historical struggle by capital to lengthen the working-day as long as possible while labour struggle to shorten it. In the final chapter of part three, chapter 11, Marx concludes this investigation of labour and work under capitalism by returning to where he began. Marx returns to his considerations of the capitalist labour-process and of the problem of work as the conscious life-activity of the labourer. As Marx writes,

> Within the process of production, as we have seen, capital acquired the command over labour i.e., over functioning labour power or the labourer himself. Personified capital, the capitalist, takes care that the labourer does his work regularly and with the proper degree of intensity.[49]

Marx reiterates the character of the theoretical movement made here in order to capture this reality: 'If we consider the process of production from the point of view of the simple labour-process', we will only ever see labour as 'the mere means and material of his own intelligent productive activity'.[50] However, 'it is different as soon as we deal with the process of production from the point of view of the process of creation of surplus-value'.[51] Rather than human alienation, it is the commodity-form that stands at the base of this operation, that 'simple transformation of money into the material factors of the process of production', which 'transforms the latter into a title and a right to the labour and surplus-labour of others'.[52] It is this original social relation, and its reflection in those concepts described by Marx throughout, that underpins the control of capital over labour, not any kind of subjective alienation. It is these social rela-

---

48   Ibid.
49   Marx 2013, p.212.
50   Marx 2013, p.213.
51   Ibid.
52   Ibid.

tions that produce the effect observed by Marx in which the means of production, 'instead of being consumed by him as material elements of his productive activity ... consume him as the ferment necessary to their own life-process': a life-process irreducible to the greed of individual capitalist, but dictated by the social laws inherent to capital accumulation, where 'the life-process of capital consists only in its movement as value constantly expanding, constantly multiplying itself'.[53] This social relation, this antagonism between capital and labour at the base of the capitalist labour process, is irreducible to the subjectivity of the individual capitalist as human subject, but instead only 'mirrors itself in the consciousness of capitalists'.[54]

Thus, it is possible to see the theoretically anti-humanist character of the development of Marx's critique of labour and its place within the analysis of capitalism. In the *1844 Manuscripts*, the concept of labour describes simply the activity of human beings and explains capitalism as existing to the extent that this labour is alienated from the human subject. However, in *Capital Volume I*, this limited definition is broken with and instead new concepts replace the concept of labour on its own: labour-power, labour-time, the labour-process, abstract labour, concrete labour, necessary labour, surplus labour and the working day. By using these concepts, in conjunction with other important concepts such as fixed capital, variable capital and surplus-value, Marx is able to describe capitalism in terms of *exploitation*, where these variables are all adapted in order to increase the maximum yield of surplus-value by the capitalist. In this way – and in a way that was precisely forbidden by the theoretically-humanist concept of alienation in the *1844 Manuscripts* – the presence of social relations now burst onto the stage. The adaptation of these variables is socially grounded and is the subject of the *class struggle* which now emerges before the eyes of the reader, as the capitalist struggles to extend the working day as far as possible in order to maximise the expenditure of surplus-labour by the worker and therefore increase as far as possible the yield of surplus-value; and as the worker struggles against these moves, in order minimise this period of surplus-labour and have the working day be comprised as much as possible by the labour necessary for their own reproduction.

---

53   Ibid.
54   Ibid.

2 A 'Politics of Labour'

An observable change in the concept of labour takes place in the development of political theory in the works of Marx and is crucial in allowing Marx to explain the political character of class struggle as a social relation. The reading completed in this section will demonstrate the extent to which the visible change in the concept of labour in Marx's writings is reflected in Marx's ability to pronounce what Étienne Balibar calls a "politics of labour".[55] The essence of this politics of labour is located primarily in the emergence of class struggle as a concept, and the importance of this concept for thinking through the possibilities of communism and communist revolution in the form of a political materialism. The reading completed here demonstrates the extent to which, as the concept of labour changes in Marx's writings – and as the theoretically anti-humanist operation that makes this possible, develops – this is reflected in alterations to Marx's theory of politics.

In order to demonstrate this, it is necessary to observe the relationship in Marx's writings between the concept of 'labour' and that of the 'social' relation. In reconstructing Marx's political anthropology, Balibar has emphasised the importance of the concept of the social relation, as it provides the material basis for Marx's political theory. This is because, as Balibar writes:

> Marx makes the *relation* or the *relationship* both what 'engenders' or constitutes for each subject its own individuality, lived in a more or less conflictual way, and what makes this individuality immediately 'dependent' on all the other individualities, following the way in which they have been instituted.[56]

This permits a particular indeterminacy of social relations within Marx's thought, crucial for pronunciation by Marx of any kind of communist politics. Balibar argues that this indeterminacy is the central characteristic of the 'social relation' in Marx, a characteristic which 'thus makes them "plastic" or susceptible to being realised in turn in a multiplicity of "interactional" situations'.[57] Crucially, this indeterminate character of the social relation is guaranteed, theoretically, by Marx's anti-humanism. As Balibar explains, the social relation for Marx cannot be reduced to 'a *simple relation*, which "relates" individuals to one

---

55   Balibar 1994, p.118.
56   Balibar 2020, p.143–4.
57   Balibar 2020, p.145.

another',[58] but rather must be interpreted as an ongoing process of transformation, as 'the activation of the "transformability" or the "changeability" inherent to social relations'.[59] Crucially, the concept of labour is of great importance in allowing Marx to guarantee the political materialism that he grounds in this notion of the social relation. Balibar gives this political materialism the name of a 'politics of labour', where the concept of labour itself emerges in order to name the indeterminacy and transformability of the social relation itself:

> *Communism is a politics of labor*, not only as a struggle of workers aspiring to 'government by the working class', but, more profoundly, as a recomposition of politics starting from the very activity of labor, as a reciprocal transformation of politics by labor and labor by politics.[60]

This reading will track the elaboration of this politics of labour, arguing that its purchase as a political theory is evident in – and dependent upon – the theoretically anti-humanist abandonment of the simple concept of labour in the writings of Marx and Engels. Important political concepts, such as class struggle, emerge precisely out of this theoretical operation and become crucial for the pronunciation of this political materialism.

In the works of the Young Marx, this political materialism is nowhere to be found. According to Balibar, this is because Marx had yet to make a break with the dominant ideologies of nineteenth century political theory, continuing to reproduce these ideologies in his own thinking about communism and revolution. In these early works, the 'social' character of the social relation is not the one of complex indeterminacy described by Balibar, but one synonymous with a view of politics as human transformation, guaranteed of course by a theoretically humanist concept of labour. As Althusser argues, 'everything that is "social" designates, not the structure of social *conditions* and the *labour-process* or the process of the realization of value, but the externalization/alienation (via as many mediations as you like) of an originary essence, Man'.[61] Returning to the *1844 Manuscripts*, this is evident in the way in which Marx brings together the idea of the 'social' with the simple concept of labour expounded in the previous section. He describes labour as:

---

58   Balibar 2020, p.148.
59   Balibar 2020, p.145.
60   Balibar, 1994, p.118.
61   Althusser 2003, p.288.

> The production of the object of human activity as *capital* – in which all the natural and social characteristics of the object is *extinguished*; in which private property has lost all its natural and social quality (and therefore every political and social illusion, and is not associated with any *apparently* human relations); in which the *selfsame* capital remains the *same* in the most diverse natural and social manifestations, totally indifferent to its *real* content.[62]

Labour, as expressed in private property, is described by Marx as being 'extinguished' of, or having 'lost' all of its 'social' and 'natural' characteristics due to its economic form. The political remedy to this state of things, therefore, is the return to labour of these lost social characteristics. Communist politics is described here by Marx in terms of 'the complete return of man to himself as a *social* (i.e. human) being',[63] where 'society is the complete unity of man with nature – the true resurrection of nature – the accomplished naturalism of man and the accomplished humanism of nature'.[64] As Marx continues:

> The abolition of private property is therefore the complete *emancipation* of all human senses and qualities, but it is this emancipation precisely because these senses and attributes have become, subjectively and objectively, *human*. The eye has become a *human eye*, just as its *object* has become a social, *human* object – an object made by man for man. The *senses* have therefore become directly in their practice *theoreticians*. They relate themselves to the *thing* for the sake of the thing, but the thing itself is an *objective human* relation to itself and to man, and vice versa.[65]

There is no political materialism forthcoming in these passages because, for the Young Marx, the 'relation' is only 'social' to the extent that it is 'human', opposed to its alienation in the economic. The simple concept of labour, as a human relation, forbids Marx from pronouncing the materialism of communism as a politics, because the exploitation of labour is not described as a relation of class struggle, but as one of human alienation.

However, Marx begins to unsettle some of these assumptions with the development of political theory in *The German Ideology*. As Balibar has demon-

---

62 Marx 1981, p.77.
63 Marx 1981, p.90.
64 Marx 1981, p.92.
65 Marx 1981, pp.94–5.

strated, and echoing Althusser's own insights, *The German Ideology* as a text represents a site both of continuity and trouble with regard to the continuation of this ideological schema in Marx's work. It is a text in which the indeterminacy of the social relation begins to emerge, as Marx 'sought to transcend the amphibology of externalist and internalist interpretations of the category of *social relation* ... between a pure structuralism and pure philosophy of intersubjectivity'.[66] The relationship between this new definition of 'social relation' occurs alongside the simultaneous emergence of a new concept of labour. The relationship between these two theoretical developments occurs most prominently in the section dedicated to the analysis of the 'social division of labour'. At first glance, there is language used in this section to talk about work and labour which would seem to fit quite comfortably with the *Manuscripts*. For example, Marx writes that:

> The division of labour offers us the first example of the fact that, as long as ... activity is not voluntarily, but naturally, divided, man's own deed becomes an alien power opposed to him, which enslaves him instead of being controlled by him.[67]

Following this is the famous assertion that whilst capitalism enforces this division of labour so that each person is 'a hunter, a fisherman, a shepherd, or a critical critic, and must remain so if he does not want to lose his means of livelihood', the political aim of communism is to collapse this division, so that people may 'hunt in the morning, fish in the afternoon, rear cattle in the evening, criticise after dinner ... without ever becoming hunter, fisherman, shepherd or critic'.[68] Found here are the remnants of an idea of the 'social' expounded in the *Manuscripts*, and the idea that work as a social and human activity is not carried out autonomously, but is something which human beings are compelled to do, given particular economic circumstances. As Marx continues, 'this fixation of social activity, this consolidation of what we ourselves produce into a material power above us ... is one of the chief factors in historical development up till now'.[69]

This 'alienation', however, takes on a different character to that of the *Manuscripts*. In the *Manuscripts*, that which was alienated was described by Marx in terms of the 'life-activity' of the human subject, the 'species-being' of that

---

66 Balibar 2017, p.154.
67 Marx and Engels 1976, p.47.
68 Ibid.
69 Marx and Engels 1976, pp.47–8.

subject and of labour as the very quality which marked that subject 'human'. In *The German Ideology*, though there are some similarities in the language, these references to species-being disappear and are replaced by new terms that indicate, instead, the existence of the *social relation*. This takes place alongside a change to the concept of labour, which shifts from one that describes the simple interchange between man and nature, to a more complex articulation which describes a set of social relations that exist between individuals within society:

> The division of labour also implies the contradiction between the interest of the separate individual or the individual family and the common interest of all individuals who have intercourse with one another. And indeed, this common interest does not exist merely in the imagination, as the 'general interest', but first of all in reality, as the mutual interdependence of the individuals among whom the labour is divided.[70]

Interestingly, Marx here indicates the existence of material social relations and the role of these relations in determining the appearance of work in society. Crucially, it is this reality, this necessary interdependence of individuals – not the species-being of the human subject – which Marx describes as undergoing a process of 'alienation'. But this alienation is not transcendental: it is an alienation in the state. For instance, Marx writes that the state is to be thought of as 'an illusory community, always based, however, on the real ties existing in every family conglomeration and tribal conglomeration – such as flesh and blood, language, division of labour on a larger scale, and other interests'.[71] Moreover, that labour is now configured as a set of material relations, reflected in the state, allows Marx to pronounce the ways in which the state reflects, not the alienation of the human subject itself, but *class struggle*. Marx writes that 'it follows from this that all struggles within the state ... are merely illusory forms ... in which the real struggles of the different classes are fought out among one another'.[72] Consequently, this produces in Marx a new theory of politics:

> It follows that every class which is aiming at domination, even when its domination, as is the case with the proletariat, leads to the abolition of the old form of society in its entirety and of domination in general, must

---

70 Marx and Engels 1976, p.46.
71 Ibid.
72 Marx and Engels 1976, pp.46–7.

first conquer political power in order to represent its interest in turn as the general interest, which in the first moment it is forced to do.[73]

Though imperfect, in these passages Marx moves away from an idea of communism as a simple 'negation of the negation',[74] as the negation of man's alienation: communism is now a political project which must be targeted at the transformation of the very political structures in which the relations between individuals in society are reflected in an illusory form. Communism moves from a moralistic politics of overcoming human alienation, towards the development of a politics based upon the recognition of existing material social relations. As Marx says, 'the proletariat can only exist *world-historically*, just as communism, its activity, can only have a "world-historical" existence'.[75] The human individual does not disappear from Marx's formulations at this point, but its existence is qualified as being 'world-historical ... directly linked up with world history',[76] and not as a quality which emanates from any essential, subjective characteristics.

Balibar has clarified how, in this example, the elaboration of Marx's political theory owes a debt to theoretical anti-humanism. Though the language of 'man' still remains, Marx's political project expresses a complexity which forbids 'any possibility of defining the human *before* having described the multiplicity of *different ways* of relating human beings or relating to the human'.[77] These passages demonstrate that, contrary to the definition of human subjectivity elaborated in the *Manuscripts*, '"human beings" (or "men" in traditional usage) *only exist in the plural*',[78] and what matters most is the fluctuating and historically determined relations that exist between them. Marx's reconstitution of the concept of labour within *The German Ideology* was an important part of the reformulation of his political theory: the displacement of the human subject made necessary the analysis of the role of the state and of class struggle in the achievement of communism as 'the real movement which abolishes the present state of things'.[79]

Though gestured towards here, Marx's reformulation of the 'social' – and the assessment of this reformulation in the interests of advancing a theory of polit-

---

73   Marx and Engels 1976, p.47.
74   Marx 1981, p.101.
75   Marx and Engels 1976, p.49.
76   Ibid.
77   Balibar 2017, p.150.
78   Ibid.
79   Marx and Engels 1976, p.49.

ics – is completed in the *Manifesto*. Here, the concept of the social is untied from any equivalence with the human subject. For example, Marx writes that 'to be a capitalist is to have not only a purely personal but a social *status* in production'.[80] Nowhere here does a theory of human nature or human subjectivity enter in order to describe the 'social' character of production. Marx instead emphasises the *social relation* ('his real conditions of life, and his relations with his kind'[81]) arguing that it is the setting-in-motion of these relations that give rise to the historical character of production:

> Capital is a collective product, and only by the united action of many members, nay, in the last resort, only by the united action of all members of society, can it be set in motion. Capital is, therefore, not a personal, it is a social power.[82]

The concept of labour is an important one in allowing Marx to explain the nature of this social character of capital. Marx again makes a distinction between labour as a human activity and labour as a social relation, but does not say that the former is in anyway alienated in the latter, but rather, and perhaps for the first time, that we are dealing here with two *separate* ideas. As Marx explains, in the move towards communism:

> We by no means intend to abolish this personal appropriation of the products of labour, an appropriation that is made for the maintenance and reproduction of human life, and leaves no surplus wherewith to command the labour of others. All that we want to do away with is the miserable character of this appropriation, under which the labourer lives merely to increase capital, and is allowed to live only in so far as the interest of the ruling class requires it.[83]

With this shift away from the simple concept of labour, the possibility of observing and analysing the social character of both labour and capital, emerges for Marx. Untied from theoretically humanist concepts such as alienation and personification, Marx is able here to forward an analysis of labour and capital that pushes their social character to the forefront of investigation:

---

80 Marx and Engels 2002, p.236.
81 Marx and Engels 2002, p.223.
82 Marx and Engels 2002, p.236.
83 Ibid.

a social character that is observed, *par excellence*, through the concept of class struggle. As Balibar has explained, it is the emergence of class struggle that sets the *Manifesto* apart from the *The German Ideology*:

> It is clearly no longer a case of representing the revolutionary proletariat as situated *beyond* any existence as a class, in a mass of de-individualized individuals, as *The German Ideology* would have it. On the contrary, the concept of class struggle must be extended to the revolutionary process itself in order to *think the revolution within the class struggle* (and not the class struggle within the immanence of revolution).[84]

The concept of class struggle opens up the space for the pronunciation of a political materialism and the possibility to consider communist revolution not simply as a final 'negation of the negation',[85] a final overcoming of human alienation, but as a historical process, grounded in historically determined social relations. By centralising labour as a social relation and in the theoretical movement away from the simple concept of labour towards the analysis of labour as social relation, the concept of class struggle is permitted to emerge in Marx's writing and with it, the political materialism Balibar identifies.

3 Labour and Ideology

The concept of labour not only plays an important role in permitting Marx's consideration of political struggle. It is also an important concept in the development of a theory of ideology and of ideological struggle within Marx's work as well. In this final section, the reading completed here will demonstrate the role of 'labour' in providing Marx with a theory of ideology and, in particular, the link between ideology and the political domination of one class over another. The importance of this thesis to Marx's critique of political economy is described by Althusser, who argues that, for Marx, 'one can make concessions in politics – that is known as compromise – one can forge unions in politics, but one can never forge a union with ideology'.[86] The reason for this is because of the close relationship shared between ideology and political domination: forward movement within a political materialism cannot be separated from the

---

84 Balibar 1994, pp.101–2.
85 Marx 1981, p.101.
86 Althusser 2003, p.297.

necessity of maintaining a critique of ideology. As Althusser also explains, theoretical humanism has been a particularly important weapon in the ideological arsenal of the bourgeoisie:

> When, during the eighteenth century, the 'rising class', the bourgeoisie, developed a humanist ideology of equality, freedom and reason, it gave its own demands the form of universality, since it hoped thereby to enroll at its side, by their education to this end, the very men it would liberate only for their exploitation.[87]

This reading demonstrates the role of the concept of labour, and its antihumanist critique and transformation, in allowing Marx to pronounce this link between ideology and political domination.

It is a pronunciation that begins, most polemically, at the beginning of the *Critique of the Gotha Programme*. In this text, 'labour' as concept plays a decisive role in the articulation of Marx's critique of ideology and provides the conceptual device with which Marx develops this critique. Reacting first to the assertion made within the Gotha Programme that 'labour is the source of wealth', Marx corrects this by arguing that such an assertion neglects the social relations that give this statement meaning in the first place:

> The above phrase is to be found in all children's primers and is correct insofar as it is implied that labour is performed with the appurtenant subjects and instruments. But a socialist programme cannot allow such bourgeois phrases to pass over in silence the *conditions* that lone give them meaning.[88]

The essence of this mystification, according to Marx, is theoretically humanist. It stems from the 'supernatural creative power'[89] ascribed to labour, as the source of all wealth in society. Marx identifies the source of this power as emanating from a human exceptionalism in the context of nature, where the human subject 'behaves toward nature, the primary source of all instruments and subjects of labour, as an owner, treats her as belonging to him' so that 'his labour becomes the source of use values, therefore also of wealth'.[90]

---

87 Althusser 1996, p.234.
88 Marx 1989a, p.81.
89 Ibid.
90 Ibid.

For Marx, this problem is as much political as it is theoretical. In making this assertion, Marx argues that the Gotha Programme fails to create the necessary critical distance between itself and bourgeois political economy, thereby reproducing the very ideology on which the bourgeoisie relies in order to justify its exploitation of proletarian labour-power. As Marx writes:

> The bourgeois have very good grounds for falsely ascribing *supernatural creative power* to labour; since precisely from the fact that labour depends on nature it follows that the man who possesses no other property than his labour power must, in all conditions of society and culture, be the slave of other men who have made themselves the owners of the material conditions of labour. He can only work with their permission, hence live only with their permission.[91]

Marx here demonstrates the extent to which labour as a social relation, mediated by class struggle, goes missing from the account presented in the Gotha Programme. Further still, Marx demonstrates that it does so in order to settle accounts to the benefit of the ruling class, as the idea that wealth is the supernatural creation of human labour, forgives those who own the means of production of all charges of exploitation. Marx develops this further, again introducing the role of the state to demonstrate the existence of this social relation:

> This proposition has at all times been made use of *by the champions of the state of society prevailing at any given time.* First come the claims of the government and everything that sticks to it, since it is the social organ for the maintenance of the social order; then come the claims of the various kinds of private owners for the various kinds of private property are the foundations of society, etc. One sees that such hollow phrases can be twisted and turned as desired.[92]

For Marx here, humanist ideology, bound up in a concept of labour with which the authors of the Gotha Programme have failed to dispense, is exposed as the ideological form that facilitates the domination of the proletariat by the bourgeoisie. This is because nowhere in these humanistic formulations is the power of the proletariat as a class to be found: only the power of the bourgeoisie. The power of the proletariat does not emanate from the fact that their labour

---

91 Ibid.
92 Marx 1989a, p.82.

produces wealth: it comes from the fact that they are locked into an historical antagonism with a class which exploits their labour-power. Recognition of this social relation and its determinant force over the appearance of labour in society, is a necessary precondition for the advancement of any communist politics. As Marx writes that, 'instead of setting down general phrases about *"labour"* and *"society"'* the authors of the Gotha Programme needed to 'prove concretely how in present capitalist society the material, etc., conditions have at last been created which compel the workers to lift this historical curse'.[93] In a sense, the advancement of a communist politics is closed off by the orientation of this politics around an ideological concept that is foreign to it. It is the impossibility of the coexistence between bourgeois ideology and communist politics that Marx seeks to pronounce here: an impossibility that stems from the fact that this ideology emanates from the material conditions of class domination (and that it is in fact the incompatibility between these material conditions and those of communism itself that finds itself reflected in this ideological problem).

The link between ideology and political domination is further elaborated in *Capital Volume III*, where Marx famously makes reference to the 'realm of freedom'.[94] Once more, the concept of labour emerges as an important one in allowing Marx to think this through, as Marx argues that this realm 'begins only where labour determined by necessity and external expediency ends; it lies by its very nature beyond the sphere of material production proper'.[95] This passage has captivated the imagination of critical and political sociologists of work, appearing to demonstrate Marx's acknowledgement of the link between the reduction of work and the achievement of an alternative social future. However, just as with the *Critique of the Gotha Programme*, Marx here demonstrates that the barrier which prevents the political arrival into this realm of freedom must be located through the critique of ideology. Its blocking is grounded in the mystifications of classical political economy and, in particular, their conceptualisation of the link between wealth and labour: a mystification on which the bourgeoisie is shown to have built and extended its capacity for class domination.

Chapter 48, in which this reference to the 'realm of freedom' appears, is dedicated to the analysis of 'the Trinity Formula', based on three sources of revenue found within the capitalist mode of production: profit, rent and wages. In his critique of classical political economy, Marx argues that the functionality of its

---

93 Marx 1989a, p.83.
94 Marx 1991, p.958.
95 Marx 1991, pp.958–9.

analysis depends upon a mystification, which consists in the maintenance of a separation between these three sources of revenue and of the processes that are responsible for their generation. As Marx writes:

> They appear as fruits of a perennial tree for annual consumption, or rather the fruits of three trees; they constitute the annual incomes of three classes, the capitalist, the landowning and the working class, revenues distributed by the functioning capitalist, as the person who directly pumps out surplus labour and makes use of labour in general.[96]

Indicated here is a problem within classical political economy, which not only separates out these three sources of revenue and treats them distinctly, but also, in turn, separates the process of production from that of circulation (a mystification with which Marx deals in *Capital Volume II*). Marx here argues that this separation hides the fact that the undiscovered object of classical political economy in its analysis of this trinity formula is in fact the same across all three of these revenue sources: value. As Marx writes, 'if we start by considering the disparity between the three sources, we find ... that their products or derivatives, the revenues, all belong to the same sphere, that of value.'[97]

What interests Marx for the remainder of this chapter is the ideological effects of this mystification within classical political economy. Marx argues that the primary ideological effect of this mystification is the justification of the notion that these three streams of revenue occur *naturally*, given by the nature of the means by which those revenues are generated. The capitalist of course generates profit, because the source of their revenue is *capital*; the landlord of course generates rent, because the source of their revenue is *land*; and the worker of course receives wages, because the source of their revenue is *labour*. Under the schemas of classical political economy, 'their social character in the capitalist production process, determined by a particular historical epoch, is an innate material character natural to them, and eternally so, as it were, as elements of the production process'.[98] A modality is established between the means of revenue generation and wealth, which establishes a link between this wealth and the 'natural' material qualities of capital, land and labour. In turn:

> It must then appear that it is the respective share of the earth as the original field of application of labour, the realm of natural forces, the

---

96 Marx 1991, p.960.
97 Marx 1991, p.962.
98 Marx 1991, p.964.

ready-given arsenal of all objects of labour, and the other respective share of the produced means of production (instruments, raw materials, etc.), their shares in the production process in general, that are expressed in the respective shares that fall to them as capital and landed property, or rather to their social representatives in the form of profit (interest) and rent, just as the worker's share appears to him in wages as the share of his labour in the production process.[99]

In this way, these sources of value 'appear to grow out of the roles that the earth, the produced means of production and labour play in the simple labour process'.[100] Marx here indicates the role of the simple concept of labour emergent once more, which treats the labour-process 'as proceeding between man and nature and ignoring any historical specificity'.[101]

With reference to labour and work specifically, Marx here develops an alternative understanding of the precise force which sets workers to work. Here, Marx appears to give much greater ideological flesh to what he described in *Volume I* as the 'the dull compulsion of economic relations [which] completes the subjection of the labourer to the capitalist'.[102] The dullness of this compulsion exists precisely, for Marx, in the way in which the economic relations that structure the labour-process are thought to be found in natural coincidence with the material responsible for its structure. Just as above, Marx demonstrates how classical political economy does the theoretical work of reproducing a link between the 'natural' material existence of those things found within the labour-process (the land, the raw materials, human beings, and so on), and the concurrent 'naturalness' of this labour-process itself (and with it, the wealth that it produces). As Marx explains:

> Since it is not that wage-labour appears as a socially specific form of labour, but rather that all labour appears as wage-labour by nature (presenting itself like this to those trapped within the capitalist relations of production), the determinate and specific social forms which the objective conditions of labour – the produced means of production and the earth – assume vis-à-vis wage labour (as they in turn presuppose wage-labour) coincide directly with the material existence of these conditions of labour, or with the shape that they generally possess in the actual

---

99 Ibid.
100 Ibid.
101 Ibid.
102 Marx 2013, p.516.

labour process, independent of any historically specific social form, even independent of *any* social form of this whatsoever.[103]

The evacuation of the relations of production as they are found in the immediate process of production of any social character whatsoever, helps to explain the dull compulsion that they exercise over those subject to them. All labour is presented as wage-labour to those 'trapped within the capitalist relations of production'. The ideological core of this operation is the 'coincidence' that is established between the nature of the labour-process and the 'natural' character of its constituent parts, with this coincidence facilitating the evacuation of any social characteristics from this relation. Crucially, Marx demonstrates the extent to which theoretical humanism is the framework of this ideological operation.

With the separation of these three sources of revenue comes also the production of particular subjectivities: tied to profit, rent and wages are the capitalist, the landlord and the worker respectively. The only way to sustain the separation of these revenue streams is, in the same ideological breath, to *personify* these revenue streams in a way that further underscores the 'natural' character of this separation. In other words, the existence of these subjects coincides with the conditions of the process responsible for the production of these revenues, in a way that justifies their existence and separation as self-evident. As Marx writes:

> Just as the products become an independent power vis-à-vis the producers in capital and in the capitalist – who in actual fact is nothing but personified capital – so land is personified in the landowner, he is the land similarly standing up on its hind legs and demanding its share, as an independent power, of the products produced with its aid; so that it is not the land that receives the portion of the product needed to replace and increase its productivity, but instead the landowner who receives a share of this product to be sold off and frittered away.[104]

The implications of this ideological mystification within classical political economy, which begins with a 'natural' separation of revenue streams within the capitalist mode of production, is shown here by Marx to have an interpellating effect, enrolling at its side a set of subjects through which these economic

---

103   Marx 1991, p.963.
104   Ibid.

relations are personified. It results in the creation of what Marx describes as a 'bewitched and distorted world',[105] where capitalists, landlords and workers appear as the 'bearers'[106] of a set of naturalised economic relations.

This ideological schema, which turns not only on the 'natural' connection between the labour-process and its component parts, but also on the 'personification' of these relations within the existence of concrete individuals, is described as the precise ideological force by which the social relations of capital are 'reified' and impressed upon the consciousness of the subject:

> Capital-profit (or better still capital-interest), land-ground-rent, labour-wages, this economic trinity as the connection between the components of value and wealth in general and its sources, completes the mystification of the capitalist mode of production, the reification of social relations, and the immediate coalescence of the material relations of production with their historical and social specificity: the bewitched, distorted and upside-down world haunted by Monsieur le Capital and Madame le Terre, who are at the same time social characters and mere things.[107]

This is why Marx was right to remonstrate the authors of the Gotha Programme for their insistence on the natural link between labour and wealth. It is demonstrated here that this ideology is, of course, socially grounded, in relations of exploitation that are necessarily mystified within the discourse of classical political economy. As Marx explains, it is for this reason that 'the actual agents of production themselves feel completely at home in these estranged and irrational forms of capital-interest, land-rent, labour-wages, for these are precisely the configurations of appearance in which they move and with which they are daily involved'.[108] The bourgeoisie has a political stake in this state of things, for the continued justification of this arrangement allows for the justification of their own social position: 'This formula also corresponds to the self-interest of the dominant classes, since it preaches the natural necessity and perpetual justification of their sources of income and erects this into a dogma'.[109]

What Marx produces here is a theory of ideology which demonstrates its role in facilitating and reproducing the domination of one class over another. The evacuation of 'labour' of all of its social content and its continued interpreta-

---

105   Marx 1991, p.966.
106   Ibid.
107   Marx 1991, pp.968–9.
108   Marx 1991, p.969.
109   Ibid.

tion as the result of a set of 'natural' circumstances, is not simply a theoretical error but an ideological production which emanates directly from the material conditions of society. Through an ongoing critique of the concept of labour, Marx is able to demonstrate this fact. The theoretically anti-humanist nature of this critique has also been made evident here, with the humanist character of this ideology particularly important in its maintenance and reproduction. This humanism is experienced in an apparent 'naturalness' of the social relations of exploitation. Marx here demonstrates the importance of the critique of ideology, expressed through a critique of labour, in bringing out this reality and with it the reality of the social relations responsible for its production.

4 Conclusion

The reading completed in this chapter has demonstrated the extent to which the possibility for Marx to produce a materialist theory of work, politics and ideology has stemmed from a theoretically anti-humanist critique of the concept of 'labour'. Marx's explosion of the simple concept of labour is a vital theoretical operation which, through the production of a multitude of new concepts, allows Marx to describe the precise social relations that explain work under capitalism. The nature of this operation is theoretically anti-humanist, evident in the shift from 'labour' as a simple concept describing an exclusive human activity, towards a number of new concepts intended to describe the social (that is, class) character of capitalist production. Relatedly, this critique of labour also plays an important role in providing Marx with a definition of social relations, which informs the development of a political materialism in his writings. This is evident primarily in the movement from a concept of labour that is theoretically humanist, describing a determinate relation between human beings and nature, towards a concept of labour that reflects a more complex and indeterminate transformation of relations between individuals: with the subjective status of those individuals defined, precisely, by the setting in motion of these social relations. The critique of the concept of labour also permits Marx's development of a theory of ideology, demonstrating the extent to which humanist ideology permits the domination of one class over another, and showing how the critique of this ideology permits the exposure of this fact and of the precise material relations responsible for its production.

It is therefore clear that, if the concept of labour is to have any value in the forwarding of Marxist theory, it is precisely in this way: at the centre of a critical theoretical operation that is anti-humanist in its character. There is no Marxist concept of labour. Rather, the concept of labour finds its place at the centre of

Marx's critique of political economy, useful in the pronunciation of material social relations only to the extent that it undergoes a philosophical transformation, critique and explosion. As Althusser argues, it is for this reason that 'in order to think the nature of "labour", *one has to begin by thinking the structure of the social conditions (social relations) in which it is mobilized*'.[110] It is the theoretical operation completed by Marx here which allows for this to take place and for the material social conditions of work under capitalism to be available for analysis and, crucially, change.

Despite this, Marxism as a theoretical endeavour has not always remembered these lessons, and this is particularly the case when it comes to Marxism's dealings with the topic of work and labour. In the next chapter, the book turns to the treatment of work and labour within the Marxist critique of work, in order to problematise the persistent reproduction of theoretical humanism throughout its various formulations. It will be important to pinpoint where and to what extent the importance placed upon the critique of labour within Marx's critique of political economy has been discontinued at various stages within these critiques of work, as this will facilitate greater depth in subsequent critiques of this same discontinuation in political sociologies of work today.

110 Althusser 2003, p.290.

CHAPTER 3

'Social Labour' and the Critique of Work in Marxist Theory

Across many contemporary contributions to Marxist theory, the critique of work and labour has been persistently haunted by the problem of theoretical humanism. Nowhere is this more evident than in the deployment of the concept of 'social labour'. This concept – a concept which gestures towards the innately collaborative qualities of human labour that lie at the basis of all human societies – not only provides the basis for the observation and diagnosis of the problem with work under capitalism (that work's innately collaborative characteristics have been necessarily alienated in capitalist social relations), but also offers the framework for a politics designed to address and correct this problem (if work's collaborative characteristics can be re-organised and re-asserted by workers, a new society can be constructed). However, this concept of social labour is a problem insofar as it produces a theory and politics of work that tends towards a view of class struggle and social relations anchored in an ideology of the human subject. 'Work' finds itself defined and observed in the collaborative interchange between human individuals: a definition which conditions the critique of capitalism as a force observable primarily in the subjective alienation of the human worker. Furthermore, this conditions any emerging politics, as the objective of class struggle is then interpreted as the quest for the negation of this alienated condition, its success observed first and foremost in subjective transformation rather than social change.

The argument forwarded in this chapter is that the ideological weight of the concept of social labour emanates from a tension present in Marx's elaboration of this concept between the works of his youth and his maturity. In focusing on the first and second notebooks of the *Grundrisse*, it is evident that the concept of social labour, though certainly marking a break with earlier concepts, at best fails to shed the ideological weight of the early works entirely, and at worst remains something of an artefact of these early works which persists through Marx's maturity. Nevertheless, the concept itself is a site of tension in Marx's work, existing at the point of departure between the theoretical humanism that conditioned the formulation of his early ideas and the materialism that conditioned Marx's epistemological break.

Given the troubled legacy of this concept of social labour, the persistence of this concept within contemporary contributions to the Marxist critique of work and labour means that, to varying degrees, these contributions have inherited this tension. In order to demonstrate this, the chapter will analyse the ways in which the concept of social labour provides the ideological pin that holds theory and politics together in four key contributions to the Marxist critique of work: E.P. Thompson's historical sociology; Harry Braverman's labour process theory; Michael Hardt and Antonio Negri's sociology of immaterial labour; and André Gorz's post-work thought. Though certainly not an exhaustive list, the legacy of these influential contributions continues to be lived in many contemporary political sociologies of work. In each of these cases, the chapter demonstrates how the concept of social labour both implicitly and explicitly allows these authors to hold a theory and politics of work together. The concept of social labour, in each instance, provides these authors with means by which to think the problem with work under capitalism and its potential political remedy, together. However, this reproduces a tendency within Marxist thought about work in which the nature of class struggle and its reflection in social relations is either mis-represented or mystified by this ideological concept.

Before this, the chapter will re-trace Althusser's critique of social labour, found in his text *The Humanist Controversy*. Althusser's argument in this piece is that work and labour act as an allegory for the human subject within Marxist theory, where the material study of the value, exploitation and class struggle reflected in the concept of labour-power is substituted for an ideological discourse of labour as the social activity of human beings, characterised by an experience of human alienation.

1   'Social Labour'

The concept of 'social labour' finds its origin at the intersection of historicist and humanist ideology, observed in the insistence on the historical tendency of human beings to collaborate in their labour as a 'social' activity. Althusser points towards, for example, recent discoveries in the field of human palaeontology which argued that the condition of human evolution was the existence of a human ancestor who 'stood upright, so that its hands were free to fashion rudimentary tools under conditions which, it seems reasonable to suppose, were not "individual" but social'.[1] As Althusser continues, 'we see straight away the interest that this discovery can hold for historical materialism', as it makes

---

1 Althusser 2003, p.284.

it possible to '"bridge the gap" between present-day human societies and the animal origins of the human species, since they seem to show that the human species comprised, from its beginnings, creatures living "together" and producing rudimentary tools'.[2] Althusser identifies discoveries such as these forming the basis of an emerging ideological operation in Marxist theory that 'consists in giving Theoretical Humanism a new "lease on life"': the conceptual basis of this operation was 'labour ... or the apparently more "Marxist", but in fact equivalent, notion of "social labour"'.[3]

The concept of social labour insists on two main points: first, that labour is the essential activity of the human subject and; second, that it is by virtue of this activity that this subject enters into relations with other subjects, making history as it does so. Althusser describes its ideological schema in the following way: 'Essence of Man = labour (or social labour) = the creation of Man by Man = Man, Subject of History = History as a process whose Subject is Man (or human labour)'.[4] This notion of social labour is located in the works of the young Marx, who 'defines this labour in terms of its originary act, the (Feuerbachian) externalization of the Essential Forces of the individual producer'.[5] In this way, the word 'social' in this concept does not refer to material social relations, rather to the externalisation of this essence in labour, in production and in history:

> The adjective 'social' in the expression 'social labour' ... designates, in the Manuscripts, the effect or phenomenon or manifestation ... of the generic character of Man contained in the originary act of externalization/alienation of the essence of Man, which is present [in] the worker's labour.[6]

For the young Marx then, the concept of social labour was useful insofar as it facilitated his holding together of a theory and politics of labour under capitalism: that is, the definition of an initial problematic (labour under capitalism is alienated essence) and the formulation of a solution (revolution as the historical overcoming of this alienated condition, completed through labour itself). As Marx wrote, communism was 'the positive transcendence of private property as human self-estrangement, and therefore as the real appropriation of the human essence by and for man; communism therefore as the complete return

---

2 Ibid.
3 Althusser 2003, p.286.
4 Ibid.
5 Althusser 2003, p.288.
6 Ibid.

of man to himself as a social (i.e. human) being'.[7] The problem with this, of course, is that this schema unfolds not on the terrain of material social relations, but on the terrain of human essence and human subjectivity: 'Everything that is "social" designates, not the structure of social conditions and the labour-process or the process of the realization of value, but the externalization/alienation (via as many mediations as you like) of an originary essence, Man'.[8]

Though it shares the ideological characteristics of the Young Marx, the concept of social labour is a product of the move towards Marx's more mature writings. In particular, this section focuses on Marx's elaboration of this concept in the preparatory notes for *Capital*, known collectively as the *Grundrisse*. Just as Althusser argues in relation to texts such as *The German Ideology*, it is evident in the below passages from the *Grundrisse* that Marx finds himself on the threshold of a theoretical change, reflected in a persistent tension between two problematics at the core of this notion of social labour: namely, one of capitalist social relations, and one of human labour. This tension, when not resolved, finds itself reflected in the theoretical humanism that persists through more contemporary Marxist theory when it encounters this concept.

The focus here is on the 'chapter on money' across the first and second notebooks of the *Grundrisse*. What must be made clear is that the Marx found on these pages is not the Young Marx and evidence of the theoretical antihumanism that characterises his mature political economic works is easy to find. 'Individuals', writes Marx, 'although their relationships appear to be more personal, only enter into relations with each other as individuals in a particular determination'.[9] This determination is observed by Marx in 'certain narrow relations of production' between social classes, and it is for this reason that Marx is able to say that individuals 'are not the products of nature but history'.[10] What is evident, in sentences such as these, is a different lexicon from that found in the early works of Marx, where the nature of the human subject is not taken for granted or assumed, but observed as the determination of historical social relations of production. This is, of course, the theoretical antihumanism that conditions Marx's explosion of the simple concept of labour as discussed in the preceding chapter.

However, these ideas find themselves in tension with Marx's elaboration of the concept of social labour. With this concept, Marx wants to explain the way in which human labour is generalised such that it can find itself represented

---

7   Marx 1981, p.90.
8   Althusser 2003, p.288.
9   Marx 1986, p.100.
10 Marx 1986, p.99.

in a universal form, specifically in the form of money. In what will be the early sketches of Marx's theory of commodity fetishism, Marx relies on the concept of social labour in order to demonstrate the social realities reflected in money. Social labour, for Marx, describes, essentially, the relations of mutual dependence that exist at the basis of any human society. Social labour describes the fact that individuals can neither produce nor consume in isolation from one another and that both production and consumption necessarily bring individuals into relations with one another. As Marx writes, 'the production of each individual producer is dependent upon the production of all the others, as also the transformation of his product into means of subsistence for himself has become dependent upon the consumption of all the others'.[11] This immanent inter-connection between individuals is the basis of the *social* relation that emerges between them: 'The absolute mutual dependence of all individuals, who are indifferent to one another, constitutes their social connection'.[12] Marx wishes to highlight this because he is here formulating a critique of the classical political economic notion of 'private interest', by demonstrating the fact that interests, private or otherwise, can never emerge in true isolation. As Marx writes,

> Private interest is itself already a socially determined interest and can be attained only with the conditions laid down by society and with the means provided by society, and is therefore tied to the reproduction of these conditions and means. It is the interest of private persons; but its content, as well as the form and means of its realisation, are given by social conditions that are independent of them all.[13]

The argument that Marx seeks to forward here, in the chapter on money, is that the money form within the capitalist mode of production is expressive of a generalised measure of this social labour. In doing so, Marx attempts to explain the material realities of exchange-value, arguing that 'the objectification of the general, social character of labour ... makes the product of labour an exchange value and gives the commodity its money quality, which, in turn, implies a money subject existing outside it and independently of it'.[14] The concept of social labour is therefore central to Marx's explanation of exchange-value and its reflection in the money form within the *Grundrisse*. Problematically, there is

---

11   Marx 1986, p.93.
12   Marx 1986, p.94.
13   Ibid.
14   Marx 1986, p.105.

evidence of the persistence of certain theoretically humanist tropes in Marx's explanation of this process, in particular the persistence of a theory of alienation.

One of the first signs of this is the continuing suggestion within Marx's writings here that social labour in some way represents a pre-existent social relationship between human individuals, conditioned by their activity. This is evident, for example, when Marx writes that 'relationships of personal dependence (which originally arise quite spontaneously) are the first forms of society, in which human productivity develops only to a limited extent and at isolated points'.[15] Here, Marx insinuates that the 'social' character of labour finds itself most organically expressed at this early stage of human society, upon which later forms develop. As well as this insinuation of social labour as a pre-existing relation, Marx also finds difficulty in sustaining the notion that these relations are not simply individual relations. For example, he describes social labour as a relation between 'universally developed individuals, whose social relationships are their own communal relations and therefore subjected to their own communal control'.[16] The persistence of these assumptions is not accidental: rather, it is crucial in allowing Marx the theoretical space to explain how social labour is transformed and becomes reflected in money as exchange-value.

In explaining this process, the theoretical humanism implicit in these original assumptions persists into the explanation of exchange-value. Where social labour is reflected in exchange value, Marx says that social labour takes on the appearance of 'something general in which all individuality, all particularity, is negated and extinguished'.[17] Marx continues, saying that 'this is indeed a condition very different from that in which the individual, or the individual extended by a natural or historical process into a family and a tribe (later community), directly reproduces himself from nature'.[18] Having established social labour as something pre-existent and taking place between concrete individuals, Marx then must rely on this language in order to explain the generalisation of social labour within the money form. In order to explain this further, Marx resurrects a concept of alienation:

> The social character of the activity, as also the social form of the product and the share of the individual in production, appear here as something alien to and existing outside the individuals; not as their relationship to

---

15   Marx 1986, p.95.
16   Marx 1986, p.99.
17   Ibid.
18   Ibid.

each other, but as their subordination to relationships existing independently of them and arising from the collision between indifferent individuals. The general exchange of activities and products, which has become the condition of life for every single individual, their mutual connection, appears to the individuals themselves alien, independent, as a thing.[19]

With this movement, Marx describes labour as becoming something 'not *directly* social, not the offspring of association distributing labour within itself'.[20] In this way, as Marx continues, 'the *private exchange* of all products of labour, capacities and activities, stands in contradiction ... to the free exchange of individuals who are associated on the basis of common appropriation and control of the means of production'.[21] What these passages demonstrate is that, even in Marx's mature economic writings, this concept of social labour carries with it persistent humanist ideological tropes that make their way into Marx's explanation of important political economic concepts such as exchange-value.

As demonstrated in the preceding chapter, Marx achieves this generalisation of human labour with other concepts in the final version of *Capital*, particularly in Volume I, such as 'abstract labour' and 'labour-power', used to describe this commodification of labour and its reflection in exchange-value. The concept of social labour does not entirely disappear from *Capital* but, as Lise Vogel has demonstrated in her analysis of Marx's writings, becomes expressed in terms of 'socially necessary labour' and its relationship to the value of labour-power. For Vogel, 'in *Capital* ... this small concession to the notion of a natural physical minimum has all but disappeared, and the "historical and moral element" plays the principal role'[22] as the determination of social labour as corresponding to any natural or pre-existing relation is more convincingly overcome and replaced with a formulation that centralises the role of historical social relations.

It would be inaccurate to say that Marx, in these passages in the *Grundrisse*, succumbs entirely to theoretical humanism in elaborating this concept of social labour. As indicated in the opening of this section, Marx carries through with much greater consistency and precision the theoretical anti-humanism that says that 'individuals, although their relationships appear to be more personal, only enter into relations with each other as individuals in a particular

---

19 Ibid.
20 Marx 1986, pp.95–6.
21 Marx 1986, p.96.
22 Vogel 2013, p.69.

determination'.[23] The most that can be said here is that the movement beyond theoretical humanism is either *unsuccessful* or *incomplete* when it comes to this concept of social labour. This is problematic, however, because what is evident is that when those disciples of Marx took up this concept as they found it, throughout the twentieth century, much of the ideological weight that Marx himself failed to do away with in producing this concept, found its way into these more contemporary analyses as well.

2 Theory, Politics and 'Social Labour' in the Marxist Critique of Work

The concept of social labour is therefore the site of an important tension in Marx's work, which he had in some way or another to resolve. Problematically, where this concept persists in the work of those who came after Marx, this tension itself is carried through, and with it, its ideological consequences. In contemporary contributions, the persistence of this concept is particularly evident where Marxism tries to hold theory and politics together in its thinking about work. The concept of social labour is a particularly useful – if, of course, obstructive – ideological bridge between the theoretical analysis of the problem of work under capitalism and the necessary political intervention required to correct this problem. The problem with this concept is that it forces Marxism to think a theory and politics of work on the terrain of human subjectivity, observing its application in subjective changes to the human individual and their labour. This diverts its theoretical attention away from material social relations and, in turn, removes these relations from the crosshairs of political intervention.

In contributing to this effort, the chapter moves through a reading of four important contributions to the Marxist critique of work. The concept of social labour appears differentially across all of these examples and produces different effects in each. In some of these examples, the concept is explicitly deployed; in others it 'lurks behind the theoretical scenes'[24] of the critique of work. But in each example, it is precisely at the point where theory and politics are held together that this concept emerges and does its work, providing them with an analysis of capitalism and an opportunity to think its political overcoming. Though crucial for the functionality of these discourses, where the concept of social labour emerges it reproduces particular shortcomings and

---

23   Marx 1986, p.100.
24   Althusser 2003, p.261.

oversights by moving this critique away from the field of social relations and towards the human subject.

2.1   'Experience', Labour and Class

E.P. Thompson's historical sociology of work has maintained an important role in Marxist critiques of work and labour today. Thompson's historical sociology has provided the sociologist of work with a theoretical framework through which to view class as an experiential relation, formed between individuals where their work intersects with culture, politics and ideology. Michael Burawoy argues that Thompson's work demonstrates how 'the so-called economic realm is inseparable from its political and ideological effects, and from specifically political and ideological "structures" of the workplace'.[25] The value of Thompson's writing, for Burawoy, finds its place in demonstrating social class as something that emanates from the ways in which concrete individuals, concrete workers, behave within these structures, emphasising that 'there is no "objective" notice of class prior to its appearance on the stage of history. Acting on the historical stage has to be conceived of as a moment in the constitution of class'.[26]

In looking first at this definition of labour and class in Thompson's work, it is possible to observe the implicit and unspoken presence of the concept of social labour lurking behind the scenes of his theoretical system. Thompson describes both labour and class as the unfolding of subjective *experience* and the expression of historical social relationships that exist between concrete individuals, between 'men as they live their own history'.[27] As Thompson writes:

> Class happens when some men, as a result of common experiences (inherited or shared), feel and articulate the identity of their interests as between themselves, and as against other men whose interests are different from (and usually opposed to) theirs.[28]

For Thompson, these common experiences are found *par excellence* in the forms of 'social' collaboration, cooperation and kinship that emerge between human labourers. Thompson describes, for example, the 'common occupa-

---

25   Burawoy 1985, p.39.
26   Ibid.
27   Thompson 1991, p.10.
28   Thompson 1991, pp.8–9.

tional and social tensions'[29] and the 'long traditions of the urban artisans and tradesmen'[30] that characterised the social relationships between workers in the long run-up to the Industrial Revolution. With these early statements, Thompson describes an existing co-operation between 'the self-educated journeyman ... the printer, the shopkeeper, the engraver or the young attorney',[31] that indicate a social character to labour in England, held together by a sharing of common historical and subjective experiences. Problematically, it is this imprecise definition of social class as existing in the subjective 'experiences' of concrete individuals that guides Thompson's holding together of theory and politics and leads it into problems.

First, it is the establishment of this basis of social labour that allows Thompson to think through the unique intervention of Jacobinism and the ideologies of the French Revolution. Jacobinism was a powerful political idea in England precisely because it was able to capture the essence of this existing shared experience between these workers. According to Thompson, 'it precipitated a new agitation, and certainly this agitation took root among working people, shaped by new experiences, in the growing manufacturing districts'.[32] The political orientation of Jacobinism as an ideology – one that stressed collaboration and involvement between every citizen, 'based on the deliberate belief that every man was capable of reason and of a growth in his abilities'[33] – mapped onto the social experience of labour and class experienced by workers in England that prioritised precisely the same attributes. It was for this reason that Jacobinism was a success and why socialism, in '[shifting] emphasis from political to economic rights', succeeded only in reinforcing 'distinctions of class and status'.[34]

Socialist ideology was not the primary cause for the fall of Jacobinism and the failure of any revolution it promised: for this, Thompson looks to the Industrial Revolution. According to Thompson, the Industrial Revolution introduced 'a profound alienation between classes in Britain', which undid many of the shared social relationships that had previously existed between workers of different kinds and saw 'working people thrust into a state of *apartheid* whose effects ... can still be felt to this day'.[35] The defining intervention made by the

---

29   Thompson 1991, p.23.
30   Thompson 1991, p.27.
31   Thompson 1991, p.23.
32   Thompson 1991, p.27.
33   Thompson 1991, p.201.
34   Ibid.
35   Thompson 1991, p.195.

Industrial Revolution, for Thompson, was precisely its interruption of social labour and the previously-existing social relationships that it had reflected (an interruption evident in the defeat of Jacobinism as ideology). For Thompson, this is evident in the ways in which the struggles of workers that 'provoked the most intensity of feeling were very often ones in which such values as traditional customs, "justice", "independence", security or family-economy were at stake'.[36] Exploitation emerges for Thompson precisely at the point where social labour is interrupted: 'as old customs were eroded, and the old paternalism was set aside, the exploitative relationship emerged supreme'.[37] In this way, 'the process of industrialization must, in any conceivable social context, entail suffering and the destruction of older and valued ways of life'.[38] The establishment from the outset of a theory of social labour, emanating from the collaborative experience of individual workers, provides Thompson with the ground from which to explain the rise of Jacobinism as a politics, but also from which to pronounce the precise crime of capitalism and its industrial intervention, resulting in the defeat of this politics.

However, it is precisely because of the fact that labour and class are located in the realm of subjective experience and not in ideology *per se* that Thompson is able to articulate the working-class politics that emerges and develops throughout the Industrial Revolution. It is because the collaborative characteristics of human labour exist in the subjective experiences of these workers that new political ideologies – in particular, those of Chartism and Luddism – are able to emerge and take shape. It is in this way that Thompson argues that the industrial working class that would emerge 'was not the spontaneous generation of the factory system', but was the result of a social labourer pushing back against the imposition of a new industrial regime, of 'the freeborn Englishman ... the inheritor of Bunyan, of remembered village rights, of notions of equality before the law, of craft traditions'.[39] The existing social relationships between individuals, emanating from their subjective experience of labour as a social activity, provides the theoretical ground from which to observe the emergence of working-class politics and its development.

By virtue of his reliance on this concept of social labour, there is never any burden on Thompson to explain the precise conjuncture into which Jacobinsim as an ideology intervenes. Thompson's historical sociology begins with

---

36   Thompson 1991, p.222.
37   Thompson 1991, p.223.
38   Ibid.
39   Thompson 1991, p.213.

an imprecise 'social' relationship between labourers, based on shared traditions, culture and *experiences*, which Jacobinism adequately reflects, and which industrial capitalism effectively subsumes and alienates. The social situation that industrial capitalism inherits and subsumes appears in Thompson's work to have always-already existed. The concept of social labour sees this oversight forgiven in Thompson's work, as social relations need only be interpreted in terms of the subjective experience of collaboration between individual workers. It is this subjective *experience* of class, conditioned at all times by the pre-existing 'social' connections between labourers, that provides Thompson with the window through which to observe the subsequent resistance of workers to the impositions of an emerging industrial capitalism. It produces a humanist theory and politics of labour, where the *experience* of co-operation and alienation between these labourers constitutes their class condition and that the political intervention *par excellence* of the working class was the subjective *articulation* of this experience through ideologies like Jacobinism, Luddism and Chartism. The notion of a pre-existing 'social' relationship between workers – defined by their inter-subjective *experience* of class – is a restatement of the ideological concept of social labour and, as is evident, provides the conceptual grounding through which Thompson thinks theory and politics together in his historical sociology of work. Problematically, it resolves itself in an imprecise understanding of both class struggle and of the social relations of work reflected in this struggle, which are at all times mediated by the experience of the working subject and its mirror-image in politics.

2.2   *De-skilling and the Labour Process*

Harry Braverman's labour-process theory has been an important theoretical component within contemporary sociologies of work for some time. Braverman's focus on the labour-process, on the process through which both commodities and value are materially produced, has provided the sociology of work with a conceptual repertoire through which to observe and explain the relationships between workers and employers and chart the sociological content of these relationships. Erik Olin Wright saw the potential of Braverman's work for sociology, celebrating its ability to 'go beyond a simple, positive account of societies as they are, and develop a critical theory of societies as they might become'.[40] Wright's key focus is 'Braverman's discussion of the progressive separation of conception and execution [which] is at root an argument about the

---

40   Wright 1981, p.57.

loss of the capacity of workers to control the labour process',[41] arguing that here lies the sociological explanation for the production and accumulation of value.

The concept of social labour comes into play within this particular strand of Braverman's thought, explicitly deployed in the articulation of the theory of *de-skilling*. Braverman's problematic – of a labour-process that continually de-skills human labourers in order to facilitate their continued exploitation – relies on a concept of social labour from its outset, providing the normative theoretical ground from which to observe this problem. De-skilling is observed in the historical separation of human workers from the collaborative and therefore 'social' characteristics of their activity, with the notion of social labour used by Braverman as the conceptual standpoint from which to view this historical process. It is also through this concept that Braverman can hold this theory of deskilling together with a proposed political intervention, where the objective of class struggle is reformulated as the struggle to reclaim autonomy over 'skill' and the traditions embedded within it. Problematically, in beginning his inquiry with the notion of social labour, the theory of de-skilling is grounded in the observation of a historical and subjective separation of workers from the autonomous and deliberate engagement in work as a 'social' activity, as opposed to the material social relations that describe work under capitalism.

Braverman's reliance on the concept of social labour is evident first and foremost in his definition of labour and the labour-process. The primary quality of human labour, for Braverman, is its conceptual and deliberate quality: 'Human work is conscious and purposive, whilst the work of other animals is instinctual'.[42] Human labour's essential quality is located in the link that exists between the ability of the human brain to conceive of an idea and of the human hand to execute that idea. This specifically human activity, grounded in human consciousness, is responsible for the creation not only of humanity as subject, but of human societies themselves: 'Labor that transcends mere instinctual activity is thus the force which created humankind and the force by which humankind created the world as we know it'.[43] In this way, Braverman argues that labour is an inherently 'social' activity:

> Each individual of the human species cannot alone 'produce in accordance with the standard of every species' and invent standards unknown to any animal, but the species as a whole finds it possible to do this, in part through the social division of labor. Thus the social division of labor

---

41 Wright 1981, p.69.
42 Braverman 1974, p.46.
43 Braverman 1974, p.50.

is apparently inherent in the species character of human labor as soon as it becomes *social labor*, that is, labor carried on in and through society.[44]

For Braverman, de-skilling begins with the intervention of the capitalist into this process. De-skilling finds its root in the division, not only of labour, but of the *individual*, where the unity of conception and execution at the core of the human's deliberative act of labour is interrupted and separated: 'While the social division of labor divides *society*, the detailed division of labor divides *humans*', which Braverman describes as 'a crime against the person and against humanity'.[45]

Theoretically, this poses a particular problem for Braverman, observed in the counterposition of 'social labour' with its alienated capitalist form. Braverman in fact argues that this very counterposition is the starting-point for scientific management itself, which launches 'not from the human point of view but from the capitalist point of view'[46] of the labour-process. It is only from this 'capitalist' point of view that it becomes both necessary and possible to separate the unity of conception and execution found in human labour. Braverman argued that this amounts to a *dehumanisation* of labour and of the labour-process:

> This dehumanization of the labor process, in which workers are reduced almost to the level of labor in its animal form, while purposeless and unthinkable in the case of the self-organized and self-motivated *social labor* of a community of producers, becomes crucial for the management of purchased labor.[47]

'Management' and the control of the labour-process is therefore positioned by Braverman as precisely the management of this process of dehumanisation. Scientific management functions by maintaining this process of dehumanisation, 'not interested in the person of the worker, but in the worker as he or she is used in office, factory, warehouse, store, or transport processes ... the human being is here regarded as a mechanism articulated by hinges, ball-and-socket joints'.[48] Machinery and the development of technology furthers this separation and intensifies the dehumanisation of the worker, confining them to 'a blind round of servile duties in which the machine appears as the embodiment

---

44 Braverman 1974, p.72, emphasis added.
45 Braverman 1974, p.73.
46 Braverman 1974, p.86.
47 Braverman 1974, p.113, emphasis added.
48 Braverman 1974, p.179.

of science and the worker as little or nothing'.[49] Though 'absolutely incomprehensible from the human point of view',[50] the continued separation of the capacity for conception and execution at the core of human labour becomes the necessary project of capitalist management of the labour-process.

Crucially, the history of de-skilling told by Braverman through the concept of social labour is reflected in the problem of monopoly capitalism at which he arrives towards the end of the text. For Braverman, monopoly capitalism – and the forms of work in the service-sectors, in clerical and managerial work and in teaching and education that characterised this particular arrangement of the labour-process – is the reflection *par excellence* of this historical process of de-skilling. Braverman observes in the emergence of monopoly capitalism the most developed alienation of human workers from the 'social' qualities of their labour, facilitated by new technologies and machinery that accelerate this process ever further. For the worker of monopoly capitalism, the task is:

> No longer adaptation to the slow round of seasonal labor in an immediately natural environment, but rather adaptation to a speedy and intricate social machinery which is not adjusted to social humanity in general, let alone the individual, but dictates the rounds of production, consumption, survival, and amusement.[51]

Problematically, the grounding of this analysis in the concept of social labour (and its alienation) is productive of a political recommendation emblematic of a vulgar 'economistic-humanism',[52] in which the historical task of the proletariat becomes the re-discovery of the skill crystallised in these technologies and their putting to use towards more progressive ends. As Braverman writes, 'the worker can regain mastery over the collective and socialized production only by assuming the scientific, design, and operational prerogatives of modern engineering'.[53] Such a politics, like the worst examples of today's accelerationism, tends to overlook the social relations contained in these machineries and treats them as neutral tools to simply be directed by a newly conscious working subject.

Evident in Braverman's historical analysis of de-skilling is a tendency towards the disappearance of social relations from his account, reflected in an

---

49   Braverman 1974, pp.194–5.
50   Braverman 1974, pp.205–6.
51   Braverman 1974, p.287.
52   Althusser 2014a, p.36.
53   Braverman 1974, pp.444–5.

analysis of monopoly capitalism that is observed primarily in the heightened alienation of human individuals from the 'social' characteristics of their labour. It is for this reason that Michael Burawoy, in his critique of Braverman, argued that he in fact 'mourns the eclipse of the bourgeois individual' as it disappears under capitalism and crafts a 'functionalist' politics based on its rediscovery.[54] Braverman's theoretical humanism facilitates his forgetting of the social relations contained in technology and accelerated productive development, producing an unjustified optimism in Braverman based on the political redirection of modern engineering by a more conscious proletariat towards the creation of a more progressive labour-process.

2.3 The Sociology of Immaterial Labour

The work of Michael Hardt and Antonio Negri, particularly developed in *Empire*, has proven to be a popular and common reference within contemporary political sociologies of work. In particular, they have provided sociologists of work with conceptual devices with which to think about emancipation and revolution within a sociological situation – at least in the Western world – where the traditional industrial proletariat has been displaced by a new demographic, emblematic of today's post-Fordist labour markets. For Kathi Weeks, for example, Hardt and Negri's work has opened up the refusal of work as 'a path of separation that creates the conditions for the construction of subjects and whose needs and desires are no longer as consistent with the social mechanisms within which they are supposed to be mediated and contained'.[55] The secret to this is contained within the shift to 'immaterial labour' and the social labour contained inherently within its completion. The concept of social labour is the precise one that allows for Hardt and Negri to privilege immaterial labour as the precursor to a crisis of value and as a subsequent site of revolution: a privileging that necessarily obfuscates important social relations from view.

For Hardt and Negri, work under contemporary capitalism is characterised by the presence of 'immaterial labour.' A decided shift away from the production of material, tangible commodities within defined territorial boundaries (such as the factory), towards the immaterial production of knowledge, communication and emotion across the edifice of the 'factory-society'[56] defines capitalism in post-modernity. In what Hardt and Negri describe as a 'sociology

---

54   Burawoy 1985, p.56.
55   Weeks 2011, p.100.
56   Hardt and Negri 2001, p.247.

of immaterial labour',[57] they point towards a changing landscape of work under contemporary capitalism, based primarily on the production of services rather than physical commodities. Hardt and Negri define this type of work as 'immaterial labour', in that it 'produces an immaterial good, such as a service, a cultural product, knowledge, or communication'.[58] The work that they describe here includes 'a wide range of activities from health care, education, and finance to transportation, entertainment, and advertising. The jobs for the most part are highly mobile and involve flexible skills'.[59] There are two main features of immaterial labour. First, there is the immaterial labour at the centre of the burgeoning communications and information-technology sectors, the concrete act of which involves the 'manipulation of symbols and information'.[60] Second, immaterial labour is found in the production of emotions or affects, common in customer-focused services, observed concretely in the production of 'a feeling of ease, well-being, satisfaction, excitement, or passion'.[61]

In order to articulate the importance of the immaterial, Hardt and Negri need the concept of social labour. Immaterial labour is important for Hardt and Negri because it is productive of *relations* between individuals at numerous stages: be these relations facilitated through the production of communication and knowledge within the digital economy; or affective relations through the production of services dedicated to the delivery of emotional labour. In these ways, precisely through the reproduction of relations based on communication, knowledge and affect, contemporary capitalism is reproducing the conditions of *life itself*, a phenomenon that Hardt and Negri seek to capture through the concept of social labour:

> In postmodernity the social wealth accumulated is increasingly immaterial; it involves social relations, communication systems, information, and affective networks. Correspondingly, *social labor* is increasingly more immaterial; it simultaneously produces and reproduces directly all aspects of social life. As the proletariat is becoming the universal figure of labor, the object of proletarian labor is becoming equally universal. *Social labor* produces life itself.[62]

---

57 Hardt and Negri 2001, p.289.
58 Hardt and Negri 2001, p.290.
59 Hardt and Negri 2001, p.285.
60 Hardt and Negri 2001, p.292.
61 Hardt and Negri 2001, pp.292–3.
62 Hardt and Negri 2001, p.258, emphasis added.

Precisely through the immaterial nature of social labour, Hardt and Negri surmise that today, 'we participate in a more radical and profound commonality than has ever been experienced in the history of capitalism'.[63] It is precisely here that the revolutionary opportunity within this new way of working presents itself.

The revolutionary capacity of the new proletariat is contained in the production of a 'general intellect', made up of the communicative and affective relations immanent to immaterial labour: 'General intellect is a collective, social intelligence created by accumulated knowledges, techniques, and know-how'.[64] The revolutionary opportunity is to be grasped here, in the capacity of the new proletariat to take control of these relations of communication and affect, 'managed by the multitude, organized by the multitude, directed by the multitude – absolute democracy in action'.[65] Problematically, the initial framing of this direction through the concept of 'social labour' sees this political directionality reflected in a humanist politics of *subjective transformation*. This means not simply the refusal of work, but rather:

> What we need is to create a new social body, which is a project that goes well beyond refusal ... we need also to construct a new mode of life and above all a new community. This project leads not toward the naked life of *homo tantum*, but toward *homohomo*, humanity squared, enriched by the collective intelligence and love of the community.[66]

For Hardt and Negri, 'postmodernization or informatization today marks a new mode of becoming human'[67] as immaterial social labour fulfils its function of human subjective production. In this way, it is 'the constitution of new bodies, outside of exploitation' that emerges as the 'fundamental basis of the new mode of production'.[68] For Hardt and Negri, what is at stake here is nothing less than the 'recognition of the new human condition'[69] thrown into being by the communicative and affective relations of immaterial labour.

In holding theory and politics together through the concept of social labour, Hardt and Negri reproduce a theoretical humanism in their analysis. George

---

63   Hardt and Negri 2001, p.302.
64   Hardt and Negri 2001, p.364.
65   Hardt and Negri 2001, p.410.
66   Hardt and Negri 2001, p.204.
67   Hardt and Negri 2001, p.289.
68   Hardt and Negri 2001, p.410.
69   Hardt and Negri 2001, p.291.

Caffentzis confirms this view, arguing that 'though it looks like the machines are eliminating the humans in this period of capitalism ... a new "humanism" arises from these anti-humanist Marxists claiming the renewed indispensable importance of knowledge in humans'.[70] This humanism (among other ideologies) necessarily obfuscates certain social relations from view, allowing Hardt and Negri to observe unique characteristics in immaterial labour which undermine capitalism's ability to measure, value and discipline this labour: characteristics that cannot be justified when this labour is placed in the context of broader social relations. The concept of social labour permits Hardt and Negri to privilege immaterial labour as both prompting a crisis of value and measurability under capitalism and providing the launch pad for revolutionary intervention. But as Caffentzis argues, this produces an impoverished view of the social relations of work which, when analysed closely, do not confirm the historical privilege placed on this type of work (for example, contemporary capitalism does not appear to struggle too much to find ways to quantify, measure and discipline various types of 'immaterial' labour within contemporary labour-processes). It is precisely humanist ideology – found in the apparently 'social' nature of immaterial labour – that provides this privilege and not the social relations themselves: a problem which goes undisturbed by the arrangement of their analysis around the concept of social labour.

2.4 The Crisis of Work

The work of André Gorz has very recently found renewal among a new collection of interlocutors within the sociology of work. Gorz provides a politics based on the reduction and refusal of work and a critique of the fact that 'the obligation to paid employment so often precludes the possibility of engaging in activities that are genuinely creative, collaborative and useful'.[71] At the core of this is Gorz's diagnosis of a 'crisis of work' with the advent of the 'post-industrial' society. For Gorz the initial identification of the 'social' characteristics of human labour allows him to pronounce the significance of the alienation that defines the work of post-industrial society. Politically, the task of the 'neo-proletariat'[72] is to create a new space in which the social characteristics of labour can be recaptured and autonomously controlled: a space that must, according to Gorz, exist outside of 'work' as it is known.

For Gorz, the concept of social labour is particularly important in defining work as both a social and a political activity. For Gorz, '"work" must therefore be

---

70 Caffentzis 2013, p.111.
71 Frayne 2015, p.23.
72 Gorz 1983, p.70.

understood, as in Hegel, as the activity by which the human being externalizes his being ... as "sensuous-practical activity", as "appropriative shaping of one's own objective world".[73] In this sense, human labour is defined as the reflection of human subjectivity in objective social relations between individuals, and as the subject produces these objective relations in co-operation with others, they acquire 'a sense of him- or herself as an autonomous subject possessing practical freedom'.[74] The problem facing Gorz, in the context of an emerging 'post-industrial' society that is characterised by de-territorialised, highly mechanised and increasingly immaterial forms of production, is whether work, even in its alienated form under capitalism, can any longer retain any of these 'social' qualities. As Gorz writes:

> The question, however, is to what extent this conception of work, handed down to us essentially by the skilled industrial workers of the nineteenth century (workers who were still close to artisan production, and had a complete grasp of manufacturing *procedures* and the *products* to be made), can apply to the largely de-materialized, pre-determined, specialized work which is the predominant form in today's macro-social space – a form of activity which has no purchase or influence either on the way it is performed or on the final purpose it is to serve, and is commonly referred to simply as 'work'.[75]

The answer to this question, for Gorz, is that it cannot. As Gorz writes, 'instead of being the worker's mode of insertion *into a system of universal cooperation*, work is now the mode of subordination to the machinery of universal domination'.[76] In an argument similar to that of Braverman, Gorz argues that it is the separation of the worker from its capacity for autonomous thought and decision-making inherent to the act of labour, which characterises this heightened form of alienation. For Gorz this lack of subjective autonomy is reflected in the evanescence of the social power of human labour, which introduces a political problem:

> In the first place, the worker's labour no longer involves any power. A class whose social activity yields no power does not have the means to take power, nor does it feel called upon to do so. In the second place

---

73   Gorz 2012, p.55.
74   Ibid.
75   Gorz 2012, pp.55–6.
76   Gorz 1983, p.71, emphasis added.

work is no longer the worker's own activity. In the immense majority of cases, whether in the factory or the office, work is now a passive, pre-programmed activity which has been totally subordinated by the working of a big machinery, leaving no room for personal initiative.[77]

The heightened alienation of the worker from the 'social power' of their activity – incubated in their ability to autonomously direct this work – poses a political problem for the proletariat as revolutionary subject. In post-industrial society, the proletariat becomes 'no more than a vague area made up of constantly changing individuals whose main aim is not to seize power in order to build a new world, but to regain power over their own lives'.[78] In this way, this neo-proletariat is politically unequipped to confront the conditions of contemporary capitalism, fraught as they are, and thus cannot emerge as a revolutionary subject: 'The crisis of the industrial system heralds no new world. Nothing in it is indicative of a redeeming transformation ... the society disintegrating before our eyes heralds no new order'.[79]

This characterises what Gorz identifies as a 'crisis of work'. As a consequence of these developments, this proletariat finds no social characteristics at all in the work that it does and therefore no route towards a revolutionary political intervention. Work is in 'crisis' for Gorz insofar as it has become an activity saturated of all social and political potentialities, with the subjective category of 'worker' or 'proletarian' suffering a similar fate. Thus, Gorz argues that the political intervention of the proletariat must be launched from an alternative site, one that exists outside of the sphere of 'work' as defined under contemporary capitalism. This crisis forms the essence of Gorz's 'post-work' thought and in order to think through both the implications of this crisis and the potential political remedy to it, Gorz relies once more on the concept of social labour.

Gorz's post-work politics turns on the struggle to locate and create a space outside of 'work' in which the social characteristics of human labour can flourish and therefore become *powerful* once more. As Gorz wrote, 'there is no social space in which "true work" ... can deploy itself in such a way to *produce society* and set its stamp upon it. *It is this space we have to create*'.[80] For Gorz, this has to be pursued *outside* of 'work', outside of the traditional political arena of the industrial proletariat, as 'the desire for liberation *in* work presupposes a practical experience of autonomy, but the workers are objectively and subjectively

---

77 Gorz 1983, p.67.
78 Gorz 1983, p.75.
79 Ibid.
80 Gorz 2012, p.57.

denied this by work which deforms and mutilates their sensuous-practical faculties'.[81] The name that Gorz gives to this project of locating a new space in which both the 'social' characteristics of human labour could be relocated, is a 'politics of time':

> The development of free activities which are no longer *work* (in the sense this term has come to assume) obviously cannot be produced simply by reducing working hours. It requires a *politics of time* which embraces the reshaping of the urban and natural environment, cultural politics, education and training, and reshapes the social services and public amenities in such a way as to create more scope for self-managed activities, mutual aid, voluntary co-operation and production for one's own use.[82]

It is clear that the concept of 'social labour' looms large in the political project offered by Gorz, crucial for holding the theory and politics of work together in Gorz's thinking. The concept of social labour provides Gorz with his initial definition of work as a human activity, emanating from its distinction from 'work' in its waged capitalist form. It is precisely because of the 'social' characteristics of human labour that Gorz refuses 'to extend the notion of "work" to autonomous activities and work-for-oneself',[83] as work under capitalism is defined by its *lack* of "social" qualities. In the same breath, the political intervention offered by Gorz to remedy this situation turns on the celebration of the 'social' qualities of human labour and the struggle to locate these qualities in forms of activity that escape the capitalist wage-labour relation. It is only through this concept of 'social labour' that the simultaneous critique and celebration of 'work' can be held together at the core of Gorz's politics. It is the only way that the demand of the proletariat 'to liberate themselves *from* work as it exists and find *in* work as great a potential for self-determination as possible'[84] makes sense.

The problem with this formulation is that, in relying on this concept of social labour in order to construct a post-work vision in this way, Gorz produces a view of the space 'outside' of work as in some way devoid of class struggle and class antagonism, as a neutral space in which the naturally collaborative qualities of human labour go on undisturbed. This undermines the political potentialities that Gorz filled such a space with, for if the space outside of work is devoid of

---

81   Gorz 2012, p.58.
82   Gorz 2012, p.61.
83   Gorz 2012, pp.60–1.
84   Gorz 2012, p.64.

class antagonism or class struggle, then it is devoid of the very motor of social change that such a politics requires. This is a problem reproduced in contemporary post-work thought too, which tends too often to attempt to develop a post-work society as one devoid of class antagonism and therefore evacuated of the very motor that would bring about progressive social change. As Frederick Pitts and Ana Dinerstein have argued, 'nowhere in the popular imaginary of post-work or post-capitalist society does class struggle feature, when it is only by means of this that a post-capitalist society can be accessed at all'.[85] The persistence of the concept of social labour in the critique of work can be found at the origin of this oversight, which has persisted into political sociologies of work today.

3 Conclusion

By way of a conclusion, it is possible to observe the ways in which the persistence of the concept of social labour within Marxist theories of work and labour tends towards the reproduction of theoretical humanism within these critiques. The consequences of this ideological reproduction differ between the accounts covered in this chapter. For Thompson, social labour provides the basis for understanding class as a cultural or ideological *experience*, which complements his avowed humanism, but produces an idealist interpretation of the relations of production. For Braverman, social labour provides a normative definition of human labour, the mental and physical division of which provides the view of the emergence of the capitalist labour-process. However, it privileges the social relation as a relation between concrete individuals, producing a misleading symmetry between the control over one's own labour and control over the labour-process itself. In the sociology of Hardt and Negri, social labour is mobilised to explain the revolutionary potential of immaterial labour and the 'general intellect' produced through the socialisation of communicative and knowledge-based capacities inherent within its completion. In so doing, it tends towards the reproduction of a theory of social change which privileges subjective transformation, covering an over-emphasis on the novelty of the relations of production apparently inaugurated by post-modern capitalism. And in the work of Gorz, social labour provides the basis for the refusal of work, offering a normative definition of human activity which can escape the wage-labour relation and offer the ground for an alternative basis of class

---

85 Pitts and Dinerstein 2017, p.4.

power. Problematically, Gorz celebrates a notion of human labour that in some way escapes class struggle and social relations entirely, thereby erasing the very mechanism capable of achieving such a post-work world in the first place.

It is for these reasons that Althusser was sceptical of the role of this concept of social labour within Marxist theory. The reading of this concept within Marx's *Grudrisse* reveals its mischievousness, in many instances compatible with his mature political economy, but often responsible for the reintroduction of theoretically humanist notions and thus of detrimental analyses. This, coupled with the critique of the four contemporary contributions covered in this chapter, reveals that which Althusser originally argues in *The Humanist Controversy*: that the concept of social labour, if it is to be useful in any way for Marxist theory, must be subject to a great deal more theoretical and philosophical work. Its uncritical acceptance or reproduction within these contemporary contributions allows the humanist ideology inherent within its assumptions to pass into the theoretical frameworks of these accounts, in a way that distracts from or distorts the view of important social relations.

As indicated throughout, the legacies of these contributions have continued in many more contemporary discussions within the sociology of work. It is therefore important to track and expose how the humanist ideological tropes often reproduced by these accounts have found themselves reproduced in the political sociologies of work today. The remainder of the book will undertake this task, beginning in the next chapter with an emerging 'post-work' discourse within the sociology of work.

CHAPTER 4

Theoretical Humanism and the Post-work Imaginary

The focus of this chapter is upon one of the more popular contemporary discourses within the sociology of work today, here described as the 'post-work imaginary'. The proponents of this discourse argue that amid a landscape of crisis and uncertainty with regards to work and employment in the Western world, the opportunity for a transition towards a post-work society exists and should be the focus of political attention today. The argument forwarded here is that this discourse presents a flawed analysis of work under capitalism today, reproducing particular assumptions about work and employment which, far from breaking with the dominant paradigm of how work is thought about, reproduces it in damaging and problematic ways. The chapter argues that it is a persistent theoretical humanism, reflected in both the epistemological and political arrangement of this discourse, which is responsible for these oversights, by bracketing important social relations and shifting the object of its analysis towards the human subject.

Althusser had his own critique of those who fetishized the promises of automation and imagined a world without wage-labour delivered on the back of technological advancement alone. In *On the Reproduction of Capitalism*, he writes:

> Here the imaginations of our utopian thinkers, apologists for neo-capitalism and reformists start churning and promise us the moon (either the disappearance of classes or communism) just as soon as automation becomes universal ... because automation will put an end, 'to all intents and purposes', to nearly every intervention by labour-power ... and, consequently, to the exploitation of labour-power! Let us be serious.[1]

For Althusser, such technological fetishism is a problem because it risks overlooking the complexity of capitalist social relations and their reproduction, in favour of a more simplified technological determinism (and its mirror-image, humanist determinism, their cooperation described by Althusser as

---

[1] Althusser 2014a, p.30.

an 'economistic-humanist ideology'[2]). Natalia Romé revisits and extends this critique of 'reformism', arguing that alongside a theoretical determinism, the interlocutors in this current of thought are guilty of 'a certain "politicist" optimism: a fetishism of popular *demands*, taken immediately as political, blind to the complex ensemble that reigns over concrete historical formations in the struggle of the bourgeois class in its antagonism toward the working-class struggle'.[3] In this way, Romé emphasises how these theoretical problems become reflected in the production of a programme of political demands: a relationship which will be particularly important in this analysis of the post-work imaginary as a political sociology.

The critique of theoretical humanism within the post-work imaginary focuses on these two problems, a theoretical problem and a political problem, arguing that at the core of both is an epistemological arrangement which emphasises the human subject over the social relations of capitalism. The result, this chapter argues, is the production not of a sociology of work (a sociology, as defined by Mario Tronti, as a 'science of society',[4] the object of which is the social relations of society) but an *anthropology of the working subject* (an ideological discourse focused primarily on the alienation of the worker and its psychological and cultural effects). But before this, the chapter takes some time to establish both the precise sociological conjuncture from which this post-work imaginary claims to emerge, and the criticisms of this current that have emerged in recent years.

1   A Brave New World of (Post-)work

At the turn of the twenty-first century, Ulrich Beck describes and predicts the emergence of a *Brave New World of Work*: one in which globalisation and advancing technological development has created a condition of precariousness and vulnerability among the workers of the Western world. As Beck writes of this new world of work, 'for a majority of people, even in the apparently prosperous middle layers, their basic existence and lifeworld will be marked by endemic insecurity'.[5] Everywhere, the availability of secure, regular and formal employment opportunities is disappearing, with the contemporary employment market dominated by jobs that prioritise 'flexibility' and 'self-employment.' Techno-

---

2   Althusser 2014a, p.36.
3   Romé 2021, p.46.
4   Tronti 2020, p.48.
5   Beck 2000, p.3.

logical advancements are heightening these conditions of insecurity, as 'rising unemployment can no longer be explained in terms of cyclical economic crises; it is due rather to the successes of technologically advanced capitalism'.[6] Over twenty years on from Beck's predictions, the world of work he envisaged appears to correlate ever-more accurately to the contemporary landscape of work. Today's sociologists of work have brought Beck's brave new world to life, presenting a world of work with increasingly mobile working populations, vast unemployment and a heightened experience of precariousness and risk: all inaugurated by the productive and technological development of capitalism.

Global proletarianisation continues apace with an increasing number of potential wage-labourers enlisted within the world's industrial reserve army. In 2020, the International Labour Organization (ILO) reported expectations that over the next decade the world's urban population is set to grow by 126 per cent, a growth which will be reflected in a shift in the global division of labour, with fewer agricultural workers and greater numbers of workers employed in service industries.[7] Typically, these types of work tend to engender more informal employment arrangements. The ILO reported that in 2019, 60.1 percent of the world's employed workers were working informally.[8] With the onset of the Covid-19 pandemic, the consequences of these changes within the world of work were further pronounced. Total employment fell globally by 114 million during the pandemic, with this caused by workers losing full-time hours and taking up informal, part-time or zero-hours employment, or by simply losing their jobs altogether.[9] Not everyone worked from home during the pandemic, with this condition more often than not the privilege of well-paid professional workers. As Marco D'Eramo wrote at the time, 'the privileged lock themselves in houses with fast internet and full fridges, while the rest continue to travel on crowded subways and work elbow-to-elbow in contaminated environments'.[10] This indicates a growing inequality among the world's workers, with workers in particular industries and particular parts of the world enjoying vastly different working conditions than others. At the same time, as vast swathes of the workforce began to work from home, questions were raised about the nature of work, where people work and the role of technology in facilitating different or possibly even less work. Weighing up both the obstacles and opportunities presented by the pandemic, Farruggia et al. argue that 'the pandemic has

---

6 Beck 2000, p.2.
7 International Labour Organization 2021a.
8 International Labour Organization 2021b.
9 Ibid.
10 D'Eramo 2020, p.26.

demonstrated that many prefer remote work arrangements; that office work is not an inevitable fact of white-collar life; and that productivity is not necessarily reduced when work takes place in the home'.[11] Remote working and the technological developments that make this work possible, also raise another characteristic problem of this new world of work: automation. It is estimated that up to 49% of the world's activities in work could be automated immediately with technology that is currently available. Moreover, by 2030, 30% of all jobs in Britain are predicted to be at risk of automation and 38% of jobs in the United States.[12]

There have been a number of contemporary sociological interventions into this discussion of this emerging world of work, particularly from those rooted in the sociology of work, employment and industrial relations. Changes in the labour market conditions have often been positioned in the context of developing economic trends, collected in discussions of the 'gig economy', the 'platform economy' or 'crowdworking': working arrangements in which 'employees complete short-term, on-demand work assignments (i.e. "gigs") across a variety of employers'.[13] Inaugurated within these economic shifts have been shifts in the characteristics of work and employment in advanced capitalist economies, including the emergence of more informal working arrangements (such as part-time, zero-hours and fixed-term employment) and the rise of self-employment among contemporary workers. Alongside this has been the charted development of 'involuntary' or 'false' self-employment, where the risks normally shouldered by employers are transferred onto individual workers, but these workers do not enjoy the autonomy of the traditionally self-employed, with their work still controlled by an employer. In these situations, employers will treat their workers, 'through high levels of control and other markers of employee status, such as long standing obligations between the parties, integration and dependency – as employees, while giving them none of the protections that individuals with formal employee or worker status enjoy'.[14] Though often couched in the language of 'autonomy', 'freedom' or 'flexibility', the proliferation of informal working arrangements such as these 'allow organizations to shift the costs of employment and economic risk onto their workers, all the while removing them from important employment-bound social security benefits and social insurance programs'.[15]

---

11   Farruggia, Jones, and Siravo 2020, p.20.
12   Cole 2017.
13   Schroeder, Bricka, and Whitaker 2021, p.1.
14   Cruz, Hardy, and Sanders 2017, p.276.
15   Moisander, Groß, and Eräranta 2018, p.393.

Whilst recognising the challenges posed by this new world of work, one of the defining features of an emerging base of post-work thought within contemporary sociology today is the simultaneous recognition of an opportunity for humanity's liberation from work within this situation. The unsettling of the dominant work arrangement by things like informal employment and automation confirms the fact, for these post-work thinkers, that work is not an immovable institution within contemporary society, but that its existence is open to being radically changed. Paul Mason writes, 'we lie at a moment of possibility: of a controlled transition beyond the free market, beyond carbon, beyond compulsory work'.[16] The unique characteristic of this period of capitalist development is the centrality of information and of highly developed machinery in contemporary production. Though it is true that this new form of production exists at the epicentre of the contemporary crisis of work, it is also responsible for the development of new social forces that continuously escape its grasp. For the thinkers of this post-work imaginary, it is in the struggle over these social forces that the future will be written. For whilst technological advancement exacerbates global inequalities and the proliferation of poverty, it also produces the precise conditions through which the transition beyond these things is possible. As Nick Srnicek and Alex Williams write, 'rapid automation, expanding surplus populations and the continued imposition of austerity all heighten the need to rethink work and prepare for the new crises of capitalism'.[17] The contemporary post-work imaginary pivots on the idea that workers can take advantage of developing technologies, automate production and thus liberate themselves from the drudgery of work.

For Mason, the anchor of the new post-work imaginary is the abundance and availability of *information* in the twenty-first century. For Mason, information fundamentally alters (and undermines) the mechanics of capitalist production in a way that it is unprepared for. According to Mason, 'information technology, far from creating a new and stable form of capitalism, is dissolving it: corroding market mechanisms, eroding property rights and destroying the old relationship between wages, work and profit'.[18] This argument rests on the fact that unlike traditional forms of production which were based upon a principle of scarcity and were therefore dictated by the laws of supply and demand, contemporary production is anchored in information as a raw material that transcends the problem of scarcity. With traditional 'material' commodities, their consumption is often limited to one individual consumer at a time. The

---

16   Mason 2015, p.290.
17   Srnicek and Williams 2015, p.86.
18   Mason 2015, p.112.

same, however, is not true with information. The ability to 'copy and paste' information means that information-based commodities have the potential to be enjoyed by multiple consumers at the same time without their supply ever diminishing. As Mason writes, 'once you can copy and paste something, it can be reproduced for free. It has, in economics-speak, a "zero marginal cost".'[19] According to Mason, the mechanics of capitalist production are set in motion by the laws of supply and demand governed by the problem of scarcity. With information-based production, this problem is transcended and the anchor of capitalist production is therefore in crisis: 'Until we had shareable information goods, the basic law of economics was that everything was scarce. Supply and demand assumes scarcity. Now certain goods are not scarce, they are abundant – so supply and demand become irrelevant.'[20]

The characteristic ability of information to transcend the problem of scarcity means that, according to Mason, the social relations of capitalism encounter a severe difficulty in controlling it in the way that they had other resources. In relation to resources such as land or fossil fuels, it had been much easier for the capitalist class to maintain a monopoly over these resources, due in part to the scarcity of these resources. However, it has become increasingly difficult for capitalism to maintain control over information in the same way, due to its ability to transcend scarcity and be shareable in ways that other more 'material' resources could not have been. Despite attempts made by capitalism to control this new resource – such as the implementation of copyright law or the hiding of information behind paywalls for example – Mason uses the proliferation of peer-to-peer and open-access platforms, based fundamentally upon information, in order to describe capitalism's inability to control information as a resource. The emergence of websites such as Wikipedia and open-access operating systems such as Android, which are based upon the open sharing of information are evidence, according to Mason, of subversive forms of production taking place within the capitalist economy: 'Decentralized action by individuals, working through cooperative, voluntary forms of organization. It is producing new forms of 'peer-to-peer' economics, in which money is either absent or not the main measure of value.'[21] Crucially, these subversive forms of production fundamentally challenge the organisation of work under capitalism. The wage-labour relation disappears, as the free and open access to information subverts the economic necessity and coercion that previously guided the wage-labour relation of traditional capitalism: 'It is not money the

---

19   Mason 2015, p.117.
20   Mason 2015, p.119.
21   Mason 2015, p.128.

participants are exchanging. They are in effect exchanging gifts'.[22] It is here that Mason locates the roots of a postcapitalist transition: in subversive forms of production anchored in a fundamental reorganisation of work.

The abundance of information not only facilitates cooperative working, but it also underpins the forward march of automation. Srnicek and Williams argue that information is the driving force of the contemporary machinery of capitalism: a reality which, they argue, has great emancipatory potential. Srnicek and Williams observe the historical development of capitalism in its tendency to continually automate ever-greater parts of its production process. From the mechanisation of agricultural labour and craftwork in the nineteenth century, the displacement of skilled workers in the twentieth century by machines and office technologies and the growing automation of mass-production thereafter signify the developmental stages of capitalist production. Today, the presence of information in production defines a new era of capitalist production, with automation markedly different from that which went before:

> The most recent wave of automation is poised to change this distribution of the labour market drastically, as it comes to encompass every aspect of the economy: data collection (radio-frequency identification, big data); new kinds of production (the flexible production of robots, additive manufacturing, automated fast food); services (AI customer assistance, care for the elderly); decision-making (computational models, software agents); financial allocation (algorithmic trading); and especially distribution (the logistics revolution, self-driving cars, drone container ships and automated warehouses).[23]

Crucially, for Srnicek and Williams, the presence of information means that automation in the twenty first century has moved into jobs and employment sectors that would have otherwise been impossible to mechanise. Work once thought uniquely human, such as care work or work involving cognitive processing, is now, thanks to the abundance of information, potentially open to automation. As Srnicek and Williams write, 'complex communication technologies are making computers better than humans at certain skilled-knowledge tasks, and advances in robotics are rapidly making technology better at a wide variety of manual-labour tasks'.[24]

---

22 Mason 2015, p.129.
23 Srnicek and Williams 2015, pp.110–11.
24 Srnicek and Williams 2015, p.111.

This emerging tendency of capitalist development towards the automation of vast swathes of work, combined with the ability of information-machines to produce wealth without human labour, presents society with the foundation for the full abolition of work. Whereas past movements have been founded upon the resistance to capitalist development, Srnicek and Williams argue that 'the tendencies towards automation and the replacement of human labour should be enthusiastically accelerated and targeted as a political project of the left'.[25] According to Srnicek and Williams the liberation of vast swathes of humans from work, combined with the proliferation of information sees capitalism incubate particular social forces that are beyond its control: 'This is a project that takes an existing capitalist tendency and seeks to push it beyond the acceptable parameters of capitalist social relations'.[26] Crucially, embracing automation alone is not sufficient for emancipation: rather, the free time that automation would inevitably open up, in order to escape the dystopia of perpetual poverty and precariousness, must be reinforced by a source of income untied from participation in wage-labour.

Srnicek and Williams complement their demand for automation with a demand for the implementation of a universal basic income (UBI). As automation reduces the demand for human workers, Srnicek and Williams argue that free time will surely increase, but that 'this free time will be of little value if people continue struggling to make ends meet'.[27] The concept of a UBI is premised on the payment to each individual, without means-testing, of a basic salary or income, regardless of the employment status of that individual. According to Srnicek and Williams, it must fulfil three conditions: 'It must provide a *sufficient* amount of income to live on; it must be *universal*, provided to everyone unconditionally; and it must be a *supplement* to the welfare state rather than a replacement of it'.[28] The fundamental aim of the UBI is not simply to provide an income for those liberated from work by machines, but also to necessarily alter the social position of work, decentralising it as the fundamental activity of societal value. The UBI will remove the tendency to value people only by virtue of the economic contribution that they make to society, allowing people both the time (thanks to automation) and now the resources (money through the UBI) to experiment with alternative social arrangements and activities: 'It transforms precarity and unemployment from a state of insecurity to a state of voluntary flexibility'.[29]

---

25   Srnicek and Williams 2015, p.109.
26   Ibid.
27   Srnicek and Williams 2015, p.118.
28   Srnicek and Williams 2015, p.119.
29   Srnicek and Williams 2015, p.121.

The abundance of information, the automation of the labour process and the implementation of a UBI form the 'material' bedrock of the post-work imaginary: that is, the strategy for physically reducing the amount of work completed by human beings and satisfying their needs thereafter. But accompanying these 'material' considerations are those that Srnicek and Williams identify as 'political' considerations: those which underpin not simply the appearance of the labour process, but the cultural and political *positioning* of work itself. As Srnicek and Williams write:

> The most difficult hurdles for UBI – and for a post-work society – are not economic, but political and cultural: political, because the forces that will mobilise against it are immense; and cultural, because work is so deeply ingrained into our very identity.[30]

The discussion of the potential to automate production and thereby move into a post-work society has prompted further considerations of the role of work in society and culture which is a prominent but often under-discussed element of the contemporary post-work imaginary.

For example, David Frayne's central argument pivots on the fact that even in the midst of such technological possibilities, the compulsion to work remains central to people's lives and to the orientation of society and politics more generally. For Frayne, critical social theory has been preoccupied with 'trying to figure out why, in a time of unprecedented technological possibility, people's lives [are] still characterised by toil and repression'.[31] For Frayne, the freeing-up of greater amounts of time for people through automation can only be successful alongside a cultural struggle against the dogma of work and the idea that work should define an individual's place in society and the value of their contribution to it. The value of the post-work imaginary, for Frayne, is not just the struggle against the inherent inequalities crystallised in contemporary forms of work, but more importantly the struggle against 'the celebrated prominence of work in the cultural, ethical and political life of advanced industrial societies'.[32] The 'material' elements of the post-work imaginary – full automation and the establishment of a UBI – are useful only insofar as they facilitate this cultural struggle.

For others like Peter Fleming, any effective post-work imaginary must immediately combat the way in which work itself has come to animate the human

---

30   Srnicek and Williams 2015, p.123.
31   Frayne 2015, p.34.
32   Frayne 2015, p.14.

body, dictating its behaviour in all walks of life: jobs 'are detached from their basis in productive utility and work becomes the wandering reference point for everything else. Not a concrete activity but an abstract and diffuse prism through which all of life is myopically evaluated and managed'.[33] By stressing this material detachment, Fleming does not discount the usefulness of automation and the UBI in the achievement of a post-work world, but stresses that their success is dependent upon the consideration of work as a cultural and psychological force as well as a material one. For David Graeber, this finds its crystallisation in the phenomenon of 'bullshit jobs': jobs so detached from any material utility that their meaning is unclear or non-existent. In fact, Graeber argues that these 'bullshit jobs' are the product of an ineffective cultural struggle against the dogmatism of work, as developing automation, rather than reducing the amount of 'bullshit jobs' available, has in fact led to their increase:

> Rather than allowing a massive reduction of working hours to free the world's population to pursue their own projects, pleasures, visions, and ideas, we have seen the ballooning of not even so much of the 'service' sector as of the administrative sector, up to and including the creation of whole new industries like financial services or telemarketing, or the unprecedented expansion of sectors like corporate law, academic and health administration, human resources, and public relations.[34]

Set out here are the parameters of the contemporary post-work imaginary. Its material pillars appear to be the abundance of free information, the technological development of machinery and the establishment of a UBI, designed to replace the expenditure of human labour-power entirely within the labour process. It is complemented by a cultural and psychological struggle against the dogmatism of work in society and a reorganisation of the social principles that prioritise work as *the* valued human activity. Together, this post-work imaginary thinks it both possible and necessary to transition into a post-work, post-capitalist society where human beings are freed of the responsibilities of production and in which the social inequalities tied historically to this responsibility, are actively undermined.

---

33   Fleming 2017, p.154.
34   Graeber 2013, para. 4.

2 The Problem with Post-work

Before analysing the theoretical humanism of the political sociology presented above, it is important to lay out some of the existing critiques of this discourse. The main argument of the critiques presented here is that the post-work imaginary leaves unthought certain important social relations which lead it into particular theoretical difficulties: including the reproduction of productivism, the treatment of machines and technology as neutral forces of production, or an over-emphasis of the novelty of precariousness or informality as characteristics of contemporary work.

Within the sociology of work, there is the recognition of the need for a more 'scientific' approach to the study of work, that would be in keeping with the spirit of the Althusserian project advanced in this book. There is an acknowledgement that many of the concepts used to critique work today mystify important social relations in their operation, which require further elaboration before these concepts can be deemed useful. For example, Charles Umney argues that work is too often thought about with an individualistic notion of class, betraying the Marxist concept of class as the bearer of a matrix of important social relations:

> When talking about class, our objective should not be simply to provide a comprehensive categorisation of groups of people and the differences between them, but *to consider how the interactions between people with different economic roles affects the working of society as a whole*, from the experiences people have at work, to the development and application of technology, to the economic and social policies pursued by governments.[35]

Kathi Weeks has also recognised this problem in the formulation of the post-work imaginary. Far from offering a radical theoretical perspective from which to re-think work, Weeks argues that this contemporary post-work imaginary is still caught up in an epistemological arrangement that complements the existing order of capitalist social relations and thus the images of work that spring from them. As Weeks writes,

> Although they may appear to be categories of nonwork, they fail to escape the imaginary of productivity or the models of the subject that would

---

35 Umney 2018, p.21.

deliver it. My point is that because these notions of work's refusal are still under the sway of its ethics, the models of nonwork they generate are too locked within the orbit of work as we now know it to push us very far beyond its gravity.[36]

Together, both Umney and Weeks recognise that much of the contemporary critique of work and the post-work imaginary that has emerged from it, fail to offer a break with a prevailing arrangement of knowledge responsible for work's dominant conception.

This is productive of a number of problems within post-work thought. One of the first points of tension is the post-work imaginary's treatment of automation and technology. A prevailing critique of this post-work imaginary is that there exists a *tendency* within this post-work imaginary to forget the class character of technology, machinery and information and treat it as a neutral resource as opposed to a product of definite and unequal social relations. It is not true to say that the class character of machinery and technology is totally ignored by the theorists of the post-work imaginary. For example, Srnicek and Williams argue that one of the fundamental failures of the Soviet Union was its lack of appreciation for the class character of the capitalist productive machinery that it attempted to repurpose for the construction of a communist society: 'The ambitious plan to conquer the capitalist means of production ran aground on the reality that power relationships are embedded within technologies, which cannot therefore be infinitely bent towards purposes that oppose their very functioning'.[37] However, when it comes to the imagination of social futures based upon the emancipatory potential of productive technologies, this tendency emerges and the post-work thinkers forget their own lessons. Whilst there is a critical analysis of 'traditionally' capitalist technologies such as machinery, 'new' technologies such as data and information are treated as though they extend beyond the grasp of capitalist social relations and therefore provide a firm basis for social emancipation. For example, Mason discusses data and information in the context of 'a revolution in the way we process, store and communicate information ... [that] has started to corrode the traditional property relations of capitalism'.[38]

For a number of critics, such a position relies on a particular ignorance of the unequal social relations bound up in these new technologies. For example, Spencer writes that 'the authors fail to recognize how digital technologies are

---

36 Weeks 2016, pp.257–258.
37 Srnicek and Williams 2015, p.151.
38 Mason 2015, p.142.

themselves products of unequal power – they are not neutral as such, but rather created, harnessed and reproduced under conditions where power resides with capital, not labour'.[39] Aaron Benanav argues that the significance of automation as the cause of new socio-economic problems is overstated and that the links between declining demand for human labour-power and the advanced development of productive forces is not so clear-cut: 'What automation theorists describe as the result of rising technological dynamism is actually the consequence of worsening economic stagnation, following on decades of manufacturing overcapacity and underinvestment'.[40] Pitts further develops this critique, arguing that the fetishism of information and data in this way sees productive technology stripped of its class character and reduced to a set of quantitative economic exchanges: 'Postcapitalists like Mason would have us believe value relates not to abstract social forms, but quantities of inputs and outputs. Indeed, their politics of the future depends upon it'.[41] Tellingly, this is the precise criticism that Althusser made in his own confrontation of post-work thinkers: 'While the capitalist mode of production does indeed produce objects of social utility, it produces them only under the aegis of very specific relations of production ... that simultaneously make them relations of *exploitation*'.[42] Emerging here are the consequences of ideology upon the post-work imaginary, as key social relations of work are mystified for the benefit of a particular analytical direction.

Another consequence is the reproduction of productivist notions of work and labour throughout the post-work imaginary: something to which Weeks alludes in her initial criticism above. Despite Srnicek and Williams' insistence that 'there can be no return to Fordism ... premised on the production paradigm of the orderly factory environment', the stomping ground of the 'white (male) workers',[43] it is precisely these parameters of productivism that the post-work imaginary reproduces and reinforces. Its disproportionate concentration on the forces of production 'bears out a disavowed productivist temptation towards the factory'[44] in the post-work imaginary. Here again, in the thinking of technology in relation to potential post-work futures, the relationship of class struggle to the appearance and deployment of machinery disappears and the post-work imaginary reproduces a productivist image of work

---

39   Spencer 2017, p.145.
40   Benanav 2020, p.39.
41   Pitts 2017, p.333.
42   Althusser 2014a, pp.30–1.
43   Srnicek and Williams 2013, para.17.
44   Pitts 2017, p.333.

as a set of value-producing material operations, with the social relations and other material operations that exist outside of this definition (but nonetheless contribute to its appearance) completely obfuscated from view. As Pitts and Dinerstein write:

> The post-work literature is productivist insofar as it sees 'work' as the central relation of capitalist society and not as the antagonistic relations of property, ownership and subsistence that logically and historically precede a society in which most people are compelled to sell their labour to live, nor the specific kind of results assumed by the products of that labour in the market. In so doing it remains locked within a capitalist understanding of what is productive and what is not, despite professions otherwise.[45]

Paradoxically, the post-work imaginary at once criticises contemporary capitalism for concretely deciding what is and is not productive (prioritising wage-labour activities over other activities of social utility such as poetry, art and care for example) and then, in the same movement, unwittingly emphasises that it is the productive forces of capitalism, in particular information and automation, that are the sole location of productive activity. It celebrates activity outside of work but overlooks its own reproduction of capitalist productivist ideology by fetishizing the forces of production as the most important site of productive activity. In this way, the post-work imaginary overlooks its own reinforcement of capitalist ideology: 'Despite different politics, our present-day post-work dreamers desire much the same flat-white future as the so-called "productivity ninjas" that spring from the Silicon Valley subculture of pop-optimism and personal optimisation'.[46]

Weeks has drawn greater attention to this oversight, particularly in relation to key demands of the post-work imaginary such as automation and the UBI. For if a UBI is to be, as Srnicek and Williams argue, a 'fundamentally feminist proposal',[47] then it cannot begin with the question of 'work' but *must* begin with the question of reproduction. In *The Problem with Work*, Weeks argues that reproduction is not only missing from dominant post-work imaginaries but provides an altogether more useful starting-point for thinking about post-work society. Weeks shows that dominant post-work imaginaries struggle in

---

45 Pitts and Dinerstein 2017, p.4.
46 Pitts and Dinerstein 2017, p.7.
47 Srnicek and Williams 2015, p.122.

their objective to trouble the ideological and cultural centrality of work in society, primarily because they reproduce these ideological notions by upholding the false separation between the relations inside work and those outside of it. A feminist consideration of reproduction, however, does a much better job at this, because it problematises this false division and forces attention towards the actual source of work's cultural domination: namely its social relations, that extend *beyond* the factory walls. For Weeks, this is the value of feminist campaigns in the mid-to-late twentieth century, such as the Wages for Housework Movement:

> By naming part of what happens in the family as work, the demand for wages confounds the division between work as a site of coercion and regimentation and the family as a freely invented site of authentic and purely voluntary relations.[48]

In drawing attention to the fact that the family and reproduction more generally is regulated by unique social relations, dominant pillars of the post-work imaginary such as the UBI suddenly become ineffective, as the problem with reproduction is not simply that it is unwaged but the fact that change to the relationship between capital and labour alone is insufficient in ending capitalist exploitation.

A third problem with the post-work imaginary is its insistence on the novelty of the current appearance of work under capitalism, often emphasised through concepts like 'precariousness'. For those like Guy Standing, precariousness is the defining characteristic of the contemporary crisis of work, the reduction of which is centralised as one of the key aims of automation and the UBI. Standing uses precariousness as a way of defining the existence of an entirely new class in society. The 'precariat,' according to Standing is 'a growing mass of people – potentially all of us outside the elite, anchored in their wealth and detachment from society – in situations that can only be described as alienated, anomic, anxious and prone to anger'.[49] However, as Alberti et al. write, the description of class on the basis of precariousness alone precludes particular social relations and ideologies that ultimately define and describe class experience: 'Class, however, is about more than classification. The relationship between labour and capital is a dynamic one: the imperatives of capital accumulation lead to new and constantly evolving demands on workers

---

48 Weeks 2011, p.129.
49 Standing 2016, p.28.

and governments'.[50] In this way, precariousness is not a particularly helpful pivot of analysis because 'there is no one group for whom precarity is a unique hallmark; precarity is instead theorized as inherent to all labour-capital relationships, to varying degrees'.[51]

This last point on 'varying degrees' of precariousness is important to stress as well, because the notion of precariousness as a new or unique phenomenon also precludes gendered and racialised voices for whom this condition has been the norm rather than the exception. In relying on precariousness as the defining characteristic of the crisis of work, it reproduces a particular Eurocentrism, focused on an immediate change in circumstances to an otherwise stable social norm. In other words, precariousness describes an aberration from the stable, secure and formal forms of employment that were predominant in Europe during the twentieth century. But this is precisely the point: these stable forms of employment were a European phenomenon not a global one and relied implicitly on the precariousness of other, much larger populations, such as women and the colonised. Contrary to the assertions of the post-work imaginary, 'if we look at capitalism in a wider historical and geographical scope, it is precarity that is the norm and not Fordist economic organization'.[52]

Neilson and Rossiter's argument precedes much of the literature discussed in relation to the post-work imaginary, but its argument is nonetheless applicable to the problematisation of the latter's discourse. Neilson and Rossiter acknowledge a disproportionate presence of the concept of precariousness and precarity in the development of Western social science, emerging particularly in the early twenty first century, in which it is fetishised as the defining concept of contemporary considerations of work and subjectivity within sociological analyses. As Neilson and Rossiter write in relation to this emerging discourse, 'at base was an attempt to identify or imagine precarious, contingent or flexible workers as a new kind of political subject, replete with their own forms of collective organization and modes of expression'.[53] The problem with this discourse is that the concept of precariousness is not centralised in the same way in sociological critiques developed outside of North America and Western Europe, as 'precariousness' does not present itself as a discernible and unique characteristic of work in other parts of the world. Neilson and Rossiter argue that this is because 'precariousness' is a fundamentally Western phenomenon that describes a deviation from a brief period of stability in the history of West-

---

50 Alberti et al. 2018, p.449.
51 Ibid.
52 Neilson and Rossiter 2008, p.54.
53 Neilson and Rossiter 2008, p.52.

ern capitalism, whilst precariousness never came and went for the rest of the world: rather, it was described simply as work. As the post-1945 welfare state disintegrated in Western Europe, the concept of precariousness and of post-Fordism came into fruition in Western social science. But these terms are more descriptive of the inward-looking nature of Western social science as opposed to the sociology of work itself. The post-work imaginary is founded in precisely the same Western intellectual movement, routinely locating the contemporary crisis of work in the decline of the welfare state, the emergence of neoliberalism and the shift to post-Fordist or post-industrial economic eras: 'The 1970s created a major shift within these general conditions, away from secure employment and unwieldy industrial behemoths and towards flexible labour and lean business models'.[54]

This is problematic because it demonstrates that the post-work imaginary, even in attempting to decentralise traditional considerations of work, continues to reinforce them. It is an exclusionary consideration of work that overlooks racialised and gendered forms of work, instead concentrating on work as a mutual, albeit antagonistic, relationship between worker and employer. The post-work imaginary's critique of capitalism – a mode of production they define as 'the relationship between proletariat and employers, with waged work mediating between them'[55] – is levelled on the basis of a very particular, closed and modern conceptualisation of work imbued with the very ideological characteristics of the concept from which they themselves are trying to break. In the context of Neilson's and Rossiter's argument, the post-work imaginary here fails to problematise the precise ideologies that normalise dominant considerations of 'work' in the first place and the social relations they reflect: 'The dominant theorization of post-Fordism leaves no room for the construction of new forms of political subjectivity or the invention of new institutional forms'.[56]

In what follows, the chapter looks to interrogate the precise epistemological arrangement that allows for these oversights to remain in place. The following section demonstrates that the persistence of a theoretical humanism throughout the post-work imaginary is responsible for the bracketing of social relations in such a way as to facilitate and perpetuate these oversights within its analysis of work under capitalism.

---

54   Srnicek 2016, p.34.
55   Srnicek and Williams 2015, p.92.
56   Neilson and Rossiter 2008, p.58.

3 The Theoretical Humanism of Post-work Thought

In order to analyse the source of the shortcomings outlined above, it is important to focus on two important aspects of the post-work discourse: first, the *object* or *problematic* that concerns its social scientific enquiry; and second, the reflection of this theoretical problematic in practice (in politics). This section of the chapter demonstrates that the post-work imaginary relies on a theoretically humanist problematic, one which produces *not a sociology of work but an anthropology of the working subject*. The centrality of this problematic eclipses what could be a sociological analysis of the problem of work today behind an ideological problem of the alienation of the human subject from its activity. It is the profound alienation of the human subject from their activity that defines the problem with work today and necessitates its urgent sociological analysis. Secondly, and relatedly, this post-work imaginary is shown to reflect this problematic in its construction of politics and its imagination of an alternative social future. Due to the centrality of its ideological problematic, strategies for the abolition of work do not find themselves targeted at the wage-labour relation or its connected social relations, but instead prioritise the re-introduction of the human subject with their activity as the precondition of effective political strategy.

3.1 The Theoretical Problem

The sociological backdrop upon which this discourse unfolds is one which apparently demonstrates a world of work undergoing significant shifts. The rapid development of the forces of production places the widespread automation of work on the horizon, leading to particular socio-economic problems including 'deindustrialisation' and the 'hollowing-out' of the labour-market. Relatedly, these developments are linked to a growing precariousness of work which see full-time and secure forms of employment give way to more informal, part-time and irregular employment relations. As demonstrated above, the novelty of these developments has been subject to significant and sustained scrutiny. However, these oversights remain relatively undisturbed because they sit within a theoretical discourse whose object is not 'work' (that is, the social relations that underpin the worker's experience of the working day) but the working human subject. It is precisely because the focus of this discourse is not squarely upon the social relations reflected in the contemporary problem with work – the analysis of which has cast light on these oversights – that these assumptions surrounding automation and precariousness can pass relatively unchallenged.

The evidence for this claim is found first in the initial problematisation of work itself. Within the sociology of post-work, the 'problem with work' is very specifically defined. It is not a problem of the social relations of work that these thinkers are interested in, but rather a disturbance, brought to light by the 'sociological' conditions of automation and precariousness, in the relationship that has hitherto existed between human beings and their labour. Peter Fleming observes the alienation of the human subject today in the culture of meaningless over-work that has come to pervade the automated post-industrial societies of advanced capitalism. In the face of important sociological changes, work has become merely 'ceremonial', in which 'beautiful human faculties [are] totally unused but still observable in the shadow form they take of acute anxiety, high blood pressure and an early death, all caused by doing fuck all rather than something meaningful'.[57] For David Frayne, the problem is an untethering of the link between work and social belonging. Developments in productive technology have meant that 'growing numbers of the people suffer because their labour power is no longer useful for the generation of private profit', with this group existing 'either without work entirely, or functioning as a reserve-army of low-paid, insecure workers'[58] within the new 'gig economies' of European labour markets. However, society itself has not adapted to these changes, reproducing this same cleavage between human experience and the societies to which these human subjects belong: 'The social construction of work as a key source of income, rights and belonging is unswerving. Yet what is also clear is that, for vast numbers of people, work is becoming an increasingly *unreliable* source of these things'.[59] Guy Standing has described the effective ejection of masses of workers from mainstream employment markets into a 'precariat' class which not only must subsist on less work, but experiences a heightened separation from their society as a result: 'When employed, they are in career-less jobs, without traditions of social memory, a feeling they belong to an occupational community steeped in stable practices, codes of ethics and norms of behaviour, reciprocity and fraternity'.[60] The problem with work today is here constructed as a problem of the alienation of the human subject from their society, underpinned by the steadfast importance of work to their social identity in the context of a society decreasingly dependent upon human labour.

The genealogy of this problematic passes not only through the works of the Young Marx but also through the post-work thought of those like André Gorz, examined in the previous chapter. For Gorz, not only was work disappearing from society as manufacturing industries declined and moved offshore, but

---

57 Fleming 2017, p.140.
58 Frayne 2015, p.38.
59 Frayne 2015, p.43.
60 Standing 2016, p.20.

the service-based work that was taking its place implicated a far-greater and more damaging form of alienation. As Gorz wrote, 'the old notion of work is no longer valid, the subject assumes a critical distance not only from the product of his work but from that work itself, regards that work as something other than his own activity'.[61] Gorz therefore argued that the possibility of transforming this type of work into something over which the proletariat would take historical control and put to the service of its own liberation, was quickly vanishing: 'In present conditions … neither the material possibility nor the subjective capacity for a transformation of work into autonomous activity exists'.[62] The disappearance of work from human society left fewer and fewer opportunities for an industrial proletariat, whose subjective identity was tied so closely to its labour, to realise itself in that society.

The pronunciation of this problem with work relies on an operational contradiction between two definitions of 'work': the alienated form of work evident in capitalist society; and its normative form, characterised by autonomy and self-determination. Gorz expounded this distinction in his writing:

> It is precisely this type of activity, which is not – or not entirely – my own activity, to which the term 'work' refers today. 'Work' is distinct from 'autonomous activity' and, indeed, from 'work-for-oneself.' Neither of these latter can any longer be regarded as modes of the former. By 'work,' we no longer mean all the forms of sensuous-practical activity by which a subject gives objective expression to his or her being, but a particular type of activity which is neither autonomous nor immediately useful to the person performing it.[63]

This distinction theoretically structures Gorz's problematisation of 'work' under capitalism and his refusal 'to extend the notion of "work" to autonomous activities and work-for-oneself'.[64] Crucially, *it is the relation of the activity to the human subject* that provides the functional hinge of this distinction, rather than any difference in the social characteristics of these activities. The post-work imaginary has today reanimated this humanist distinction in order to ensure the operationality of its critique, centralising the human subject as the object of these definitions, in place of the social relations of work.

---

61 Gorz 2012, p.59.
62 Gorz 2012, p.57.
63 Gorz 2012, pp.59–60.
64 Gorz 2012, pp.60–1.

Frayne argues that 'we can define true, meaningful work as work in which people are allowed to carry out tasks in accordance with their own technical, aesthetic and social criteria'.[65] However, Frayne juxtaposes this 'true' definition of work with its capitalist form, arguing that 'the obligation to paid employment so often precludes the possibility of engaging in activities that are genuinely creative, collaborative and useful'.[66] Frayne here echoes the Gorzian distinction between 'work' as the capitalist social relation of wage-labour ('paid employment') and the more humanist definition of 'work' as conscious or collaborative human activity, with the capacity for useful, self-directed human labour positioned as the imperative condition of this distinction. The same distinction is made by Fleming, when he writes that under capitalism work has become a 'crude political artefact',[67] in which it has become 'decoupled from its original purpose of labour, which ought to be about securing our collective needs so that we can do other things like relaxing, art, inventing, thinking or whatever'.[68] Standing also describes this distinction in his juxtaposition of 'labour' and 'work' (a more Arendtian rather than Gorzian distinction), with the former pertaining to the wage-labour relation and the latter to 'that most human of activities'[69] of collective and collaborative work. Evident here is that this post-work imaginary, in defining work and its problematic nature in contemporary capitalism, must reify and centralise the figure of the human subject, observing its functional definition of 'work' in the relationship enjoyed by this subject to its own activity.

For the interlocutors of the post-work imaginary, the problem with capitalism today is that, as a consequence of its development, it further alienates and subsumes the last remaining characteristics of autonomous human labour, animating them through the wage-labour relation and further marginalising any possibility to engage in 'truly' conscious and self-directed activity. For Frayne, work today is characterised by 'the normalisation of a new form of alienation',[70] in which previously-protected characteristics of human life valorised in autonomous human activity – 'their emotions, their personalities and their individuality'[71] – find themselves reified in the service-industries of post-industrial capitalism. This focus on 'emotional labour' is a key feature within

---

65 Frayne 2015, p.63.
66 Frayne 2015, p.23.
67 Fleming 2017, p.143.
68 Fleming 2017, pp.142–3.
69 Standing 2016, p.221.
70 Frayne 2015, p.52.
71 Frayne 2015, p.53.

this sociology of post-work: the exploitation of which was first described by Arlie Hochschild as the process by which 'the worker can become estranged or alienated from an aspect of self – either the body or the margins of the soul – that is *used* to do the work'.[72] Discussing its place today, Jamie Woodcock writes that 'whether sending "humorous" text messages or making emotionally persuasive phone calls, it appears that human labour remains essential to the process, especially when sales are involved', but that 'the use of emotions by low-paid workers is, in any case, rarely a genuine human experience',[73] relying on an observation of emotional alienation in order to pronounce the problem with work today. Relatedly, Carl Cederström & Peter Fleming cite the rise of 'human resources' departments and efforts to manufacture and regulate the emotional output of contemporary workers as efforts to subsume the organic sociality of human labour into the wage-labour relation: 'Their aim is clear. Not only to make us do something we would rather shun, but also make us want to do it'.[74]

By virtue of its focus upon alienation, and upon the separation that emerges between the human subject and its 'genuine' emotion or activity, the sociological object of 'work' finds itself displaced for an anthropological object, namely 'the human subject.' A theoretical tendency now emerges within the sociology of post-work as the social grounding of the problem of work begins to give way to a more humanist ideological grounding, where work is observed less as a problem of material exploitation and more as a problem of subjective estrangement. In Frayne's analysis, wage-labour as a problem of the exploitation of labour-power gives way to wage-labour as a device to 'exploit the workers' selfhood',[75] with its aim not the accumulation of capital but limiting the individual autonomy of the human worker. For Cederström & Fleming, 'the real fault-line today is not between capital and labor. It is between capital and life'.[76] In this formulation, class struggle and its reflection in capitalist social relations gives way to a new dialectic between 'capital and life', between capitalist social relations and human subjectivity.

3.2 *The Political Problem*

Given the epistemological orientation of the post-work imaginary – one organised around the ideological principle of the human subject and the observation

---

72   Hochschild 1983, p.7.
73   Woodcock 2019, p.71.
74   Cederström and Fleming 2012, p.9.
75   Frayne 2015, p.62.
76   Cederström and Fleming 2012, p.7.

of its alienation at work – the political imagination germinated therefrom is equally constrained by these same epistemological coordinates. The post-work imaginary that emerges from this initial theory is one that focuses its attention primarily on this human subject, constructing a political strategy designed to attack and correct the alienated condition of this subject. This, once more, is a problematic development, as the social relations of work – and the class struggle that has, historically, underwritten any and all changes to these relations – is eclipsed behind a moralistic political strategy aimed at redressing the feelings of alienation and meaninglessness that characterise the life of the working subject today.

For Srnicek and Williams, the project of post-capitalism appears oftentimes as one of subjective transformation. Though they try to insulate themselves from charges of theoretical humanism ('There is no "true" essence to humanity that could be discovered beyond our enmeshments in technological, natural and social webs'[77]), the success of their demands for full automation and the institution of a UBI appear conditional on a simultaneous transformation of the human subject and a reconstruction of the relationship between this subject and the society in which they live: 'Such a project ... potentiates the conditions for a broader transformation from the selfish individuals formed by capitalism to communal and creative forms of social expression liberated by the end of work'.[78] Mason, in his contribution to the postcapitalist discourse, argues that the rise of 'immaterial' commodities such as data and information, brought on by advancements in productive technologies, have the capacity to liberate and accentuate 'our human desire to make friends, [and] build relationships based on mutual trust and obligation, fulfilling emotional and psychological needs'.[79] It is also found in the post-work vision offered by Mareile Pfannebecker and J.A. Smith, who argue that 'any prospective post-work society would require nothing short of a thoroughgoing overhaul of all values ... as well as new definitions of the "care of the self" and of human flourishing'.[80]

The genealogy of this humanist political imaginary is again helpfully curated and applied in the work of Gorz and his consideration of a post-work future. Gorz argued that the imagination of an alternative social future beyond work relied on the ability to reorganise how time is allocated and spent within society: a project he called a 'politics of time'.[81] Gorz argued that a post-work future

---

77   Srnicek and Williams 2015, p.180.
78   Srnicek and Williams 2015, p.176.
79   Mason 2015, p.130.
80   Pfannebecker and Smith 2020, p.91.
81   Gorz 2012, p.61.

relied on the ability to greatly reduce the amount of time society spent on 'heteronomous' activity (wage-labour, or work as defined by capitalism), in favour of expanding the time available for workers to engage in 'autonomous' activity (self-directed labour).[82] The achievement of this societal re-organization of time lay at the core of Gorz's imagination of a post-work society:

> The development of free activities which are no longer *work* (in the sense this term has come to assume) obviously cannot be produced simply by reducing working hours. It requires a *politics of time* which embraces the reshaping of the urban and natural environment, cultural politics, education and training, and reshapes the social services and public amenities in such a way as to create more scope for self-managed activities, mutual aid, voluntary co-operation and production for one's own use.[83]

Importantly, the main target of this politics of time was the creation of a space for subjective transformation: the space for an alternative subjective development opened up by a more voluntary and autonomous engagement in work-for-oneself. The 'crisis of work' for Gorz was therefore not simply a crisis of the employment market, but also a crisis of the emancipatory potential of work itself ('The transformation of work – of *all* work – into an autonomous activity was, according to Marx, the meaning of communism as a lived historical horizon'[84]). The heightened alienation experienced by the proletarian at work was, for Gorz, too great, meaning that the opportunities for self-realisation and liberation *within work as workers* had diminished significantly. The only alternative was to therefore expand the space outside of work and develop a new subjective identity tied not to the heteronomous act of wage-labour but to the autonomous act of work-for-oneself: 'There is no social space in which "true work" – which, depending upon circumstances, I prefer to call "work-for-oneself" or "autonomous activity" – can deploy itself in such a way to *produce society* and set its stamp upon it. *It is this space we have to create*'.[85]

Frayne engages directly with Gorz's ideas, arguing that the model of a 'politics of time' offered by Gorz represents something around which a post-work society should continue to be organised. Frayne argues that this must hinge on a significant reduction of working-time, as 'an increasing amount of free-time will allow people to forge new relations of co-operation, communication and

---

82   Gorz 1983, p.97.
83   Gorz 2012, p.61.
84   Gorz 2012, p.56.
85   Gorz 2012, p.57.

exchange, and thereby become participants in the construction of their own futures'.[86] For Fleming, the post-work imaginary is characterised in terms of an 'escape': of formulating social spaces and social relationships that escape or exit their subsumption by capitalism in some form or another. Fleming argues that an 'abrupt and finalising "break" with capitalist routine appears to be one of the main ways that people resist and refuse neoliberal pan-capitalism today'.[87] Within the post-work imaginary, these socio-political visions of rupture with old working relations and the forging of new and more organic forms of activity tend to coalesce around a number of strategies. These include the implementation of new social policies such as a UBI – the payment of a standardised, weekly or monthly income to each citizen regardless of their existing income – which would 'be beneficial in tilting human activity towards forms of work that are not labour and enabling many to have greater control of their time'.[88]

This theoretical humanism persists in the conception of how this alternative social future will be achieved. For Frayne, the freedom of the human subject to pursue conscious and self-directed forms of work (that is, the reversal of the human subject's initial alienation by capitalism) is the precursor to significant social change that sees the ultimate reduction of wage-labour as a whole. As Frayne argues,

> The guiding ideal of social development would be the extent to which people were free to pursue and develop a range of interests and capacities. With more time to ourselves, we would have more time to work for ourselves, and hence would no longer depend on the economic sphere to cater to our every need.[89]

In this formulation, the compulsion to engage in waged-labour (expressed in the 'dependence on the economic sphere') emanates from the inability to engage in conscious, self-directed labour (from human alienation). Thus, the ability to reduce the societal dependence on the economic sphere and thus reduce the burden of wage-labour emanates from the ability of the human subject to re-establish control over those qualities of its work that have previously been alienated from it: a re-establishment that becomes the 'guiding ideal of social development'. In this formulation, the autonomy of the human subject becomes the *historical precondition* for the achievement of social change: in

---

86   Frayne 2015, p.222.
87   Fleming 2017, pp.219–20.
88   Standing 2016, p.311.
89   Frayne 2015, p.221.

other words, it is as a consequence of the initial re-establishment of the connection between the human subject and the self-directed qualities of this subject's own labour that the post-work imaginary, as a blueprint for a social movement, will come to pass. It is a problematic formulation because, when organised in this way, it provides a narrative of social change that is increasingly decoupled from class struggle and from strategies of social change grounded in the material alteration of social relations. As Frayne concludes, the post-work imaginary is one organised around the 'inventiveness of people', developing 'their own conceptions of pleasure, sufficiency, wealth and well-being, fit for a less work-centred society'.[90]

For Cederström and Fleming, the social transition into a post-work future rests in what they describe as a 'symbolic suicide',[91] committed by the working subject under capitalism. For Cederström and Fleming, the success of the post-work imaginary hinges on the ability to kill off the alienated working subjectivity created under capitalism, in favour of a different and more autonomous subject, more attached to the qualities of human life and labour. As they explain:

> If capital and life have become indistinguishable, then how could we know, taste or feel the latter? This is precisely what the symbolic suicide aims to achieve, to rethink life from the perspective of death. It is only by killing ourselves, as we know it, that we could start anew.[92]

Fleming builds on this idea in a later text, arguing that the battleground of the future of work and capitalism will unfold in the creation of a new social subjectivity following the 'death' of *homo economicus* as the expression of contemporary subjectivity under capitalism. Fleming offers a somewhat pessimistic image of the current state of subjectivity, arguing that both exploitation and resistance have been subsumed by its logic, leaving little subjective space for the creation of an alternative: 'Hopes of an escape and exit have quietly moved from a clean theory of freedom to a universalised economy of being alone'.[93] According to Fleming, escaping this pessimism is dependent upon escaping the alienated form of human subjectivity associated with this existence and searching for 'new inhabitants'[94] to take its place.

---

90 Frayne 2015, p.232.
91 Cederström and Fleming 2012, p.67.
92 Cederström and Fleming 2012, p.66.
93 Fleming 2017, p.255.
94 Ibid.

THEORETICAL HUMANISM AND THE POST-WORK IMAGINARY 125

Standing argues that precarious work is the reflection of precarious subjectivity and that the improvement of work in society relies on the improvement of the social and political life of the human subject. Standing argues that 'our happiness comes primarily from the work, leisure and play we undertake outside our labour, and from the income security we obtain from a job, not from the job itself'[95] and that the freedom of the human subject to think and act in accordance with its autonomous desires, resolves itself in an emancipatory social future: 'Freedom comes from being part of a community in which to realise freedom in the exercise of it. It is revealed through actions, not something granted from on high or divined in stone tablets'.[96] Other accounts, such as that of Nic Murray, argue that social and political alternatives not only emanate from human autonomy over work, but also human autonomy over speech. Work under capitalism has, Murray argues, alienated the way in which workers discuss stress, anxiety and mental health, encouraging workers to be open about these stresses whilst using this as a method of directing the work of its workers. Murray's answer to this is observed subjectively, in the individual's ability to 'press pause, seek to regain control over the discourse and steer the conversation towards more radical ends', with a view to developing collaborative discourse and unearthing 'the more radical aims that lie on the other side of silence'.[97] For Mason, the success of postcapitalism is firmly observed in the subjective alteration necessitated by digital commodities and free-flowing information today. Mason argues these advancements in the forces of production are 'making it possible for a cooperative, socially just society to emerge',[98] carried into being on the back a 'new kind of person, the networked individual, who is the bearer of the postcapitalist society that could now emerge'.[99]

In these ways, it is evident how the initial theoretical problem which sees the analysis of work take the form of an anthropology, is reflected in a political moralism which observes its success in the achievement of a subjective transformation. These two problematics cooperate in the production of a theoretical humanism at the centre of the post-work imaginary. It is in the shadows cast by this ideological operation that the theoretical shortcomings of this discourse – discussed above, primarily located in the bracketing of important social relations – are allowed to pass and sit comfortably within its formulations. The novelty of the sociological conditions said to precipitate this post-work imagin-

---

95 Standing 2016, p.243.
96 Standing 2016, p.288.
97 Murray 2019, p.58.
98 Mason 2015, p.143.
99 Mason 2015, pp.143–4.

ary are grounded not in the emergence of new material realities, but simply in the observation of new forms of human alienation and in the prospects of subjective transformation. As this theoretical humanism is dismantled, the novelty of the post-work imaginary gives way, leaving only the theoretical shortcomings of this discourse behind.

4 Conclusion

It's evident that, though the post-work imaginary presents an exciting and attractive vision for the future, its analysis of the present conjuncture is significantly flawed. Capitalist social relations of various kinds find themselves bracketed or rendered invisible within this imaginary, which sees this discourse over-emphasising both the novelty of the present 'crisis' of work and also the political opportunities presented by this crisis. This chapter has argued that the crux of this problem ought to be located in the persistence of theoretical humanism throughout this discourse. The post-work imaginary overlooks important social relations because the object of its analysis is not these social relations, but the individuals and concrete subjects implicated in these relations. The post-work imaginary reduces work and, consequently, post-work politics, to a subjective phenomenon that takes place at the individual level, observing social and political relations as relations between concrete subjects. This produces a flawed problematisation of work that focuses on the alienation of the human subject from their labour, and thus a political programme based on the correction of this alienated condition. In these two formulations, the social relations of work are pushed to the side in favour of a focus on the human subject, and it is within this arrangement that the various theoretical shortcomings with this imaginary are allowed to pass without problem.

Althusser's initial scepticism of the tendency to fetishise automation as a motor of social change therefore appears well-founded. By applying the principles of Althusser's critique of theoretical humanism to the post-work imaginary, this chapter has revealed the extent to which the shortcomings of this discourse are theoretical and ideological in nature. Some contributors have acknowledged this and attempted to offer corrections in their analysis of technology, work and class struggle. Gavin Mueller argues that when it comes to thinking about technology and work, 'the problem of technology is not simply that it alienates us from Being, or from authentic experiences', but rather 'the problem of technology is its role in capitalism'.[100] Re-orienting the analysis of

---

100   Mueller 2021, pp.6–7.

the relationship between work and technology in this way therefore requires a theoretically anti-humanist approach, in order to emphasise and prioritise the analysis of the social relations of capitalism in this analysis, as opposed to the concrete individuals implicated in these relations alone.

In the next chapter, the book follows the problem of theoretical humanism into feminist sociologies of work. A similar problem emerges in which the specific social relations responsible for the gendered exploitation of reproductive labour are hidden behind a theoretical and political framework which prioritises the relationship between reproductive labour and the human subject. The problem of contemporary capitalism is analysed within feminist sociologies as a problem of subjective alienation, with a moralistic politics offered as a potential solution. In what follows, the book analyses this problem through the reconstruction of an anti-humanist feminism in order to bring these theoretical and political problems into relief and observe their consequences upon feminist sociologies today.

CHAPTER 5

Social Reproduction and Theoretical Anti-humanism

This chapter continues to track the problem of theoretical humanism through feminist sociologies and the analysis of reproductive labour. Contemporary feminist sociologies of reproductive labour have, this chapter argues, organised themselves around a theoretically humanist problematic, observed primarily in the alienation of women from the 'emotional' or 'intimate' characteristics of reproductive labour. Particularly as globalised markets have emerged as the predominant mechanism for the regulation and exploitation of reproductive labour – visible in the emergence of new global 'trades' in domestic services, sex work, surrogacy and tissue donation – feminist sociologies have sought to emphasise the unique danger presented by these markets by emphasising the propensity, at their core, to commodify uniquely human tendencies to care and nurture. This chapter argues that this theoretically humanist problematic at the core of these feminist sociological approaches undermines their analysis of the material relationship between class and gender in the exploitation of reproductive labour. The humanist ideological core of these approaches causes these authors to over-state the uniquely alienating character of the work involved in these new trades, in a way that causes particular theoretical problems. These problems include a moralistic critique of the 'unnatural' characteristics of these types of work which overlooks existing Marxist-feminist attempts to denaturalise *all* types of reproductive labour in order to subject them to analysis and critique; and, consequentially, an effort to 'protect' wage-labour from its contamination by these unnatural forms of work through a resistance to classify these activities as work at all. The latter problem not only reinforces key social relations of capitalist exploitation, but again overlooks existing Marxist-feminist efforts to position women as workers so as to analyse and mobilise their historical and political power. Therefore, the chapter investigates the anti-humanist potential of a theoretical shift away from ideological notions of alienation, emotion and intimacy, towards a theory of social reproduction.

Social reproduction theory is a strand of feminist thought, informed by Marxism, that originated during the second wave of the 1970s. It has, however, continued to develop and is an important and growing component of contemporary theoretical feminism. To speak of the social relations of work under capitalism, one must speak too of the relations that govern the *reproduction* of work. To describe what takes place when the worker and the capitalist meet, it is not enough to describe the relations that govern the division of labour within the factory walls, of the absorption of surplus-value at the close of the labour process or the payment of wages. Because these social relations are not relations of the workplace alone: on the contrary, they demand reproduction within spaces and amongst actors who fall outside of this traditional productive arena. To describe the *reproductive* relations contained herein is the *only* way to fully describe the social relations of production and of capitalism more generally. As Tithi Bhattacharya describes it:

> It is an approach that is not content to accept what seems like a visible, finished entity – in this case, our worker at the gates of her workplace – but interrogates the complex network of social processes and human relations that produces the conditions of existence for that entity.[1]

The Althusserian tradition is familiar with a concept of reproduction, notably in Étienne Balibar's contribution to *Reading Capital* and at the core of Althusser's *On the Reproduction of Capitalism*. However, the analyses of reproduction forwarded in these examples can be said to fall short of an analysis of the reproduction of those social relations ideologically excluded from the realm of 'production' proper. It was, rather, a vanguard of Marxist-feminists who opened up reproduction and sexuality '*historically* ... pointing out that reproduction can be understood "in the last instance" not only in an economic way, but in a way that takes into account the entire conditions for the "perpetuation of the worker"'.[2]

The chapter follows Lise Vogel, Natalia Romé, Kathi Weeks and Susan Ferguson in their argument that social reproduction theory represents an important theoretical framework through which to re-orient feminist theory today. In particular, it follows these authors in their observation of the (necessarily) theoretically anti-humanist nature of this theoretical re-orientation. In concluding this chapter, social reproduction theory will be positioned as an important theoretical perspective through which to counter the most damaging aspects of the theoretical humanism that currently persists within feminist sociologies and thereby articulate a more materialist understanding of reproductive labour today.

---

1 Bhattacharya 2017, p.2.
2 Power 2017, p.227.

1   A 'Crisis' of Feminism?

Much as Althusser sought to make his intervention at a point he described in terms of a 'crisis of Marxism', it may be appropriate to say that contemporary discussions surrounding social reproduction theory have emerged in the context of a crisis of feminism: that is, at a point in which feminist thought has reached a theoretical impasse, which, if it hopes to move past, must go through a process of radical re-orientation and possible rupture. In her discussion of the correspondence between Maria Macciocchi and Louis Althusser, Imogen Woods has indicated the existence of this crisis, in the form of a mismatch between feminist theory and struggle. Just as Macciocchi sought to work through the mis-match between theory and practice within the context of the Party, Woods has argued that a similar moment has presented itself again in the context of feminist struggle: the struggle must 'begin with the class and an understanding of the class that is developed from listening rather than assumption. Before plastering demands as our slogans, we need to understand the specific conjucture we are organising'.[3] The question is, then, that of the nature of this obstacle. As it was for Marxism, theoretical humanism and humanist ideology represents a significant component of this contemporary crisis, as even Macciocchi herself recognised: 'Marxism is not a 'humanism' ... less moralism and more politics. More truth, and less ambiguity'.[4]

The implications of theoretical humanism within the context of feminist thought and strategy are convincingly (though not always explicitly) articulated by Lise Vogel, in her discussion of socialist feminism in her book *Marxism and the Oppression of Women*. In a similar register to Althusser, Vogel argues that at the core of this crisis of feminism is a theoretical problem expressed in a poor reading of Marx, in which moral categories are favoured over scientific concepts. Vogel describes a situation in which 'theoretical underdevelopment combined with a certain moralism and strategic opportunism to create a great deal of confusion', in which 'the terms productive and unproductive, which Marx used as scientific-economic categories, were invested with moral overtones'.[5] In much the same way as Althusser, Vogel argues that it is important to undertake a particular – one might say, guilty – reading of the works of Marx and Engels in order to draw from their work the concepts necessary to develop

---

3   Woods 2022, para.14.
4   Macciocchi 1973, p.31.
5   Vogel 2013, p.22.

a strategy that is suitable and appropriate for the aims and ends of socialist feminism today: that is, in order to 'hear what they actually said'.[6]

Vogel is clear that the crisis of socialist feminism about which she writes emanates from an abandonment of materialism in favour of idealism, synonymous with the evacuation of feminist theory of Marxist concepts. As Vogel writes, 'despite its commitment to socialism, socialist feminism's different starting point often leads to a theoretical emphasis divergent from that of Marx and Engels'.[7] This tendency towards idealism is observed by Vogel in the greater persistence of humanist ideology within feminist thought. This takes a number of forms. On the one hand, it can be seen through a repeated refraction of feminist demands through discourses of bourgeois political anthropology, 'which trivialises the issue of women's oppression as a mere matter of lack of rights and ideological chauvinism'.[8] On the other, it takes the form of 'a primary focus on psychology, on ideology, and on relations of hierarchy and authority',[9] that prioritises the analysis of patriarchy only to the extent that it effects an empirical and observable subject. For Vogel, the success of socialist feminism requires that it position itself more concretely in the field of materialism, with the works of Marx and Engels an important source for this orientation.

In her text *For Theory*, Natalia Romé has demonstrated the potential of an Althusserian approach to theoretical feminism in facilitating this move towards a more materialist position. For Romé, this approach 'is not in this sense a "perspective" or a discipline, but what can rigorously be called a *position* in the theoretical field; a *partisan* practice of theory that requires tracing demarcations in order to politically affect the knowledge production'.[10] Romé here echoes Althusser's insistence that philosophy is a battlefield, arguing that feminism must represent a theoretical weapon on this battlefield, fighting to establish a materialist position in the context of gendered violence and exploitation. Much like Vogel, Romé recognises that moralistic and theoretically humanist interpretations of this gendered experience too often dominate the field of theoretical feminism today. As Romé explains:

> The resurgence of essentialist and individualist forms of understanding psychic, affective, and sexual life, whose diagnoses of inequalities and injustices slide toward essentialist naturalisms or philosophical abstrac-

---

6 Vogel 2013, p.38.
7 Vogel 2013, p.37.
8 Vogel 2013, p.31.
9 Vogel 2013, p.38.
10 Romé 2021, p.95.

tions, around categories such as 'self-consciousness', 'clitoral woman', 'work', 'life,' *'ethos'*, not only leads to an indistinction and subsumption of the political in the ethical, but does so under a significant humanist emphasis that makes the very idea of feminism problematic, beyond a simple inversion of sexism.[11]

In order to combat this theoretical humanism, Romé looks to establish 'the point of view of reproduction',[12] located in Althusser's notion of reproduction as established in *On the Reproduction of Capitalism*. This point of view of reproduction turns substantially on the relationship between reproduction and 'overdetermination' established by Althusser. The concept of overdetermination allows Althusser to construct reproduction as an effect of structural causality rather than determined by any natural or subjective factors alone. In this way, 'the "point of view of reproduction" names the analytic approach that might be, in a certain way, "partisan" (for being capable of reading structure in terms of the concrete "conditions" of the situation).'[13] It is here that Romé locates the starting-point for a radical approach to social reproduction within contemporary theoretical feminisms, as 'the problem of reproduction constitutes the territory in which the ideological threat prowls the Marxist field'[14] and therefore becomes the anchor-point of feminism's position on this theoretical battlefield, particularly against its humanist adversary.

Kathi Weeks also looks to theoretical anti-humanism as a way of establishing a feminist standpoint theory capable of posing important strategic and political questions. For Weeks:

> Althusser's antihumanism provides a much needed opportunity to assess critically the legacy of socialist feminist theory. There are many examples where, despite the commitment to the Marxist conception of socially constructed subjectivity, both systems theories and standpoint theories lapse into humanist formulas.[15]

For Weeks, contemporary theoretical feminisms too often reproduce a theoretical humanism in their conceptualisation of the relationship between patriarchy and capitalism, where 'the conception of an alternative is tied to a notion

---

11 Romé 2021, p.97.
12 Romé 2021, p.51.
13 Ibid.
14 Romé 2021, p.103.
15 Weeks 2018, p.113.

of a true, authentic, original, or otherwise essential humanity.'[16] These appeals to authenticity undermine what Weeks calls 'the constructedness of the human subject – its immanence to the social world, its status as a social process'.[17] Similar to Romé, Weeks therefore recognises the potential of the relationship between overdetermination and theoretical anti-humanism for contemporary feminist thought, arguing that these two concepts provide an opportunity to break with moralistic or biological understandings of gender identity in favour of a more materialist interpretation of feminist subjectivities. As Weeks writes, 'gender identity is, thus, not determined but overdetermined: it is the unstable effect of multiple and potentially inconsistent forces of determination which are themselves overdetermined'.[18] However, Weeks finds many more limitations in Althusser's theoretical anti-humanism and the notion of history as a 'process without a subject', arguing that the end-point of Althusser's anti-humanism is the evacuation of the subject from theory entirely, rather than its simple displacement: 'Decentering the subject is one thing, eliminating subjects quite another'.[19]

When it comes to the question of work, Weeks has obviously recognised the value of developing this theoretically anti-humanist position for a feminist approach to the problem with work today. Weeks revisits the autonomist tradition and argues that it treads a theoretical line between traditional forms of socialist humanism and the theoretical anti-humanism of Althusser, leaving available a space for thinking about subjectivity rather than evacuating it from theory entirely. As Weeks writes, 'autonomists tend to shift the analytical frame from the question of individual nature to the possibilities of collective constitution, from a self to restore to selves to invent'.[20] Weeks locates the shift towards antiwork politics and the refusal of work within this ambiguity over the nature of work, at the meeting point between its scientific analysis within the capitalist mode of production and its qualitative assessment as an interpellating force. For Weeks, it is the feminism of the Wages for Housework Movement that advances this furthest both theoretically and politically, which this chapter will examine in greater detail later.

Susan Ferguson has also stressed the importance of theoretical anti-humanism when it comes to the feminist analysis of work. Ferguson demonstrates how materialist feminist analyses of work emerged from a break with

---

16   Weeks 2018, p.114.
17   Ibid.
18   Weeks 2018, p.105.
19   Weeks 2018, pp.114–15.
20   Weeks 2011, p.90.

the 'rational-humanist' feminisms of the eighteenth century, which conceptualised work as a point of moral and political elevation rather than a relation of exploitation. For the rational-humanist feminists – of whom Mary Wollstonecraft is cited as an example – work is conceptualised 'as a positive moral imperative that signalled a person's humanity, and as a potential path to independence from, and thus equality with, men'.[21] In this way, these early feminists locate women's inequality as stemming 'primarily from obstacles society puts in the way to fulfilling their potential as autonomous human beings – from legal and cultural forces denying women higher education and confining them to the household'.[22] The development of a socialist feminism is predicated on a theoretical break with this rational-humanist analysis of work, which saw the inequality of women not as the outcome of a group denied their humanity, but of one class being exploited by another: 'The problem of inequality does not lie with these facts of biology. It lies with the competitive system that organizes the production and distribution of wealth – capitalism'.[23] For Ferguson, the emergence of socialist feminism lies in the shift away from analysing reproductive labour 'as women's natural or God-given duty',[24] towards its conception as an act of *production*, 'attributing women's oppression then to the *relational dynamic* between reproductive and productive work'.[25]

Vogel, Romé, Weeks and Ferguson all contend that an integral element of the theoretical reorientation of contemporary socialist feminism is some form of theoretical anti-humanism. Particularly when it comes to the topic of work, appreciating the material realities of the intersection between gender and work, patriarchy and capitalism, relies on a theoretical break with moralistic and humanistic interpretations of reproductive labour, towards a view that Ferguson describes as 'scientific', which places reproductive labour within the context of political economy. What is evident is that within contemporary feminist discourses on the topic of work, this moralistic view is resurgent and persists within feminist sociologies today. In the following section, the chapter will demonstrate this persistence and work towards its critique.

---

21   Ferguson 2020, p.29.
22   Ibid.
23   Ferguson 2020, p.45.
24   Ferguson 2020, p.46.
25   Ferguson 2020, p.47.

2   Emotion, Alienation and Reproductive Labour

When looking at feminist sociologies of work – found at the intersection of the analysis of production and reproduction – there is an evident resurgence in this moralistic and theoretically-humanist problematic. In the context of contemporary forms of reproduction under capitalism, the sociological conjuncture is one characterised by a shift of reproductive labours from the family unit towards the market. Increasingly, globalised labour markets emerge as the contemporary social expression of reproductive labour, as new 'industries' in domestic labour, sex work, tissue donation and surrogacy see the reproduction of labour-power – and the gendered class struggle inherently reflected therein – no longer confined only to the family unit. This is characterised by Melinda Cooper and Catherine Waldby in terms of a post-Fordist shift in the appearance and organisation of reproductive labour, where 'domestic tasks, sexual services, care provision, and ... the process of biological reproduction itself have migrated out of the private space of the family into the labor market and are now central to post-industrial accumulation strategies'.[26]

In the context of these emerging political economic developments in contemporary reproduction, a theoretically humanist analysis of capitalism has emerged which observes its critique in the propensity of contemporary capitalism to centralise new strategies of human *alienation* in order to bring these new reproductive industries to pass. According to this approach, these new relations of reproduction are distinct from those of the household and the family that preceded them, by virtue of the unique and significantly heightened forms of human harm and alienation that they inaugurate. Unlike the reproductive labour of the family, so this critique goes, the manifestation of reproductive labour on global labour markets commodifies human feeling, human contact and essential human values as services to be bought and sold. 'Love', 'care', 'motherhood' and 'sexuality' all take shape as commodities in this emerging market of reproductive services, alienated from the women to whom these values belong and deployed cynically by contemporary capitalism as a source of profit. For these authors, these new forms of reproductive labour are to be guarded against and resisted as evidence of an encroaching commodification of the female body. As Hochschild wrote, 'it may not be too much to suggest that we are witnessing a call for the conservation of "inner resources," a call to save another wilderness from corporate use and keep it "forever wild"'.[27]

---

26   Cooper and Waldby 2014, p.5.
27   Hochschild 1983, p.22.

By virtue of this discourse's setting-out from a humanist problematic, it finds it particularly difficult to think production and reproduction together. As highlighted in the discussion of Vogel's work above, the key insight of Marxist-feminism has been that the social relations of production under capitalism are at all times a reflection of the relations of reproduction and that one cannot be viewed without the other. However, in this humanist argument, there is an evident resurrection of a normative division between 'work' proper and the relations that escape this definition. This normative separation becomes crucial in pronouncing the characteristics of human alienation under capitalism but makes for a limited analysis as the social relations of reproduction find themselves inevitably mystified. In this humanist analysis, there is no critique of the ways in which contemporary forms of sex work or domestic labour implicate a particular gendered class struggle which is then reflected in capitalist production more generally: rather, contemporary forms of reproductive labour are separated out from other types of 'work', as uniquely harmful expressions of human alienation that require particular strategies of resistance.

Within contemporary contributions to feminist sociology, this humanist problematic finds itself most readily expressed in the emergence of new concepts, in particular the concepts of 'emotional', 'affective' or 'intimate' labour. 'Intimacy' and 'emotion' have become increasingly popular frames of reference through which the exploitation of reproductive labour is thought about in the context of a burgeoning market economy. Contemporary capitalism and the emerging 'reproductive' industries it makes available, risk undermining the protection from the market that reproductive labour had previously enjoyed (in the private household), opening it up to commodification in ways that are uniquely dangerous. This unique danger stems from the fact that, unlike the activities of the wage-labourer, these reproductive labours correlate to distinct and specifically 'human values'[28] which, under contemporary capitalism, find themselves mobilised in the provision of a host of new reproductive services. The relationship between intimacy and labour was introduced conceptually by Arlie Hochschild with the concept of 'emotional labour', arguing that what contemporary service-industries 'sell' is in fact the emotional labour of its workers, crystallised in the maintenance of an emotionally genuine relationship between the worker and their customer in the delivery of a service. In recent years, this has been updated and expanded, particularly in notable contributions such as that of Eileen Boris and Rhacel Parreñas and their the-

---

28   Satz 2010, p.3.

ory of 'intimate labour'.[29] The concept of intimate labour 'brings together the often-separated categories of care work, domestic work and sex work, calling attention to the labour involved in tending to the intimate needs of individuals inside and outside their home'.[30] However, these concepts offer a definitively humanist framing of how reproductive labour is exploited (by emphasising the existence of pre-existing emotional or intimate human characteristics from which the reproductive labourer is alienated in the course of their work) and this section argues that this humanist framing of reproductive labour develops problematically, into a tendency which sees the gendered class relations of reproductive labour obscured or bracketed. In order to demonstrate this, this section will critically analyse some of the leading contributions to this emerging discourse.

This argument was central to Hochschild's critique in *The Managed Heart*. For Hochschild, contemporary capitalism was defined by its centralisation of what she called 'emotional labour' in its organisation of production. Hochschild described 'emotional labour' as 'the management of feeling to create a publicly observable facial and bodily display',[31] arguing that contemporary capitalism was less concerned with the production of material products, but instead was increasingly more invested in reproducing feelings of gratitude, happiness and satisfaction within an augmenting base of consumers more interested in services than commodities. Using the example of flight attendants – whom Hochschild used in the empirical studies conducted in her text – Hochschild described how through the centrality of emotional labour within contemporary production, 'the emotional style of offering the service is part of the service itself'[32] in a way that is not prevalent in earlier, more industrial forms of production (the worker's emotional attitude towards a material commodity does not have any bearing on the appearance of that commodity following its production). Synonymous with this new form of production was, essentially, a new form of alienation. Rather than separating the worker from merely the products of their labour, this new regime of capitalist production would depend upon the separation of workers from distinctively human emotional capacities. In reference to Marx's observations of wallpaper production in industrial capitalism, Hochschild described this new form of alienation:

---

29   Boris and Parreñas 2010.
30   Lee and Parreñas 2016, p.285.
31   Hochschild 1983, p.7.
32   Hochschild 1983, pp.5–6.

> The work done by the boy in the wallpaper factory called for a coordination of mind and arm, mind and finger, mind and shoulder. We refer to it simply as physical labor. The flight attendant does physical labor when she pushes heavy metal carts through the aisles, and she does mental work when she prepares for and actually organizes emergency landings and evacuations. But in the course of doing this physical and mental labor, she is also doing something more, something I define as emotional labor ... This kind of labor calls for a coordination of mind and feeling, and it sometimes draws on a source of self that we honor as deep and integral to our individuality.[33]

In this way, 'the worker can become estranged or alienated from an aspect of self – either the body or the margins of the soul – that is used to do the work'.[34] Hochschild problematised contemporary capitalism because the regimes of production that it was centralising were dependent upon the alienation and commodification of human qualities more deeply set and distinctive than the simple manipulation of tools required by manual forms of production. Human emotions and human relationships, once protected from commodification, now found themselves deployed in the service of capital accumulation, often to the detriment of the workers from whom these qualities were alienated. As Hochschild argued:

> The company lays claim not simply to her physical motions – how she handles food trays – but to her emotional actions and the way they show in the ease of a smile. The workers I talked to often spoke of their smiles as being on them but not of them.[35]

Through this argument, Hochschild problematised contemporary capitalism on the basis of its propensity to alienate and commodify basic and inherent human values – expressed primarily through human relationships and human emotions – and set these values to work in the pursuit of profit. The result, so Hochschild argued, is the production of a society in which human emotion is transformed from a genuine expression of social cohesion to simply a product of an expanding service industry. This analysis of alienation constructed by Hochschild has been reflected in contemporary social scientific analyses

---

33 Hochschild 1983, pp.6–7.
34 Hochschild 1983, p.7.
35 Hochschild 1983, pp.7–8.

of reproductive labour. The observation of this alienation provides the analytical pivot of these emerging reproductive services, which are problematised in the extent to which they demand an alienation of distinctively human emotional capacities.

This condition of alienation is evident, for example, in the employment of nannies, maids and other domestic workers. Bridget Anderson argues that the working patterns that emerge in the relationship between a domestic labourer and their employing family are much different from those of an ordinary wage-labour relationship. What is demanded from the domestic labourer in the cleaning of homes, the raising of children or the care of other family members is a particular form of emotional labour that simulates a 'genuine' familial or emotional connection that is reflected in the work that is carried out. For example, Anderson describes the way in which domestic labourers are effectively inducted into the family and are expected to develop familial emotional bonds with those family members, in order that these bonds are reflected in the quality of care delivered. Problematically, for Anderson, the emotional bond that the domestic labourer forms with their employing family is a fundamentally alienated one, which results in a disproportionate benefit for the employing family, providing them with an opportunity to exploit greater amounts of emotional labour dependent upon their needs. As Anderson writes:

> Although being a part of the family does not entitle the worker to unconditional love or support, it does entitle the employer to encroach on the worker's off-duty hours for 'favours'. In fact, many employers will invoke either a contractual or a family relationship under different circumstances, depending on what is most convenient.[36]

For Anderson, the emotional relationship forged by the domestic labourer with their employing family is exploited as a way of designing working patterns to the benefit of the employing family, played on to demand longer working hours and more imposing forms of care work, but which is not reciprocated with a similar emotional response from the employing family and is simply paid for through a wage: 'As far as the employer is concerned, money expresses the full extent of her obligation to the worker'.[37] What therefore emerges within middle-class families in North America and Western Europe is an economy of alienated emotional labour, wherein the capacities for care and compassion

---

36   Anderson 2002, p.112.
37   Ibid.

that exist within particular (often poorer) women are alienated and exploited to the benefit of (often richer) families. As Anderson writes of the domestic labourer, 'her caring engenders no mutual obligations, no entry into a community, and no real human relationship – just money': a situation which 'denies the worker's humanity and the very depth of her feelings'.[38]

In this instance, these examples of contemporary reproductive labour are considered exceptional in the extent to which they demand a form of emotional alienation more severe than normal types of work. This is true not only of examples of domestic labour, but is particularly acute in considerations of sex work. In the wake of heightened calls for the decriminalisation of sex work in Europe, social critics such as Kat Banyard argue that calls for decriminalisation and for sex work to be treated as 'work', ignore the particular and uniquely severe forms of alienation that are central to the relationship between sex workers, their clients and their 'employers.' For Banyard, sex work is different from other types of work precisely because of the intense and heightened forms of alienation – and the reflection of this alienation in sexual and gendered violence – that are inaugurated by the conditions of this industry. By drawing attention to this, Banyard hopes to expose the 'chilling absurdity of claiming that what's taking place on porn sets and in brothels can be suitably framed as an innocuous consumer transaction'.[39] Through her interviews with sex workers, Banyard describes the experience of women in the sex industry by highlighting the ways in which women are in some way separated from their sexuality as it becomes commodified and made available for sale. For example, one interviewee, 'Tanja', describes her experience as a sex worker, saying 'it was like my sexuality didn't belong to me. It was something men could take if they wanted'.[40] 'Crystal', another former sex worker interviewed by Banyard, says that 'I still feel like I lost a part of myself back there – and there's no getting her back'.[41] Banyard draws attention to these accounts of loss and separation as a way of articulating the unique harms, reflected in a form of emotional alienation, that force the thinking of sex work as separate and distinct from other forms of work. For Banyard, the sex trade codifies this alienation by 'commodifying consent', removing women's autonomy over their own sexuality by alienating it from their control and making it available to be bought and sold:

---

38   Ibid.
39   Banyard 2016, ch.2, para.18.
40   Banyard 2016, ch.2, para.24.
41   Banyard 2016, ch.2, para.51.

> If while having sex with someone you feel repulsed by them touching you, afraid of what they might do, degraded and humiliated by the sexual acts, hurt by the hateful words they're whispering in your ear, sore because he's the fifth man you've had sex with today, exhausted from it all, traumatised, abused – the fact that you'll get a bit of cash at the end does not change this fact. There is no invisible hand in the prostitution market that magically disappears the lived experience of sexual abuse.[42]

In relation to sex work, this analysis is also echoed in the context of pornography and types of sex work that differ from the selling of sex (for example the production of adult material such as magazines, films and online broadcasts). For sociologists such as Gail Dines, contemporary society is one increasingly saturated with what she identifies as 'porn ideology',[43] which not only describes the proliferation of increased popularity of pornographic images in society but, more importantly, the infection of human approaches to sex and sexuality by the ideas and values reinforced by these pornographic images. The greater involvement of women in sex industries is, for Dines, a reflection of the fact that in contemporary society, approaches to sex and sexuality have been reified in an alienated condition, where sex is routinely pictured as something to which women are only an accessory as opposed to an active participant. As Dines writes:

> Why, then, are girls and women agreeing to have sex under emotionally shallow and at times physically dangerous circumstances? ... In this hypersexualized culture, we are socializing girls into seeing themselves as legitimate sex objects who are deserving of sexual use (and abuse).[44]

For Dines, the reflection of alienated sexuality in human society is particularly damaging insofar as it reproduces dangerous attitudes towards sex not only in men (who come to see women as objects to whom the act of sex is applied) but also in women too (who come to accept that sex is not something in which they engage, but are simply involved). This reproduces a passive attitude towards the figuration of sex and sexuality in human relationships, undermining social values such as intimacy but also, more dangerously, legal considerations of consent. Therefore, for these authors, the consideration of these forms of sex work within the paradigm of 'work' overlook the fact that the mobilisation of sex

---

42 Banyard 2016, ch.2, para.20.
43 Dines 2010, p.100.
44 Dines 2010, p.117.

and sexuality within service provision implicates a heightened form of human emotional alienation that is reflected in severe societal dangers and particular types of gendered violence.

This humanist approach is also evident in confrontations with tissue donation and surrogacy. Summarising popular critical responses to emerging markets in tissue donation and surrogacy, Donna Dickenson argues that what motivates concerns in relation to these emerging markets is the prospect of the commodification and marketisation of not only the human body, but of the cells that belong to it. In particular, the way in which tissue donation separates particular cells and bodily entities away from the body, or the way in which surrogacy ascribes value to only certain parts of the body (primarily the womb and its gestational capabilities), is problematised insofar as it reproduces a particular form of subjective alienation. Here, the bodily capabilities that underpin the human capacity for care become alienated from the precise human subject and its social setting, in the sole context of which these capabilities find their importance: 'A large part of what disturbs people about commodification of the body appears to be the way in which it transforms us into objects of property-holding rather than active human subjects'.[45] For Dickenson, these concerns regarding the alienation of bodily corporeality and distinct human capacities are reflected in the political economy of surrogacy and tissue donation as 'the recipient couple views the transaction as purely monetary, while the donor mother is encouraged to think she is giving the greatest gift of all, the gift of life'.[46] Again, Dickenson here demonstrates how the concerns regarding this contemporary expression of reproductive labour are reflected in an observation of a heightened emotional alienation that is unparalleled in other types of work.

The accounts here described are evidence of an emerging theoretical approach to contemporary manifestations of reproductive labour under capitalism, which observe their analysis in the heightened and markedly severe forms of human alienation that are implicated in these developments. The quarrel with these accounts is not with the particular social and indeed disproportionately gendered harms that this theoretical approach signifies. It is clear that the contemporary constellation of reproductive relations under capitalism implicate markedly different and, in many cases, more severe instances of disproportionately gendered harm, violence and exploitation, culminating in a unique experience of the effects of patriarchal capitalist power by women. However,

---

45   Dickenson 2007, p.4.
46   Dickenson 2007, p.22.

what is evident is that the comprehension of this unique experience and its implications pivots on an initial understanding of the particular social relations that underpin this experience and the gendered class struggles reflected in these relations. It is clear that these contemporary markets in reproductive services centralise a different class relationship from that of the industrial family, implicating a gendered social division of reproductive labour that implicates not only men and women, but women and other women across transnational reproductive networks. However, in this humanist theoretical approach, the concrete knowledge of these social realities – and their expression in gendered violence – is in fact foreclosed by this theoretically humanist approach by virtue of its grounding in a problematic of human alienation and the reflection of this grounding in particular theoretical weaknesses.

In order for this humanist ideological analysis to function, it relies upon the unwitting but nonetheless problematic resurrection of a normative boundary between 'work' and 'non-work.' In observing its analysis in the heightened emotional alienation of contemporary reproductive workers, the proponents of this ideological tendency necessarily construct a normative consideration of emotion and of work itself in order to provide themselves with a point of distinction between genuine emotion and its alienated form. This is evident, for example, in Anderson's critique of domestic labour. For Anderson the heightened alienation of domestic labour is reflected in the degradation of the worker's genuine emotional and familial relationships with their own families. As Anderson writes:

> They often feel ill at ease in their home countries, where things have changed in their absence, and where they may feel that they no longer belong. When their families meet them at the airport, these women commonly do not recognize their own kin. They talk of the embarrassment of having sex with husbands who have become virtual strangers, and of reuniting with children who doubt their mother's love.[47]

This is also evident in Banyard's critique of sex work. Banyard problematises the calls for the decriminalisation of sex work and its treatment as a form of 'work' like any other, arguing that such decriminalisation would simply open sex workers up to the precariousness and informality that currently plagues contemporary employment markets:

---

47 Anderson 2002, p.110.

Basic workplace health and safety rules don't even apply to most women in Germany's legal brothels. Why? Because for them to apply an individual has to be an employee. And it is up to individual brothels whether or not they employ women or simply host them as 'independent contractors'.[48]

The theoretical approach taken by these authors sees them unwittingly reproduce a separation between 'work' and 'non-work', with the dialectical social relationship that exists between them overlooked. For Anderson, the familial space outside of work is normatively constructed as a space of 'genuine' emotion and human relationships, which allows for the description of the process of alienation that underpins domestic labour. However, this approach overlooks the fundamental lesson of feminist critiques of reproduction, which argue that behind the apparently 'genuine' emotional relationships that exist within society are always particular social relations pertaining to historical forms of production and reproduction. For Banyard, the correlation between the proliferation of the sex industry, the exercise of gendered violence and the conditions of informality of the contemporary labour market is a missed opportunity for critique, with this brief sociological critique of contemporary employment markets utilised as nothing more than a critical foregrounding to her resistance towards the decriminalisation of sex work based upon the heightened alienation that it centralises. In both of these instances, the theoretical humanism of these analyses resolves itself in the production of particular ideological limitations in which the social relations of production and reproduction are missed and overlooked in favour of an analysis of human emotional alienation.

Relatedly, the reinforcement of this normative separation often sees the proponents of this discourse uncritically or unwittingly celebrate wage-labour itself as an ideal or a 'norm', leaving the relationship that it shares with the gendered violence they have just analysed unthought. Again, in relation to domestic labour, Anderson argues in favour of the 'professionalisation' of domestic labour, writing that professionalisation serves as 'a means of giving respect to domestic workers as workers, as well as of managing the personal relationships that develop from care work'.[49] However, the idea that the wage-labour market is desirable to the extent that it respects the workers under its charge is a misnomer which, though helpful to Anderson's argument, overlooks the feminist critique of production and reproduction: a critique that demon-

---

48   Banyard 2016, ch.2, para.5.
49   Anderson 2002, p.113.

strates that part of the reason that reproductive labour is exploited is because the wage-labour relation withholds respect and economic justice from its participants. Moreover, the reach of patriarchal capitalist social relations is also left unthought by Anderson as it does not follow that the professionalisation of certain forms of reproductive labour would lead to a more egalitarian gendered division of labour across society.

Banyard's argument travels in the other direction, arguing that sex work should not be decriminalised and called 'work' but in fact should be more strictly regulated. However, Banyard makes this argument not because she recognises the reflection of gendered exploitation in the wage-labour relation itself (which makes the demand for professionalisation on its own, short-sighted); rather, Banyard unwittingly constructs an argument that defends wage-labour as a normative construct, arguing that the inclusion of sex within definitions of 'work' risks degrading the nature of work itself and the protections that 'ordinary' workers (particularly women) currently enjoy. This argument comes through in Banyard's juxtaposition of the work of sex with other 'ordinary' forms of work:

> So if 'sex work is work', then presumably if an airline company requires all its female flight attendants to offer male passengers blow-jobs, as well as drinks and snacks, that's all right? What about City firms stipulating that female employees must have sex with male clients as part of their corporate entertaining duties? OK? ... I guess if this is ordinary work then at worst the requested task is merely outside her job description?[50]

Again, Banyard's analysis points towards a critical social point, only to turn away from it in the last instance. Instead of making the argument that the contemporary appearance of sex work and the particular forms of gendered violence and exploitation that it exhibits are in fact reflected in the apparently innocuous acts of gendered exploitation that exist within 'ordinary' workplaces, the humanism of Banyard's argument forces the stopping-short of this critical point. In order to pronounce the heightened alienation of sex work and formulate this into a critical resistance to its decriminalisation, Banyard effectively forces the protection and celebration of the wage-labour relation as a form of untainted employment: an analysis that necessarily mystifies the existence of interpenetrative social relations between production and reproduction.

---

50 Banyard 2016, ch.2, para.12.

As well as resolving itself in this false distinction between work and nonwork, the humanist ideological approach also reproduces a theoretical limitation that has long haunted dominant critiques of capitalism: that is the exclusion of particular gendered actors from analyses of class struggle and social change. The objective of twentieth century movements such as the Wages for Housework Movement was to position women first theoretically and then concretely as class actors with a distinct social stake in the development of capitalism and a unique position in their ability to change this social situation. It was on this basis that the observation of housewives as 'workers' was justified. However, within this emerging ideological critique in relation to contemporary reproductive markets, this tends to be forgotten and removes the particular class agency and unique class positions that workers in these industries occupy. For Banyard the framing of sex work as 'work' and of the women involved in it as 'workers' dresses what is essentially sexual abuse, up in a 'media-friendly moniker'.[51] However, this argument misses the fact that calling sex work 'work' – in the same way that the Wages for Housework Movement defined housework as 'work' – is not a campaign to justify or simply seek compensation for the abuses suffered in these forms of reproductive labour: rather, it is to identify their position within the matrix of productive and reproductive relations essential to capitalist production, 'to make a broader point about how the wage relation operates within capitalism'[52] and thereby attribute its participants a particular class position. This position, rather than labelling them as passive victims of gendered exploitation actually empowers them as social agents with a particular and unique capability to struggle against these conditions of exploitation. This is entirely overlooked in Banyard's account, because this class position is incomprehensible: a lack of comprehension that is foregrounded by the mystification of particular social relations. For Banyard, sex workers cannot occupy a particular gendered class position, because their work is considered as cut off from the relations of production in capitalist society: as an extreme example of alienation in an underground economy rather than reflective of a deeper social situation.

In these ways, the humanist ideological approach to contemporary forms of reproductive labour is problematic and theoretically limited. By observing the critique of reproductive labour through the prism of human alienation, the proponents of this approach point towards the emergence of new gendered social harms, but provide little concrete knowledge of the precise social condi-

---

51   Banyard 2016, ch.2, para.66.
52   Power 2017, pp.224–225.

tions that underpin these harms and the potential routes out of these harms. The humanist ideological framework of this approach reproduces many of the theoretical obstacles first necessarily deconstructed by Marxist-feminist theory, relying on normative ideas of human emotion and human relationships as a way of articulating contemporary alienation and gendered exploitation, unwittingly reproducing the precise ideological mystifications beneath which gendered exploitation has typically been hidden. Moreover, rather than empowering women as agents of class struggle and social change in the context of these contemporary developments, the proponents of this analysis tend to remove the political agency of women as workers by interpreting their position as one of victimhood without conceivable escape, rather than as a position reflective of a particular gendered class constellation, the terms of which are always subject to social change. In this way, this emerging humanist ideological analysis prevents a fuller understanding of the nature of contemporary reproductive labour, whilst also obscuring the knowledge of socio-political strategies through which to combat the gendered exploitation implicated in these new arrangements.

3   Towards an Anti-humanist Theoretical Feminism: Social Reproduction Theory

The question then becomes one of how best to re-orient theoretical feminism in order to correct for this recurrent problem. For Vogel, Romé, Weeks and Ferguson, social reproduction theory emerges as a theoretical framework around which this re-orientation can be organised. As Romé argues, '*Social Reproduction Theory* has grown in such a powerful manner that it constitutes today one of the most promising ways of counteracting the lethargy of leftist thinking in this era that presents itself as post-critical'.[53] In what remains, this chapter asks to what extent the concept of 'reproduction', as developed by those within social reproduction theory, can offer a theoretical alternative to the humanist ideological concepts of 'emotion' and 'intimacy' discussed above, in order to think about the relationship between gender and work in a more materialist way.

What Vogel demonstrates is that the concept of 'reproduction' emanates from what Althusser would describe as a symptomatic, or 'guilty' reading of Marx's political economy. The concept of reproduction does not exist in simple

---

53   Romé 2021, p.93.

terms on the pages of Marx's work: rather, it must be reconstructed, through the completion of a feminist *reading* of these texts. Others, such as Shulamith Firestone, also recognise this, writing that 'Marx was on to something *more profound than he knew* when he observed that the family contained within itself in embryo all the antagonisms that later develop on a wide scale within society and the state'.[54] The task of social reproduction theory is then to reconstruct that which Marx knew but could not say as a consequence of particular theoretical presuppositions, through the very dismantling of those presuppositions. Crucially, what social reproduction theory demonstrates is that the character of these presuppositions is theoretically humanist.

Vogel demonstrates how a material critique of reproduction was hidden behind the persistence of a humanist ideology within the work of Marx and Engels, which maintained that there was a 'natural' character to the family unit and to the gendered division of labour within human societies. Marx and Engels found difficulty – particularly (but not exclusively) in the earlier works where a humanist problematic remained predominant in their works – to critically dismantle ideological notions which insisted on the biological image of men and women and the reflection of these images in the 'natural' family unit. As Vogel writes, 'in this area, they come perilously close to a position that holds biology to be destiny. A quite damaging spectre of "the natural" haunts their work, from the earliest writings to the most mature'.[55] However, through a reading of Marx's political economy, Vogel demonstrates how the foundation by Marx of a number of important concepts relied on a break with this humanist ideology, revealing in its wake the makings of a materialist theory of reproduction.

In her reading of *Capital Volume I*, there are three concepts of particular importance for Vogel in this endeavour: 'individual consumption, the value of labour-power, and the industrial reserve-army'.[56] Firstly, through the concept of 'individual consumption', Marx centralises the relationship between the renewal of the working class and the accumulation of capital. Marx makes a distinction between this individual consumption and 'productive consumption', where the latter refers to 'the bringing together of means of production – raw materials, tools or machines, auxiliary substances – and producers in a specific labour-process', whilst the former 'refers to the processes by which producers consume means of subsistence – food, housing, clothing, and the

---

54 Firestone 1979, p.20, emphasis added.
55 Vogel 2013, p.65.
56 Vogel 2013, p.66.

like – with the result that they maintain themselves'.[57] Vogel's reading emphasises that this concept of individual consumption cannot be reduced to human need, but instead refers to the reproduction of labour-power at the level of the whole class. In other words, individual consumption is not merely descriptive of a biological process of human reproduction, but to a *social process*, to the social reproduction of labour-power itself. As Vogel explains:

> Marx implies, here, a concept that would cover the maintenance not only of present wage-workers, but of future and past wage-workers (such as children, aged and disabled persons, the unemployed), including those who are not currently wage-workers but take part in the process of individual consumption (such as house-wives).[58]

Intimated here by Marx is a move away from the notion of the family unit as a 'natural' phenomenon reflective of the biology of human beings, towards a notion of the family unit as a site of social reproduction, as a structure which mediates the social process of individual consumption and the consequent reproduction of labour-power.

This fact is further emphasised by the second concept, that of the value of labour-power. Famously, Marx demonstrates that the value of labour-power 'represents the socially necessary labour required for the production of labour-power'.[59] Given that Marx has already stipulated that the reproduction of labour-power relates to individual consumption, it then follows that the value of labour-power itself bears a relationship to the individual consumption necessary for its reproduction. Vogel quotes Marx, who writes:

> The production of labour power consists in his reproduction of himself or his maintenance. Therefore the labour-time requisite for the production of labour power reduces itself to that necessary for the production of those means of subsistence; in other words, the value of labour power is the value of the means of subsistence necessary for the maintenance of the labourer.[60]

However, what again must be emphasised is the departure from any natural or biological idea of human need. These means of subsistence are not grounded

---

57 Vogel 2013, p.67.
58 Ibid.
59 Vogel 2013, p.68.
60 Marx 2013, p.115.

in any natural measure, but are *socially defined*, as 'the number and extent of his so-called necessary wants, as also the modes of satisfying them, are themselves the product of historical development'.[61] For Vogel, this again shows Marx moving away from an idea of the family unit as a natural or biological unit, towards its observation as a social structure which plays a part in determining the value of labour-power as a commodity. The entry of more family members into the wage-labour market increases the rate of exploitation; the introduction of machinery depreciates the value of labour-power and thereby accelerates this further, as the cost of subsistence is no longer covered by the wages of one earner. In these ways, the family unit is exposed as an important social mechanism in not only reproducing labour-power but mediating its exploitation too.

The final concept of the 'industrial reserve army' brings this fact into sharper relief. Again, Marx dispenses with the notion that the family unit is a natural phenomenon, instead indicating its role as a social mechanism responsible for the reproduction and maintenance of a relative surplus-population: a surplus-population that Marx deems vital for explaining the law of capital accumulation. As the drive for surplus-value sets in motion a drive towards the greater productivity of the labour-process, 'less and less human labour [has] to be set in motion in the production-process. As a result, demand for labour falls relatively, and a surplus-population of wage-workers emerges'.[62] The maintenance and reproduction of this surplus-population is therefore a social process, intimately bound up with the accumulation of capital. As Vogel explains, 'the industrial reserve-army embodies a "law of population" specific to capitalism. In this sense, Marx puts the reproduction of the working class at the heart of the capital-accumulation process'.[63]

Vogel's reading of Marx demonstrates not only how Marx implicitly founded a materialist theory of reproduction, but also shows how the theoretical operation that sets this in motion is anti-humanist in its character. It is the dispensation by Marx of the notion of the family unit and the gendered division of labour as related to natural or biological qualities that provides the space for his foundation of important political economic concepts, which help explain how capitalism exploits labour-power. However, Vogel remains critical of both Marx and Engels and does not understate the consequences of the fact that they both failed to develop these ideas due to an inability to fully break with the patriarchal ideologies that populated the thought world they occupied. As Vogel writes, 'only with the development of feminist perspectives in

---

61 Marx 2013, p.116.
62 Vogel 2013, p.71.
63 Ibid.

modern anthropology, and more especially of an approach in the social sciences that is simultaneously Marxist and feminist, have the boundaries of "the natural" in this area begun to be seriously questioned'.[64] In order to properly appreciate this fact and bring it into relief, the chapter follows Weeks and her re-appraisal of the relationship between social reproduction theory and the Wages for Housework Movement of the 1970s. For Weeks, the importance of this movement rests in the opportunity to re-evaluate the political demands that it makes available, in particular 'the project's commitment to the refusal of work'.[65] But as well as its demands, the Wages for Housework Movement provided the opportunity for a theoretical re-orientation: 'As its advocates consistently argued, wages for housework is not just a demand, it is a perspective ... an opportunity to make visible, and encourage critical reflection on, the position of women in the work society'.[66] Developing this idea, this section asks to what extent theoretical anti-humanism was important for the creation of this perspective.

Among the leading theorists of the Wages for Housework Movement were Silvia Federici, Mariarosa Dalla Costa and Selma James. Developed among the theorists of the Wages for Housework Movement is the critique of humanist ideology that is found only implicitly in Marx's dealing with the concept of reproduction. For these theorists, the main adversary is an ideological notion which says that 'housework' as a collection of socially reproductive activities – including cooking, cleaning, childcare and sex – is nothing more than the extension of women's biological capacities and their natural behaviours. As Federici writes, in this way reproductive work is 'ideologically sold to us as the "other" of work: a space of freedom in which we can presumably be our true selves'.[67] Within this movement, social reproduction theory breaks with the whole ideological representation of reproduction as a manifestation of the biological characteristics or the very *nature* of the female body, instead exposing it as the social manifestation of a particular and historical gendered class struggle.

Federici has demonstrated the extent to which these ideological themes do not float freely in the modern era but are intimately tied to the development of the capitalist mode of production. As Federici argues in her text *Caliban and the Witch*, there is an observable and important correlation between the development of the humanist fascination with the body (and the discourses of know-

---

64   Vogel 2013, p.65.
65   Weeks 2011, p.116.
66   Weeks 2011, pp.128–9.
67   Federici 2012b, p.23.

ledge that accompanied this fascination) and the process of primitive accumulation that accompanied the emergence of capitalist social relations. In the seventeenth century, humanist philosophy was taking shape in the form of a Cartesian struggle between the 'forces of Reason' ('parsimony, prudence, sense of responsibility, self-control'[68]) and 'the low instincts of the Body' ('lewdness, idleness, systematic dissipation of one's vital energies'[69]). Crucially, this philosophical struggle was reflected in the social transformation taking place at the time: a transformation that gave rise to the social relations of production and reproduction integral to the emergence of capitalism. As Federici writes:

> The battle which the 17th-century discourse on the person imagines unfolding in the microcosm of the individual has arguably a foundation in the reality of the time. It is an aspect of that broader process of social reformation, whereby, in the 'Age of Reason', the rising bourgeoisie attempted to remold the subordinate classes in conformity with the needs of developing capitalist society.[70]

According to Federici this emerging humanist philosophy was reflected in a developing gendered division of labour between men and women. The stripping of women of their rights over land, tools and other means of subsistence was justified on the basis that men, freed of reproductive obligations, were more capable of reason (and therefore closer to the human world than that of the animal kingdom) than women who were actively held back by the instincts of their bodies and its reproductive system. Indeed, the female body is here constructed 'as uncontrolled, dangerous, savage "nature"',[71] with 'control over the natural world, control over human nature being the first, most indispensable step'[72] towards bourgeois control over a newly formed class society. In this way, the 'new anthropological paradigm'[73] of the seventeenth century provided the precise ideological concepts through which to facilitate and justify the social revolution taking place at the time, in which the institution of the modern family found its beginnings.

Humanism was also the ideology through which not only economic violence but physical repression was exercised over women as the bourgeoisie attemp-

---

68   Federici 2004, p.134.
69   Ibid.
70   Federici 2004, p.135.
71   Mies 2014, p.90.
72   Federici 2004, p.140.
73   Federici 2004, p.134.

ted to discipline these newly formed reproductive labourers into their familial positions. Just as Marx described how the making of the industrial working class was preceded by the 'enforced transformation into vagabonds and paupers'[74] of those who resisted the new regime, Federici details the ways in which unproductive sexuality became criminalised by this emerging social order: new forms of moralism penalised nakedness and sexuality and decried manual labour as an unnatural occupation for women, with those who defied such moral ideologies ostracised as 'sexually aggressive shrews or even as "whores" and "witches"'.[75] This violence comes to a head with the European witch hunts which, through this lens, cannot be viewed simply as the product of an ill-educated society coming to grips with new-found knowledges but as an integral and systematic campaign of violence that was the crucial midwife of the incoming capitalist society, dependent fundamentally on the establishment of social control over the means of reproduction. As Federici writes, 'it was in the course of this vast process of social engineering that a new concept of the body and a new policy toward it began to be shaped',[76] with violence as its central pivot 'for blood and torture were necessary to "breed an animal" capable of regular, homogeneous, and uniform behavior, indelibly marked with the memory of the new rules'.[77]

Federici's social reproduction theory has argued that this history of the primitive accumulation of women, of which their violent persecution, torture and criminalisation was all a part, must necessarily be viewed in the context of the emergence of the modern family. Just as Marx writes of wage-labour in *Capital*, following this process of primitive accumulation the need for direct force disappears and the relations of reproduction are experienced as 'natural'.[78] It is precisely here where ideology serves its purpose. At the end of this process of primitive accumulation, the relationships in the modern family are not experienced as forced set of social relations but, on the contrary, appear to approach both men and women as expressions of a *natural order*: 'The image of a worker freely alienating his labor, or confronting his body as capital to be delivered to the highest bidder, refers to a working class already molded by the capitalist work-discipline'.[79]

74 Marx 2013, p.514.
75 Federici 2004, p.96.
76 Federici 2004, p.137.
77 Federici 2004, p.144.
78 Marx 2013, p.516.
79 Federici 2004, p.135.

Crucially, the same ideological constructions that facilitate the naturalisation of the social relations of the modern family, bleed into the gendering of work itself. A correlation emerges between the socio-political position of the work of men who are able to transcend the immediate physiological demands of their bodies and the work of women whose class position is defined precisely by the assumed inability of this process of transcendence. As Dalla Costa and James argue:

> The housewife's situation as a pre-capitalist mode of labor and consequently this 'femininity' imposed upon her, makes her see the world, the others and the entire organization of work as something which is obscure, essentially unknown and unknowable; not lived; perceived only as a shadow behind the shoulders of the husband who goes out each day and meets this something.[80]

This argument is further confirmed by other Marxist-feminist critiques of work and reproduction. For example, Firestone demonstrated the effect of this ideology in relation to women's experience of the Second World War, in which women were called to fill the jobs in manufacturing and manual labour left vacant by the men who had left to fight. Firestone argued that this transcendence of the household was akin to a transcendence of bodily limitations, as these women 'were temporarily granted human, as opposed to female status'.[81] In the same movement, it is this same ideological construction that contributes to the cheapening of reproductive labour. The work of women is considered an animalistic and impulsive form of work whose powerlessness derives precisely from its ties to the physiological needs of the human organism. This gendered view of the division of labour has been crucial for the development of capitalism. Because whilst men's work is considered in the form of a political act that must be encouraged through the payment of a wage, women's work, pictured as *a natural resource*, therefore requires no such encouragement or payment, and can be taken advantage of at will and free of charge: as 'a natural resource, freely available like air and water'.[82] It is for this reason that capitalism can justify the withholding of wages from those who complete reproductive labour. If reproductive labour is considered as an ever-present activity that might otherwise be wasted if not taken advantage of and organised properly, then the requirement to pay for such labour is deemed unnecessary.

---

80 Dalla Costa and James 1975, pp.37–8.
81 Firestone 1979, p.33.
82 Mies 2014, p.110.

Therefore, the definition of ideology – particularly humanist ideology – is crucial to the construction of social reproduction theory. Humanism is a pivotal ideological tool that has facilitated the original formation of capitalist social structures, the primitive accumulation of women into their positions within these structures and the maintenance of the sexual division of labour necessary for the accumulation strategies of capitalist production. Thus, the Marxist-feminist movements – such as the demand for Wages for Housework in the 1970s – are *theoretical* movements that precisely sought to cut through these ideological deployments: by *defining* them. Without this clear ideological critique in mind, the Wages for Housework movement confronts feminism as merely a 'critical ploy'[83] designed only to make impossible demands of capitalism in order to demonstrate its inadequacy. However, the struggle for Wages for Housework was more than this and is representative of a class struggle both in theory and in practice, valuable in its exposure and definition of an ideological construction which underpins the contemporary oppression of women. As Federici writes,

> *It is the demand by which our nature ends and our struggle begins because just to want wages for housework means to refuse that work as the expression of our nature,* and therefore to refuse precisely the female role that capital has invented for us.[84]

Thus, social reproduction theory has not merely constructed a critique of capitalism through the inclusion of reproduction within considerations of exploitation. Rather, it is also responsible for a fundamentally feminist critique of ideology and specifically of humanist ideology, analysing its role in the facilitation of the exploitation of women in modern capitalism.

Romé, however, points towards some significant theoretical weaknesses in this account and argues that the theory of social reproduction forwarded by Federici, though important, is inadequate in its resistance to humanist ideology. For Romé, the anti-humanist potential of social reproduction theory rests in its ability to make sense of the way in which capitalism, as a complex totality of relations operating on different temporal scales, is daily reproduced and maintained: in other words, to make sense of that which Althusser called 'overdetermination'. By centralising the reproduction of this matrix of relations, the human subject is removed as the central problematic

---

83   Weeks 2011, p.128.
84   Federici 2012a, p.18.

and history can be observed in a material rather than historicist or humanist sense. In this way, as Romé argues:

> The conceptual register of social reproduction is extended by involving in the concrete existence of these relations the superstructural configurations in which *economic causality exists as an abstract cause or as a presence (by absence) of the structure in its effects*.[85]

For Romé, this nuance is missing in Federici's version of social reproduction theory. Romé argues that Federici's theory of social reproduction focuses too heavily on the reproduction of the labour force as opposed to the *relations* responsible for the arrangement of that labour force. This, Romé argues, results in the unwitting reproduction of a historical linearity in Federici's account, where the complexity of the social reproduction of capitalism is boiled down to a series of linear interventions by the state to develop the reproduction of labour-power as a force of production. As well as a historicism, this reproduces a humanism, where the history of capitalism is observed in the organisation of the behaviour of the petty producer. Althusser observed this tendency in Marxist thought, where 'man is by nature a petty producer who cultivates nature and nature amply rewards his efforts, producing, as a result of his labour, enough to feed him – him and his little family'.[86] For Romé, this tendency is visible in Federici's formulation, where 'the result of this analysis leaves feminist political thought entangled in a specular relation, either with the bourgeois myth of the small producer or with the economicist myth of the English proletariat'.[87]

In contrast to Federici's formulation, Romé points to the social reproduction theory developed by Tithi Bhattacharya. Bhattacharya, acknowledging the persistence of the theoretical problem elaborated in this chapter, argues that more attention must be paid to *the relation* between the market and particular reproductive labours, rather than on the elaboration of a project that seeks to distinguish between them. As Bhattacharya writes:

> Several new terms have been in circulation among social theorists to describe the sphere of extramarket relations. *Moral economy, shadow economy, the social factory*, and *the unwaged work sector* are among some of the terms employed. SRT is unique in the sense that it theorizes the

---

85 Romé 2021, p.114.
86 Althusser 2020a, p.85.
87 Romé 2021, p.110.

relationship between the market and extramarket relations rather than simply gesturing toward their distinction.[88]

The success of this project, of evaluating this relation, depends upon a theory of ideology, grounded in Marxism. Bhattacharya confirms this, arguing that 'Marx argues that to try and act upon our world on the basis of an empirical or factual knowledge of reality, *as it is perceived*, involves a category mistake'.[89] This kind of vulgar empiricism, at work in the sociologies of alienation and emotion outlined above – and, for Romé at least, at work even in Federici's social reproduction theory – risks overlooking the material nature of this relation and his historical circumstances: 'The reality we perceive is only the partial truth, and ... it appears to us in a particular, historically specific form'.[90] For Bhattacharya, in contrast to the humanist and historicist ideological explanations of reproductive labour, 'we need "science" to fully grasp the phenomena that remain hidden behind this appearance of the real'.[91] Social reproduction theory, for Bhattacharya, provides the precise framework for this scientific project, containing the theoretical elements necessary to cut through these ideological forms and produce 'a rich and variegated map of capital as a social relation'.[92]

It is Bhattacharya's commitment to this project, of analysing the reproduction of capital as a *social relation* rather than as a simple empirical observation of the renewal of the forces of production, that Romé emphasises. As Romé argues:

> From Bhattacharya's developments, we can differentially deduce that the primacy of the labor force contained in Federici's program leads to a restricted reading of reproduction – one that emphasizes the reproduction of the labor force over the reproduction of the overdetermined *relation* of capital/labor.[93]

By centralising the analysis of reproduction as a relation and forwarding a critique of ideology as part of this analysis, Bhattacharya affirms that most important Althusserian principle: the primacy of the relations of production over its forces. It is this prioritisation that permits the conclusion that 'it is the

---

88   Bhattacharya 2017, p.14.
89   Bhattacharya 2017, p.15.
90   Ibid.
91   Ibid.
92   Bhattacharya 2017, p.4.
93   Romé 2021, p.114.

overdetermined "invisible time of capital" that accommodates a temporal conjunction of existing social relations in their historical, technical, institutional, cultural dimensions'.[94]

What this discussion has attempted to demonstrate is two things. Firstly, that social reproduction theory, rather than a sociology of emotional or intimate labour, provides the best grounding for a materialist analysis of reproductive labour. On this, there is consensus among the authors discussed. Secondly, that the operationality of social reproduction theory and its materialism, depends upon a theoretical anti-humanism. This has been demonstrated by Vogel, who shows how the implicit theory of social reproduction developed by Marx relied on a break with bourgeois ideologies of the 'natural'; by Weeks who points towards the social reproduction theory of the Wages for Housework Movement and whose theoretical 'position' depends on a break with humanist naturalisations of the division of labour; and by Romé who, through an appraisal of Bhattacharya's social reproduction theory, emphasises the importance of the concept of overdetermination in deconstructing humanist and historicist explanations of reproduction, beyond Federici herself.

4   Conclusion

In the context of contemporary forms of reproductive labour and the emergence of reproductive 'industries' in domestic labour, sex work, tissue donation and surrogacy, this lesson first taught by the Marxist-feminists appears to have been overlooked. This re-orientation of reproductive relations has increasingly been interpreted through a humanist ideological lens, with its unique characteristics and the particular forms of gendered social harm that it inaugurates observed in contemporary capitalism's tendency towards the greater alienation of human capacities: an alienation with disproportionate impact upon women. However, this humanist ideological reaction has been shown to in fact foreclose a fuller understanding of the social mechanics of this gendered harm, reproducing ideological obstacles that prevent the production of sociological analysis. In light of this, the chapter has demonstrated how a re-visiting of the principles of social reproduction theory, and the analysis of contemporary reproduction from the starting-point of questions of class and social relations has produced a more helpful sociological critique of contemporary reproduction, providing an understanding of the social grounding of gendered violence,

---

94   Romé 2021, p.116.

but also producing an understanding of the social grounding of those actors most appropriately poised to change these conditions.

Though there is debate over its direction, social reproduction theory has been shown to offer an alternative theoretical approach for contemporary feminist sociologies. Social reproduction theory possesses a conceptual structure that is capable of framing a materialist analysis of reproduction and reproductive labour. A key component of this structure is its theoretical anti-humanism. Across the examples relied on in this chapter, the value of theoretical anti-humanism in allowing for the production of important concepts within social reproduction theory has been demonstrated. In place of vague or moralistic ideological notions are alternative concepts that emphasise the material nature of the relation between capital and labour and how this is reflected in various forms of gendered and racialised exploitation.

In moving to the next chapter, it is evident that this ideological problematic finds itself reproduced in critical responses to the 'Anthropocene' and to emerging challenges in relation to climate change and ecological disaster. The realities of this present historical moment prompt a humanist ideological reaction, which identifies a lack of responsibility and adequate human action in the face of these ecological realities in an alienation of the human subject from its labour, upheld and reinforced by modern discourse. What is clear, however, is that this ideological argument mystifies the social relationship that exists between capitalism, work and the planet and how the realities of ecological catastrophe are not the result of alienated labour but of strategies of accumulation that have continually relied on revolutionising ways of working and on a forceful adaptation of the human relationship with nature.

CHAPTER 6

'Making' History: The Concept of Labour and the Anthropocene Discourse

The concept of labour, and the humanist ideological weight brought with this concept, are an important feature of the contemporary discourse surrounding climate change and ecological crisis in the context of the 'Anthropocene'. In order to explain the Anthropocene as a distinct geological period marked by the activity of human beings, the concept of labour emerges as an important conceptual vehicle in order to describe how human beings have *made history* through their activity upon the planet. The Anthropocene makes necessary the re-centring of questions regarding the relationship of the human subject with nature and the manifestation of that relationship within history itself. This chapter argues that a humanist conceptualisation of labour – corresponding precisely to this relationship between humans and nature – figures at the centre of a renewed theoretical humanism within the Anthropocene discourse. In this way, the Anthropocene as a geo-historical juncture, marred by planetary instability, is formulated as a problem of human labour. The concept of labour frames the problematic of the Anthropocene and also provides the foundation from which to imagine and deploy potential 'solutions' to these problems.

The proponents of the Anthropocene discourse argue that human beings have laboured in an essentially alienated condition, cut off from natural history, blindly stumbling into ecological catastrophe as a result. However, this account leaves the history of capitalism and of class struggle untouched. In order to remedy this, Marxist approaches to this topic have attempted to remedy this oversight. However, as this chapter demonstrates, the success of those approaches in overcoming the concept of labour, and thus the reliance on theoretical humanism, has been of mixed success. Where the concept of labour figures centrally in Marxist approaches to this problem – exemplified in this chapter by the work of Andreas Malm – the historical relationship between class struggle and ecological crisis is somewhat distorted as its operationality continues to rely on the existence of a conscious and deliberate human subject whose decision-making lies at the core of ecological crisis. This chapter demonstrates that it is those approaches best able to displace the concept of labour – exemplified here by the work of Jason W. Moore – that produce a more convincing analysis of the relationship between class struggle and the ecological imbalance characterised by the Anthropocene.

1   Labour and the Theoretical Humanism of the Anthropocene

The Anthropocene discourse is diverse and multi-disciplinary, covering contributions to the fields of geology, chemistry and biology as well as politics, sociology, ethics and economics under one conceptual umbrella. The term 'Anthropocene' itself originates from research conducted by Paul Crutzen and Eugene Stoermer – an atmospheric chemist and biologist respectively – in a short article for the Global Change Newsletter of the International Geosphere-Biosphere Programme (IGBP). In the article, Crutzen and Stoermer presented evidence for the Earth's entering into a new geological era, which has been shaped fundamentally by the human species as a natural force. Whilst other eras have been marked by volcanic eruptions, glacial movements or extreme cooling, the human species itself, through its activity upon the Earth, is argued to have joined this list of natural forces in ushering in the next stage of Earth's geological history. Crutzen and Stoermer argued that the Holocene epoch, a period spanning the last ten to twelve thousand years and characterised by stable global temperatures capable of sustaining life, has ended and that the contemporary geological era is that of the human: the Anthropocene.

For Crutzen and Stoermer, the start of the Anthropocene coincided with the beginning of the Industrial Revolution in Britain, with particular attention paid to the invention by James Watt of the steam engine towards the end of the eighteenth century. Other natural scientific analyses of the Anthropocene that followed have debated between themselves the 'actual' start date, with some defending the initial one agreed by Crutzen and Stoermer and others placing greater emphasis on the so-called 'great acceleration' in both human population and human consumption patterns in the middle of the twentieth century. Regardless of the start date, these natural scientists find consensus in the need to classify the current geo-historical moment as one indelibly shaped by human action:

> We learn that 30–50% of the land surface has been transformed by human action; more nitrogen is now fixed synthetically and applied as fertilizers in agriculture than fixed naturally in all terrestrial ecosystems; the escape into the atmosphere of NO [nitric oxide] from fossil fuel and biomass combustion likewise is larger than the natural inputs, giving rise to photochemical ozone ('smog') formation in extensive regions of the world; more than half of all accessible fresh water is used by mankind; human activity has increased the species extinction rate by thousand to ten thousand fold in the tropical rain forests and several climatically

important 'green house' gases have substantially increased in the atmosphere: CO2 [carbon dioxide] by more than 30% and CH4 [methane] by even more than 100%.[1]

The potential existence of the Anthropocene as a specific and 'official' geological epoch has prompted the emergence of an already quite substantial social scientific discourse dedicated to the posture of a variety of questions and theories regarding human society in relation to its new-found geological agency. As Bruno Latour writes, 'these historians are proposing the most radical term of all for putting an end to anthropocentrism as well as to the old forms of naturalism; they are thus completely reconstituting the role of human agents'.[2] Fundamentally, the possibility of the Anthropocene, and its implications in relation to the inextricable relationship between human society and planetary history, makes possible and necessary a renewed critique of the presuppositions on which social scientific enquiry has, until this point, been consistently based.

A closer analysis of the Anthropocene discourse reveals that labour and the problematisation of the historical power of human labour sits as the theoretical pivot of this emerging discourse. The emergence of the Anthropocene and the conditions of planetary instability that it brings with it are presented, fundamentally, as problems of human labour. Human interaction with nature over the last two centuries – and its manifestation in the cities, industry, agriculture and technological advancement that has come to define the appearance of human society – has, whilst bringing to pass the conditions of liberal democratic capitalism, also brought with it conditions of planetary instability. The Anthropocene brings to the attention of its observer the *power* of human labour to not only produce the marvels that have revolutionised human existence but also the planetary conditions that place this existence in real peril. The essence of this paradoxical situation is, in all instances, the labour of humanity, the activity of the Anthropos of the Anthropocene: a reality that makes absolutely necessary the figuration of this labour as the central problematic of thinking this historical epoch.

With this problem of human labour at its centre, the Anthropocene emerges as the foundation for the construction and deployment of a renewed theoretical humanism. On the one hand, the Anthropocene itself is a problem of human labour, in the ways outlined above. The conditions of planetary instabil-

---

1 Crutzen and Stoermer 2000, p.17.
2 Latour 2017, p.117.

ity that today confront humanity are a direct product of its own activity. On the other hand, however, the apparent geo-historical power of human labour in fact bolsters humanity and the human subject as a geo-historical actor. If the human subject is imbued with the power to bring the planet to the brink of ecological catastrophe then, surely, it is *the* actor with the power capable of transcending this geo-historical trajectory and charting an alternative historical path. This theoretical humanism is reflected across the Anthropocene discourse: from natural scientific considerations of 'planetary stewardship' that have built directly upon Crutzen and Stoermer's geological conclusions; to developments within the social sciences which have argued that the realities of this geo-historical moment make both possible and necessary the emergence of 'a new human condition'.[3]

The discourse of the Anthropocene is not the first time that a theoretical humanism of this type has been deployed in the formation of critical histories. In his *Reply to John Lewis*, Althusser constructs a critique of a very similar theoretical humanism emerging within Marxist-humanist critiques of labour and history. In his essay, the target of Althusser's critique is the observation of a particular historical quality within human labour: that is, the ability of human labour to *make* and *re-make* history. From a perspective of Marxist-humanism, it is easy to see the utility of this ideological notion. The idea that human labour *makes* history qualifies the notion that capitalism – as a historically specific social formation – can in fact itself be the *product* of historically alienated human labour: that is, historical activity carried out against the interests of those who completed it. Moreover, this humanist ideological consideration of labour is important because it also qualifies Marxist-humanist analyses of revolution as the ability of the human subject, now conscious of its alienated condition, to *transcend* its historical situation through the conscious application of its own historically-powerful labour. In this way, as Althusser argued, 'to make history is therefore "to negate the negation", and so on, without end'.[4]

In this humanist ideological figuration of labour and its reflection in historical progress, the precise emancipatory force of human labour exists not in its simple power of creation, but in its power of *transcendence*: that is, the ability, when confronted with particular conditions of historical existence, to overcome those conditions and chart an alternative historical path. As Althusser writes of this approach, it:

---

3   Hamilton, Bonneuil, and Gemenne 2015, p.4.
4   Althusser 2008, p.72.

> Does not endow [the human subject] with a power of absolute creation (when one creates everything it is relatively easy: there are no limitations!) but with something even more stupefying – the power of 'transcendence', of being able to progress by indefinitely *negating-superseding* the constraints of the history *in which* he lives, the power to transcend history by *human liberty*.[5]

This property of transcendence, inherent to the Hegelian humanism and historicism which Althusser critiques here, proves itself to be particularly important in the considerations of labour and history made by the theorists of the Anthropocene too. In fact, this theoretically humanist framework outlines the entire approach of the Anthropocene theorists to the problems of labour and of history. It is, on the one hand, the ability of the human subject to *make* history in the first instance that explains the emergence of the geo-historical conditions of the Anthropocene: the idea that '"we", the human species, unconsciously destroyed nature to the point of hijacking the Earth system into a new geological epoch'.[6] But on the other hand, it is the precise ability of the human subject to use this power to transcend the geo-historical conditions that confront humanity that marks an historical path out of the crisis of the Anthropocene too: 'In the time of the Anthropocene, the entire functioning of the Earth becomes a matter of human political choices'.[7]

In different ways and from varying perspectives, it is possible to observe the presence of this theoretical humanism throughout the Anthropocene discourse. For example, it finds its most simplistic reflection in the discourse of 'planetary stewardship' that emerges primarily within natural scientific approaches to the Anthropocene. Building on the original conclusions of Crutzen and Stoermer, a number of theorists within the natural scientific approach to the Anthropocene have argued that the Anthropocene marks both a moment of crisis but also a particularly useful opportunity in which to re-evaluate humanity's relationship with the planet. As Chapin et al. write, 'this unsustainable trajectory demands a dramatic change in human relationships with the environment and life-support system of the planet'.[8] These scientists observe the completion of this dramatic change in the occupation of human beings of a role as *planetary stewards*. According to these authors, humanity's ascension to a geological force in the era of the Anthropocene has not only meant that they

---

5 Althusser 2008, p.75.
6 Bonneuil and Fressoz 2016, p.XII.
7 Bonneuil and Fressoz 2016, p.25.
8 Chapin et al. 2010, p.241.

are responsible for the setting of the planet upon an unstable ecological trajectory, but also that they remain the *only force capable* of potentially reversing the effects of their actions and creating more stable climatological conditions. As Steffen et al. write, 'we are the first generation with the knowledge of how our activities influence the Earth System, and thus the first generation with the power and the responsibility to change our relationship with the planet'.[9]

For the natural scientists, the solutions to this problematic are largely techno-scientific in nature. There is an emerging consensus regarding the design and deployment of models of planetary stewardship around Rockström et al.'s model of 'planetary boundaries': the establishment of nine key ecological boundaries of differing variables (such as, for example, levels of ocean acidification, rates of biodiversity loss and the observation of ozone depletion), over which human beings become responsible for ensuring the equilibrium and sustainability. As Steffen et al. write of this approach, it is designed to 'define a "safe operating space" for humanity by analyzing the intrinsic dynamics of the Earth System and identifying points or levels relating to critical global-scale processes beyond which humanity should not go'.[10] The barriers to achieving the successful deployment of this programme are, for the natural scientists, largely problems of global governance. For these authors, fundamental alterations in international and domestic structures of governmentality are the crucial first step to successfully completing this programme of planetary stewardship. As Chapin et al. write, 'transformations involve forward-looking decisions to convert a system trapped in an undesirable state to a fundamentally different, potentially more beneficial system, whose properties reflect different social-ecological controls',[11] with Steffen et al. echoing this, arguing that 'human impacts on Earth System functioning cannot be resolved within individual jurisdictions alone; supranational cooperation is required'.[12]

This theory of planetary stewardship is a limited one, insofar as it places a great deal of faith in governing institutions such as governments, corporations or supranational bodies, without properly interrogating the particular inequalities and social harms often incubated by these institutions. It is a theory that forgets Althusser's analysis of state apparatuses as consistent reflections of the class exploitation embedded in a capitalist social formation, treating them instead as neutral institutions to be commanded at will. Moreover, as Bon-

---

9   Steffen et al. 2011, p.749.
10 Steffen et al. 2011, p.753.
11 Chapin et al. 2010, p.246.
12 Steffen et al. 2011, p.751.

neuil and Fressoz write, within the natural scientific discourse, 'everything is presented as if the environmental knowledge and initiatives of civil society did not exist'[13] and that the knowledge of this particular planetary predicament emanates exclusively from these scientists and their geological discoveries, in which the scientists appear not only 'as spokespeople for the Earth, but also as shepherds of a public opinion that is ignorant and helpless'.[14] Limitations aside, what is evident is that reflected within this theory of planetary stewardship are the ingredients of a particular theoretical humanism, which pivots on the concept of labour. The Anthropocene as a historical moment is here formulated as a product of the inherent historical power of human labour to not only shape the products that it pulls from nature (in the form of the industrial development of human society and production across the last two centuries), but also, in so doing, to shape the very nature of the raw material from which it extracts this productive capability (in the form of the ecological instability of the world which now faces this humanity). Finally, and perhaps most crucially, the knowledge of the Anthropocene catalyses the transcendent ability of human labour, of its ability to shift fundamentally and negate the constraints of this historical moment by virtue of the application of its own action in an alternative direction.

Social scientific approaches to the Anthropocene have been more successful in considering questions of social inequalities in their approach. More than this, it is argued that the Anthropocene, in forcing together human and natural histories in such a dramatic fashion in fact undermines the modern epistemological orientation on which knowledge – but also, *power* – has been based. As Hamilton et al. write, 'the Anthropocene means that natural history and human history, largely taken as independent and incommensurable since the early nineteenth century, must now be thought as one and the same geo-history'.[15] The Anthropocene therefore is expressive, for the social scientists, of an opportunity to re-interrogate notions such as 'equality', 'justice' and 'democracy' by exposing the inadequacies of a constellation of power relations now confronted with the very real dangers posed by planetary history itself:

> Human-induced climate change gives rise to large and diverse issues of justice: justice between generations, between small island-nations and the polluting countries (both past and prospective), between developed,

---

13   Bonneuil and Fressoz 2016, p.82.
14   Bonneuil and Fressoz 2016, p.80.
15   Hamilton, Bonneuil, and Gemenne 2015, p.4.

industrialised nations (historically responsible for most emissions) and the newly industrialising ones, and so on.¹⁶

Despite the fact that the social scientific approach to the Anthropocene is more developed in its considerations of power, inequality and social justice, what is evident is that the theoretical humanism of the 'planetary boundaries' approach in fact finds itself reflected – albeit with greater sophistication – in these social scientific approaches too. The adaptation of the human relationship with the planet demands the problematisation of human labour and the extent to which it itself is the reflection of the modern separation between human and natural histories. The result is an echo of the (non-sociological and non-Marxist) considerations of the natural scientists: that humans, who have laboured towards the Anthropocene, are the *only* geological agents, catalysed by the reality of their actions, capable of reformulating this relationship with nature.

The evidence of this theoretically humanist approach is located primarily in the way that labour is used to describe humanity's geo-historical emergence at the time of the Anthropocene and its discontents. This depends firstly upon the establishment of labour as *the* historical motor, which is set out well by Mackenzie Wark. For Wark, labour is an important concept for the theorists of the Anthropocene because it is descriptive of an historical motor which, though it originates from the hands of the human subject, nonetheless has interpenetrative historical effects upon both human and natural histories. The concept of labour is important because it allows for the theorists of the Anthropocene to construct a version of history that undermines the modern idea of nature as a space upon which history itself merely unfolds. Rather, the concept of labour allows for the theorists of the Anthropocene to demonstrate a *historical causality* that emerges from human labour, in its ability to shape natural history as well as its own. As Wark writes:

> Labor finds itself *in and against* nature. Labor is always firstly in nature, subsumed within a totality greater than itself. Labor is secondly against nature. It comes into being through an effort to bend resisting nature to its purposes. Its intuitive understanding of causality comes not from exchange value but from use value. Labor experiments with nature, finding new uses for it. Its understanding of nature is historical, always evolving, reticent about erecting an abstract causality over the unknown.¹⁷

---

16   Chakrabarty 2015, p.49.

In this way, the theorists of the Anthropocene can stress the central importance of human labour as a historical motor, but justify its inclusion in their anti-modern critique by showing how – by virtue of the emergence of the Anthropocene itself – it is an historical activity with implications for both humans and non-humans alike. As Wark writes, 'labor is the mingling of many things, most of them not human ... almost already a cyborg point of view, in which the human organism and its machines interleave in an apparatus'.[18] However, despite the fact that labour, thought in this way, implicates more than simply human actors or human history, the question that is left necessarily unanswered is the question of precisely *who* is carrying out this labour. The configuration of labour in this way, as a historical motor, still depends upon the existence of a human subject to carry it out.

For example, it is evident within these social scientific approaches that it is the human being – wielding this geo-historically powerful form of labour – that has *made* planetary history, albeit in a particularly unstable form. The Anthropocene, as a geo-historical moment defined by potential ecological catastrophe, is, unequivocally, the product of this human labour. The Anthropocene 'captures the realization that humanity is interfering, interacting, and communicating with the Earth's long-term systems with increasing intensity'.[19] Human action as human labour is the precondition for historical development, as 'real history only commenced when humans began to do unnatural things: cultivate crops, make tools, build cities, and create societies and cultures'.[20] What is repeatedly made clear is that, despite the fact that labour has been shown to have effects across both human and non-human histories, it is in the specifically historical character of human labour that these histories are themselves made: 'The more we interfere with resources and ecosystems, the closer we get to natural phenomena and the deeper we move "into" the new nature that arises through our actions'.[21] The Anthropocene forces humanity to confront the geo-historical power of its own labour and how it resolves itself in the appearance and trajectory not of human history alone but of natural history too.

However, it is this precise moment of confrontation that also compels the human subject to *transcend* the geo-historical conditions of the Anthropocene – conditions of its own making – and chart an alternative historical path. This transcendence of history through human labour is reflected in what the

18   Wark 2015, p.217.
19   Schwägerl 2013, p.29.
20   LeCain 2016, p.15.
21   Schwägerl 2013, p.36.

social scientists have often termed a 'new human condition': a new sense of responsibility felt by the human subject in the context of the planet and the natural world, with an alternative geo-historical trajectory emanating from this new-found responsibility. As Palsson et al. write:

> The new era, characterized by measurable global human impact – the Anthropocene – does not just imply conflation of the natural and the social, but also a 'radical' change in perspective and action in terms of human awareness of and responsibility for a vulnerable earth – a 'new human condition'.[22]

Consciousness of the power of human labour – of its inherent ability to cross both human and natural histories – underpins a new human condition in which the human subject, armed with this consciousness, transcends the present historical situation. In this way, 'the Anthropocene therefore really commences when humans become aware of their global role in shaping the earth and, consequently, when this awareness shapes their relationship with the natural environment'.[23] Despite the fact that the Anthropocene is considered an important era insofar as it presents a version of history in which human beings are neither the main nor the sole actors, the human subject nonetheless finds itself re-asserted at the centre of history in this view: it is the consciousness of the human subject as to the power of their labour that catalyses an alternative geo-historical trajectory. Though, as LeCain writes, 'humanism may never be the same again',[24] it is still very much a 'humanism' with which these theorists are concerned.

Across these examples, it has been possible to show how approaches to the Anthropocene – expressed across quite different disciplines with quite different political aims – share a central theoretical framework, the nature of which is fundamentally humanist. The central problematic with which the theorists of the Anthropocene are faced is one of human labour and the fact that its deployment over the last two centuries has resulted in the production of a particularly unstable geo-historical epoch, marred by a changing climate, biodiversity loss and ozone depletion. In the face of these realities, human labour is configured as the precise force capable of transcending this geo-historical situation and forging an alternative historical trajectory that can avoid potential catastrophe: either reflected in renewed systems of governance

---

22   Palsson et al. 2012, p.4.
23   Palsson et al. 2012, p.8.
24   LeCain 2016, p.15.

and the enforcement of planetary boundaries; or reflected in the emergence of a new human condition, wherein the human subject is conscious of their geo-historical power and aims to use it for the better.

It is evident that the Anthropocene itself is a product of human labour; and it is also evident that human labour remains the potential 'solution' to the problems presented here. What remains to be accounted for by the theorists of the Anthropocene is why, precisely, human labour over the last two centuries has resulted in the production of these catastrophic geo-historical conditions. More pressing still, this question is important because its answer points towards the precise *change* that will be necessary if humanity is to transcend these contemporary geo-historical conditions. It is here that the Anthropocene discourse relies – as many theoretical humanisms in the past have also done – on the construction and deployment of a theory of human *alienation* in order to problematise the Anthropocene. Addressing the last two centuries of human labour demands their consideration in the context of an historical alienation, the struggle against which will provide the precise geo-historical tools with which humanity can transcend the present situation.

2   Alienation, Modernity and the Anthropocene

The explanation of the Anthropocene as an unstable geo-historical manifestation of human labour, depends upon the centrality of human alienation as a theoretical problematic. For the social scientists of the Anthropocene, alienation is the precise conceptual device used to explain the geo-historical trajectory of human labour over the last two centuries, descriptive of a *distance* or *separation* enjoyed by humanity from its grounding within natural history. For these theorists, the critical analysis of this geo-historical alienation is reflected in the completion of a critique of *modernity*. These theorists argue that the geo-historical trajectory of human labour and its alienated reflection in forms of society, production, culture and history that are cut off from their grounding in natural history, has been underpinned at all times by the reinforcement of a false separation between human and natural histories at the heart of modern discourse. The Anthropocene, as a geo-historical moment, not only provides humanity with the consciousness of its geological agency, but provides the opportunity for the reflection of this consciousness in a critique of modernity and for its embedding within discourse itself. For the social scientists of the Anthropocene, the critique of modernity is a corollary critique of the geo-historical alienation of the human subject and its labour. The reflection of geo-historical consciousness within discourse is here argued to parallel the expression of this consciousness in forms of social and political action necessary to transcend the dangerous planetary conditions of the Anthropocene.

However, this problematic of alienation reproduces particular limitations that undermine the explanatory potential of this discourse. Notably, despite the centrality of the critique of modernity and the modern ideological separation between human and natural histories, this problem of alienation in fact reproduces many of the modern ideological tropes from which it seeks a break. This is visible most obviously in its re-assertion of the human subject as the central geo-historical actor in its analysis. It is the alienation of the human actor that explains the emergence of the Anthropocene, but it is also precisely the human subject, in achieving consciousness of its alienated condition (and reflecting this consciousness in its deployment of social and political strategy) that possesses the power by which to transcend these geo-historical conditions of its own making. More severely, from a sociological perspective, this story of human alienation also mystifies the social relations of human society and the extent to which they underpin any possible social or political change. As the chapter will show in due course, this mystification of social relations is particularly problematic for the implication and analysis of the social relations of capitalist production in the context of planetary crisis.

Social scientific approaches to the Anthropocene are littered with signposts that point toward the existence of a condition of human alienation. It is manifest in descriptions of the way in which human beings 'unwittingly'[25] laboured their way into the Anthropocene. As Chakrabarty writes, 'it is true that human beings have tumbled into being a geological agent through our own decisions. The Anthropocene, one might say, has been an unintended consequence of human choices'.[26] Moreover, the links between this alienated condition and the development of modernity and modern discourse are also evident in the foregrounding of this analysis. Just as Klaus Eder wrote that 'modernity's characteristic pride in dominating nature *has caused us to forget* that we are living in the culture that more or less unconsciously "forces" us into a self-destructive relationship with nature',[27] the theorists of the Anthropocene today observe a similar problematic, arguing that 'the moderns, having externalised Nature, were blind to the environmental/geological impacts of the industrial mode of development'.[28] There is a recognition, at the forefront of the Anthropo-

---

25   Chakrabarty 2009, p.206.
26   Chakrabarty 2009, p.210.
27   Eder 1996, pp.VII–VIII, emphasis added.
28   Hamilton, Bonneuil, and Gemenne 2015, p.7.

cene discourse, of a particular unconsciousness or alienation that defines the human condition and, importantly, is reflected in modernity itself.

The recognition of this condition of alienation underpins the celebration of the Anthropocene as a moment within the social sciences. In forcing humanity's consciousness as to the geo-historical power of its labour and its occupation of a position of geological agency, the Anthropocene provides an opportunity through which to undermine this condition of alienation, articulated through a critique of modernity as the concrete epistemological reflection of this alienation. As Hamilton et al. write, 'the Anthropocene represents a threshold marking a sharp change in the relationship of humans to the natural world', that is expressed in 'the "impossible" fact that humans have become a "force" of nature and the reality that human action and Earth dynamics have converged and can no longer be seen as belonging to distinct incommensurable domains'.[29] This violent coming-together of world histories necessitates the imagination of 'a new human condition and requires us to reintegrate nature and the Earth system at the heart of our understanding of history, our conception of freedom and our practice of democracy'.[30] In this way, as Bonneuil and Fressoz continue, 'the grand narrative of the Anthropocene is thus the story of an awakening. There was a long moment of unawareness, from 1750 to the late twentieth century, followed by a sudden arousal'.[31]

The social scientists of the Anthropocene pinpoint this alienated human condition in the false separation between 'human' and 'natural' histories that underpins the modern *episteme*. For the theorists of the Anthropocene, ideas of 'society' and 'nature' are themselves recent inventions of a modern discipline which has presided over a division in the production of knowledge, observing human history in one set of disciplines and discourses (the 'human sciences') and observing natural history in another, entirely separate set of discourses (the 'natural sciences'). It is through this epistemological arrangement, peculiar to modernity, that social science has arrived at the categories of 'Man' and 'Nature' as distinct entities with distinct histories:

> From Buffon to Lyell and Darwin, biology and geology extended terrestrial time to hundreds of millions of years, creating a context that was seemingly external, almost immobile and indifferent to human tribulations. In parallel with this, the bourgeois and industrial Enlightenment emphas-

---

29 Hamilton, Bonneuil, and Gemenne 2015, p.3.
30 Bonneuil and Fressoz 2016, pp.19–20.
31 Bonneuil and Fressoz 2016, p.73.

ized the value of man, the modern subject, as autonomous agent acting consciously on his history and settling social conflicts by dominating nature.[32]

Exposing the peculiarity of this epistemological orientation to modernity is the centrepiece of Bruno Latour's assertion that *We Have Never Been Modern*. Latour argues that modernity and modern knowledge are problematic insofar as they rely upon and reproduce this false separation between human and natural histories. The invention of modernity, so Latour argues, was based upon a sustained separation of human politics and society from the phenomena of the natural world, as knowledge of each was produced necessarily in isolation. As Latour writes, modern knowledge has produced a world in which 'the representation of things through the intermediary of the laboratory is forever dissociated from the representation of citizens through the intermediary of the social contract'.[33] Human history, expressed in theories of politics and society are kept at arms-length from natural history as reflected in the study of biology or chemistry. Latour's argument is that the entire modern *episteme* was based upon this fundamental separation, but that it was ultimately a false one, reproduced in order to secure the functionality of discourses of knowledge, but which had no real basis in the reality of things:

> By rendering mixtures unthinkable, by emptying, sweeping, cleaning and purifying the arena that is opened ... the moderns allowed the practice of mediation to recombine all possible monsters without letting them have any effect on the social fabric, or even any contact with it.[34]

However, with the arrival of the Anthropocene, it becomes impossible to maintain the separation between these monsters of the natural world and the social fabric of human history. The coming-together of human and natural histories implicated by the discoveries of the Anthropocene explodes the modern separation of these histories and the discourses of knowledge that were founded on this sustained separation: 'The Anthropocene does not "go beyond" this division: it circumvents it entirely. The geohistorical forces *ceased to be the same as* the geological forces as soon as they fused at multiple points with human actions'.[35] In the Anthropocene, it becomes impossible to think about 'human'

---

32 Bonneuil and Fressoz 2016, p.19.
33 Latour 1993, p.27.
34 Latour 1993, p.42.
35 Latour 2017, p.120.

and 'non-human' actors within the social and political arena, as the two are forced together and become inseparable. As Latour continues:

> Where we were dealing earlier with a 'natural' phenomenon, at every point we now meet the 'Anthropos' ... and, wherever we follow human footprints, we discover modes of relating to things that had formerly been located in the field of nature.[36]

For Latour, it is simply impossible to any longer maintain the separation of human and natural history, making necessary the explosion of modern discourse and its presuppositions. For Latour it is expressive of an opportunity to construct and deploy a critique of modernity and is 'the best alternative we have to usher us away from the notion of modernisation'.[37]

Crucially, the realities presented by the Anthropocene extend the impetus of this critique of modernity beyond mere academic interest. The Anthropocene does not simply present a conceptual or epistemic crisis in terms of modernity and its assumptions. It also presents a very real crisis in which the geo-historical existence of both humans and the planet is placed in particular danger. As Bonneuil and Fressoz write, 'while triumphant industrial modernity had promised to prise us away from nature, its cycles and its limits, placing us in a world of boundless progress, the Earth and its limits are today making a comeback'.[38] The reinforced separation between human and natural history within modernity is reflected in the real-world incapability of human beings to react to a warming climate, to rising sea levels, mass extinctions and to the increase in climate-related disasters such as earthquakes, hurricanes and floods: an incapability that is rooted, fundamentally, in an inability to *comprehend* this reality. In this way, the critique of modernity is not simply the search for better theory in the era of the Anthropocene, but also the search for a way in which to make humanity conscious of its geohistorical agency and therefore able to avert incoming ecological catastrophe.

For authors such as Latour, the focus of such an endeavour resides in the adaptation of human politics. For Latour, contemporary politics is reflective of humanity's modern alienated condition, deploying political strategies and structures in a way that remains cut off from its grounding in nature and natural history. In the modern era, Latour argues that human beings lack 'the men-

---

36   Ibid.
37   Latour 2015, p.146.
38   Bonneuil and Fressoz 2016, p.20.

tal and emotional repertoire'[39] to face the challenges of the Anthropocene. Problematically for Latour, this modern human alienation is reflected in the 'impotence'[40] of humanity when confronted with the ecological realities of the Anthropocene:

> Either we agitate ourselves as traditional political agents longing for freedom – but such a liberty has no connection with the world of matter – or we decide to submit to the realm of material necessity – but such a material world has nothing in it that looks even vaguely like the freedom or autonomy of olden times. Either the margins of actions have no consequence in the material world, or there is no freedom left in the material world for engaging with it in any politically recognizable fashion.[41]

For Latour, this human impotence stems from the spectre of the modern separation between human and natural history that continues to haunt human political strategies. As Latour argues, it is *impossible* to think politics in this condition of alienation: impossible to think politics when 'what is to be composed is divided into two domains, *one that is inanimate and has no agency, and one which is animated and concentrates all the agencies*'.[42]

The solution, for Latour is the construction and deployment of politics and forms of political agency that transcend this historical alienation and conflate human and natural histories through the distribution of political agency across human and non-human actors alike: 'Far from trying to "reconcile" or "combine" nature and society, the task, the crucial political task, is on the contrary to *distribute* agency as far and in as *differentiated* a way as possible'.[43] Crucially, however, this task remains a fundamentally human one: the task of a human subjectivity, imbued with geo-historical power and agency, to construct and deploy a form of history that embeds this political image. For example, Latour's considerations of political agency in the Anthropocene are driven fundamentally by the potential *recognition* of all non-human actors and entities by a humanity that acts as a geological force, with Latour arguing that geo-historical agency in the Anthropocene will be located by its recognition and inclusion in the historically conscious action of the Anthropos. As Latour writes:

---

39 Latour 2014, p.1.
40 Latour 2014, p.15.
41 Ibid.
42 Latour 2014, p.14.
43 Latour 2014, p.15.

This time we encounter, just as in the old prescientific and nonmodern myths, an agent which gains its name of 'subject' because he or she might be *subjected* to the vagaries, bad humor, emotions, reactions, and even revenge of another agent, who also gains its quality of 'subject' because it is also *subjected* to his or her action.[44]

In Latour's formulations, the humanity of the Anthropocene not only possesses the ability to make history but, in so doing, names the agents of this history too through its recognition – in the context of its own historical action – of actors of various kinds. Natural history comes to matter only to the extent that it becomes bound up in the historically-powerful action of the Anthropos: a binding that ascribes meaning and agency to this history. As Latour writes, 'existence and meaning are synonymous. *As long as they act, agents have meaning*'.[45]

This notion is reflected more starkly in accounts such as those of Dipesh Chakrabarty and his reconsideration of Enlightenment. In much the same way as Latour, Chakrabarty argues that the values of freedom, democracy and equality that have come to define modern, liberal politics are deployed in contemporary society in a condition of fundamental and essential alienation, in which they correspond to the false separation between human and natural histories. As Chakrabarty writes, in modernity, 'philosophers of freedom were mainly, and understandably, concerned with how humans would escape the injustice, oppression, inequality, or even uniformity foisted on them by other humans or human-made systems'.[46] In the Anthropocene, where human and natural history interpenetrate one another, this narrow conception of freedom in fact, for Chakrabarty, forecloses its fuller understanding and realisation: it is in this way that Chakrabarty poses the question, 'is the geological agency of humans the price we pay for the pursuit of freedom?'.[47] The full realisation of freedom demands its conceptual development in relation to the shared historical destiny of humans and the natural world. For Chakrabarty, it is no longer adequate to consider freedom within the confines of human societies and man-made political structures: rather, it must be a value conceived of in relation to the non-human actors who have been thrust into an inextricable relationship with humans by the Anthropocene. As Chakrabarty writes:

---

44   Latour 2014, p.5.
45   Latour 2014, p.12.
46   Chakrabarty 2009, p.208.
47   Chakrabarty 2009, p.210.

Whatever our socioeconomic and technological choices, whatever the rights we wish to celebrate as our freedom, we cannot afford to destabilize conditions (such as the temperature zone in which the planet exists) that work like boundary parameters of human existence. They have been stable for much longer than the histories of these institutions and have allowed human beings to become the dominant species on earth.[48]

Chakrabarty argues that this does not mean that these values should be abandoned: on the contrary, their achievement must be re-orientated as the central task of the human struggle against alienation. For Chakrabarty, 'the Anthropocene is about *waking up to the rude shock* of the recognition of the otherness of the planet',[49] that is, about humanity's becoming-conscious of its alienation and its struggle to redeploy these concepts of Enlightenment in the wake of this consciousness. For Chakrabarty, the answer must be the reflection of this newfound consciousness across *all* areas of life in the Anthropocene, where politics and society, and its expression in democracy, in collective action and in public discourse is at all times a manifestation of the shared historical destiny of both human and non-human actors. As Chakrabarty writes, 'for humans any thought of the way out of our current predicament cannot but refer to the idea of deploying reason in global, collective life'.[50] Just as the Young Marx argued that communism was the social manifestation of humanity's consciousness of the reflection of its own labour in nature, the Anthropocene as a geo-historical era must be, for Chakrabarty, one in which humanity similarly recognises itself in the planet as a whole: 'Logically, then, in the era of the Anthropocene, we need the Enlightenment (that is, reason) even more than in the past'.[51]

Theorists like Jane Bennett echo this in a more philosophical argument, arguing that the Anthropocene provides the context in which to re-think materialism and materialist philosophies. Bennett problematises modern considerations of materialism – particularly implicating Marx's materialism – as foreclosing the contemplation of a 'less specifically human kind of materiality' and the idea that 'attentiveness to (nonhuman) things and their powers can have a laudable effect on humans'.[52] For Bennett, the Anthropocene offers the opportunity to re-think materialist philosophy in the way that it centralises the notion that human society is not the product of isolated human action (as the

---

48 Chakrabarty 2009, p.218.
49 Chakrabarty 2009, p.55, emphasis added.
50 Chakrabarty 2009, p.210.
51 Chakrabarty 2009, p.211.
52 Bennett 2004, p.348.

modern view would have it), but in fact is the material product of a complex interplay between matter of human and non-human varieties. It is an argument for what Bennett calls 'thing-power materialism':

> Thing-power materialism does not endorse the view, absorbed from the nineteenth-century roots of the science of ecology by deep ecologists, that 'ecological' means 'harmonious' or tending toward equilibrium. To be ecological is to participate in a collectivity, but not all collectivities operate as *organic* wholes.[53]

For Bennett, contemporary philosophy reflects modern alienation, unable to think human and natural history together in its materialist vision. This version of materialism, as opposed to its modern predecessor, 'figures things as being more than mere objects, emphasizing their powers of life, resistance, and even a kind of will'.[54] In the era of the Anthropocene, this materialist vision points towards a more suitable method of philosophical comprehension in the wake of potential ecological crises. It signals the fact that planetary history is the culmination of collective action across species boundaries: a culmination that implicates not only the problems, but also the solutions of the Anthropocene. As Bennett concludes, 'these are powers that, in a tightly knit world, we ignore at our own peril'.[55]

This theoretical critique of modernity and alienation is also evident in Donna Haraway's considerations of subjectivity. Though Haraway has reservations about the name 'Anthropocene' ('surely such a transformative time on earth must not be named the Anthropocene!'[56]), Haraway recognises the present moment as one of significance, insofar as it allows for the interrogation and deconstruction of anthropocentric conceptualisations of subjectivity. For Haraway, the Anthropocene as the coming-together of human and natural histories undermines the modern humanist notion that human subjectivity is cut off from nature or other non-human entities, instead exposing subjectivity as a messy and co-created product of multiple entities. As Haraway writes, 'no species, not even our own arrogant one pretending to be good individuals in so-called modern Western scripts, acts alone; assemblages of organic species and of abiotic actors make history, the evolutionary kind and

---

53 Bennett 2004, p.365.
54 Bennett 2004, p.360.
55 Ibid.
56 Haraway 2016, pp.30–1.

the other kinds too'.⁵⁷ In the Anthropocene, the conception of subjectivity in any other way becomes inadequate, as subjectivity ceases to correlate to its modern, individualistic notion and instead has meaning only in a time of geo-historical agency: 'What used to be called nature has erupted into ordinary human affairs, and vice versa, in such a way and with such permanence as to change fundamentally means and prospects for going on, including going on at all'.⁵⁸

For Haraway, the Anthropocene is an important moment insofar as it allows for humanity to *think* beyond its alienated condition. Haraway argues that the Anthropocene is the manifestation of a particular alienated condition, in which humans are unable to think catastrophe due to the persistence of modernity and modern ideologies in the way that bodies, agents and subjects are conceived and thought to matter. As Haraway writes:

> What is it to surrender the capacity to think? These times called the Anthropocene are times of multispecies, including human, urgency: of great mass death and extinction; of unrushing disasters, whose unpredictable specificities are foolishly taken as unknowability itself; of refusing to be present in and to onrushing catastrophe in time; of unprecedented looking away.⁵⁹

For Haraway, even in her distaste for the 'Anthropocene' as a descriptive term, the value of this geo-historical moment is that, in the wake of the consciousness of humanity as to the geo-historical power located in its labour, this capacity to think returns to humanity in a way that potentially inaugurates a new way of understanding subjectivity and thus a new way of reflecting subjectivity and recognition within society and culture. In this way, the Anthropocene allows for 'making persons, [but] not necessarily as individuals or as humans'.⁶⁰

Through the examples discussed here, it is clear to see the translation of the initial theoretical humanism of the Anthropocene discourse into a critical analysis of human alienation and its reflection in modern discourse. Modernity and modern discourse have been shown here to reflect a condition of human alienation, in which the human subject has found itself essentially cut off from its grounding in natural history. The precondition for humanity's transcendence of the geo-historical parameters of the Anthropocene and its capabilities

---

57   Haraway 2015, p.159.
58   Haraway 2016, p.40.
59   Haraway 2016, p.35.
60   Haraway 2015, p.161.

in escaping potential ecological activity, demands human consciousness of the geo-historical power of its own action and the reflection of this consciousness in alternative social and political strategies. In this way, humanity finds 'the power to transcend history by *human liberty*'.[61] Therefore, the Anthropocene is not simply a moment of crisis, but celebrated here as a moment of opportunity through which humanity can – through the consciousness of its position, through its achievement of reason in the Anthropocene – chart an alternative geo-historical path.

However, this theory of alienation observed by the theorists of the Anthropocene is not unproblematic. What is evident is that the theoretical humanism of the Anthropocene discourse and its resolution in a problematic of human alienation is reproductive of a number of theoretical and ideological weaknesses that force the questioning of its analytical applicability. For example, the apparent break that the Anthropocene discourse proposes to make with modernity and modern ideology is betrayed by the re-assertion of the human subject at the centre of its theoretical critique. Despite the fact that the Anthropocene is celebrated in creating the conditions for the construction of a post-anthropocentric approach to social science, the position of the human subject as *the* defining geo-historical actor betrays this break, reflected in the reproduction of humanist ideological tropes regarding concepts such as human labour, human subjectivity and human history. In this way:

> This fable, claiming to break with the world-view of the moderns that it incriminates, in the end actually reproduces it. It proceeds from the same regime of historicity that dominated the nineteenth century and a part of the twentieth, in which the past is assessed only as a backdrop, for the lessons it yields for the future, and in representation of time as a one-directional acceleration.[62]

Moreover, by insisting upon an analysis and observation of geo-historical alienation, crucial social relations are forced to the background. Though the proponents of the Anthropocene discourse suggest the development and deployment of alternative social and political strategies for averting potential ecological catastrophe, the precise social relations (and potential social upheavals) that would foreground any such developments are obscured from view, hidden behind this ideological story of human alienation. As Palsson et al. write, 'it

---

61 Althusser 2008, p.75.
62 Bonneuil and Fressoz 2016, pp.77–8.

is remarkable how little these concepts tell us about the process, the driving forces, and the social consequences of the changes they imply'.[63]

Particularly problematic is the fact that, obscured by this humanist story of alienation are the social relations of production and reproduction inherent to contemporary capitalism. Nowhere figured in the social scientific response to the Anthropocene is the relationship between strategies of capital accumulation and the degradation of the planet. The idea that the inability of humanity to think or comprehend the crisis with which it is faced is the epicentre of human catastrophe 'are just so much ideological noise, intended to obscure the real peril that humanity is today exposed to: that is to say, the impasse that globalised capitalism is leading us into'.[64] Moreover, it is not entirely clear to what extent the social science of the Anthropocene and its notions of human consciousness directly contradicts the ideological reproductions of the contemporary capitalist class. As authors like Naomi Klein have highlighted, it is precisely within the comfort of such techno-scientific and humanist ideological reactions to the problems of climate change that capitalists such as Richard Branson – the CEO of Virgin Atlantic airways and its fleet of fossil-fuel dependent jets – and policy-makers like Al Gore – the 2000 US Presidential Candidate – locate their concern about climate change and ecological disaster. They do so, because such an anthropocentric perspective that puts the blame squarely upon the 'ingenious if unruly species'[65] of Man, foregoes the attribution of any blame to the strategies of accumulation inherent in globalised corporations or Western-democratic politics. As Bonneuil and Fressoz argue, with caution, 'the seductive Anthropocene concept may well become the official philosophy of a new technocratic and market-oriented geopower'.[66]

3   Humanism, Historicism, Marxism: Labour between 'Fossil Capital' and the 'Capitalocene'

Evident so far is the problem of the Anthropocene discourse: a theoretical humanism continues to persist through the conceptual vehicles of labour and alienation, behind which capitalism and class struggle remain hidden. The question remains as to whether or not Marxism as a theoretical response contains the potential to overcome these ideological obstacles in its own ana-

---

63 Palsson et al. 2012, p.7.
64 Badiou 2018, para.3.
65 Crist 2016, pp.16–17.
66 Bonneuil and Fressoz 2016, p.49.

lysis of climate change and ecological disaster. In what follows, this chapter will demonstrate the extent to which some of the ideological currents of the Anthropocene discourse, particularly those found within the discussions of labour and alienation, continue to persist within dominant Marxist approaches to the question of ecology, nature and climate catastrophe. In order to do this, the chapter intervenes within the discussion of two contemporary interlocutors responsible in large part for the formation of the Marxist discourse in this particular field: Andreas Malm and his notion of 'fossil capital'; and Jason W. Moore's notion of the 'capitalocene'.

Both Malm and Moore begin with a criticism of the Anthropocene discourse as it has so far been set out. Scepticism of the humanism integral to this discourse and to the definition of the human species as a geological agent frames the critique formulated by the two authors in response to this discourse. Malm writes that for the theorists of the Anthropocene, 'the "essential catalyst" and "primary reason" for the large-scale combustion of fossil fuels as it spread in the industrial era are in fact the mastering of fire by a particular primate species some half a million years ago'.[67] Alongside what Malm calls the 'Ricardian-Malthusian paradigm' which attributes climate change to humanity's attempt to overcome the problem of scarcity, the Anthropocene discourse shares a central ideological framework, based around a 'doctrine of "human enterprise"'.[68] Moore offers a similar critique, arguing that:

> The dominant Anthropocene argument assumes a standard narrative. It says that the origins of the modern world are to be found in England, right around the dawn of the nineteenth century. The motive force behind this epochal shift? Coal and steam. The driving force behind coal and steam? Not class. Not capital. Not imperialism. Not even culture. But ... you guessed it, the *Anthropos*: humanity as an undifferentiated whole.[69]

The problem with the anthropocentric view forwarded by the Anthropocene narrative is, for both Malm and Moore, that it obscures important social and class relations and their relationship to the phenomenon of climate change. Malm argues that the Anthropocene discourse finds itself in troubled waters as it misses the hypothesis that 'the relations of production – particularly those between capital and labour – enforced the selection of steam power and not

---

67 Malm 2016, p.30.
68 Malm 2016, p.36.
69 Moore 2016, p.81.

vice versa'.[70] Echoing this, Moore writes that the Anthropocene discourse 'does not challenge the naturalized inequalities, alienation, and violence inscribed in modernity's strategic relations of power and production. It is an easy story because it does not ask us to think about these relations *at all*'.[71]

Despite this recognition of the problem of humanist ideology within the Anthropocene discourse, the success of these Marxist responses in overcoming this ideology in the deployment of their own analyses is mixed. Indeed, Moore's analysis appears to do a much better job at overcoming the humanist ideological obstacles inherent within this discourse than Malm's. This is primarily because, as with the Anthropocene discourse itself, Malm's analysis begins with the concept of *labour*, reproducing the notion that fossil capital is the outcome of a particular, conscious interaction with nature by human beings. As Malm writes, in the opening lines of his text *Fossil Capital*, 'anthropogenic climate change ... has its roots *outside* the realm of temperature and precipitation, turtles and polar bears, inside a sphere of human praxis that could be summed up in one word as *labour*'.[72]

From the outset, Malm situates the phenomenon of fossil capital – that is, the emergence of a capitalist mode of production oriented around the extraction and burning of fossil fuels – within the labour process as 'the point of contact between humans and the rest of nature, where biophysical resources pass into the circuits of social metabolism, where coal and oil and gas are extracted, transported, coupled to machines: burnt'.[73] This echoes the dimensions of the theoretically humanist concept of labour discussed in chapter two. The consequences of mobilising this concept of labour become immediately clear, as Malm prefaces the launching of his investigation in the following way: 'Natural scientists have so far interpreted global warming as a phenomenon in nature; the point, however, is to trace its human origins'.[74] Malm here reproduces a synonymity between the *social* origins of climate change and its *human* origins (confirmed more explicitly elsewhere, where Malm says 'realising that climate change is "anthropogenic" is to appreciate that it is *sociogenic*'[75]): a synonymity that is too easily and uncritically reproduced within Marxist thought, as Althusser warned in *The Humanist Controversy*.

---

70 Malm 2016, p.36.
71 Moore 2015, p.170.
72 Malm 2016, p.6.
73 Malm 2016, p.19.
74 Ibid.
75 Malm 2016, p.270.

The historical detail provided by Malm certainly presents a narrative of climate change that emphasises different phenomena compared to that of the Anthropocene discourse. Through the presentation of historical data, Malm demonstrates how the shift from water to steam – or, from the 'flow' of natural energy to the 'stock' of fossil fuels like coal – was motivated by the need to capture and liberate greater quantities of labour-power and was tied intimately to the disciplining and exploitation of an emerging industrial labour force. As Malm writes, the advantage of this transition was targeted at 'overcoming the barriers to procurement not of energy, but of *labour*. The engine was a superior medium for extracting surplus wealth from the working class, because, unlike the waterwheel, it could be put up practically anywhere'.[76] The flexibility provided by fossil fuels like coal meant that factories did not need to be established only in places where water flowed freely and powerfully, but could instead be placed where reserves of labour-power existed more readily for exploitation. This is what Malm means when he says that fossil fuels 'are, by definition, a materialisation of social relations', in that they 'necessitate waged or forced labour – the power of some to direct the labour of others – as conditions of their very existence'.[77] It is therefore unfair and incorrect to say that class struggle is missing from Malm's analysis, as it is in the Anthropocene discourse. However, difficulties arise when Malm sets out to understand the nature and origin of these social relations.

Due to the centrality of the concept of labour in Malm's work, alongside the avowed historicism of the project, *Fossil Capital* reproduces a humanist interpretation of these historical social relations which privileges the deliberate decision-making of the concrete individuals who bear these relations. It is an interpretation of social relations in which their description is of 'relations into which men enter',[78] consciously and deliberately. However, Althusser reminds the reader that 'they do not enter into them the way one enters a restaurant or a political party', as human beings alone are not the primary determinants of the appearance of these relations. In significant places, Malm's analysis of fossil capital reproduces this particular ideological schema. For example, in the opening chapters, Malm sets out his interpretation of class struggle in relation to fossil capital as the way in which 'some humans introduced steam power *against the explicit resistance of other humans*'.[79] In describing the development of specific relations of production – this example explaining the reason

76   Malm 2016, p.124.
77   Malm 2016, p.19.
78   Althusser 2020a, p.71.
79   Malm 2016, p.36.

why water power ceased to develop and expand as a key aspect of the capitalist labour-process – Malm suggests that this under-development stemmed from the decision-making of individual mill-owners and 'their unwillingness or inability to submit to the *planning, coordination and collective funding* required for expansion of waterpower capacity'.[80] Explaining the shift from water power to steam power, and its utility in capturing and transforming greater populations into wage-labourers, Malm again finds the essence of this operation in the individual (and, as per the Anthopocene discourse itself, *alienated*) relation between manufacturers and workers:

> By dint of its spatial fixity, waterpower obliged the manufacturer to form *personal relations* to his hands, whether they were bound apprentices whose needs he must provide for or free labourers for whom he spun a cocoon encompassing all aspects of life, from religious instruction to basic healthcare. Estranging him from his neighbour, steam power, on the other hand, allowed the capitalist to treat his workers as 'so many old shuttles'. They could now be discarded at will, replaced with ease, left to fend for themselves on the housing market, unknown and immaterial in any other respect than as a temporarily hired capacity for labour.[81]

In all of these instances, the notion of the social relation as something into which workers and capitalists deliberately enter into, or alter for their own ends, continues to persist. In order to understand the historical development of the relations of production within fossil capital, it is important to first grasp the changing nature of the relationship between concrete individuals at various points throughout this development.

This tendency finds itself most pronounced in Malm's critique of ideology in relation to fossil capital. Malm describes the emergence of an ideological development among the bourgeoisie of the early nineteenth century, which he calls 'steam fetishism': a developing and increasingly powerful ideological synonymity between steam power and private property relations. Malm offers a hypothesis which suggests that this ideology in some way preceded the transition from water power to steam power that defines the production of fossil capital, arguing that 'it occurred *before the shift from water to steam had come near completion*'.[82] This hypothesis is problematic, insofar as it privileges the

---

80 Malm 2016, p.118.
81 Malm 2016, p.152.
82 Malm 2016, p.204.

bourgeoisie as a set of concrete agents with very particular ideas as the leading force of the shift in relations of production described by this transition from water to steam. As much is alluded to by Malm. Malm sets the scene of the emergence of steam fetishism in the context of a meeting in 1824 between some of the most important industrialists and mill owners at the time, who had come together to orchestrate a campaign to build a statue commemorating James Watt and his invention of the steam engine. It is here, in the Freemason's Hall in which they met, that Malm argues that 'steam power was ritually consecrated as *a class project*'.[83] For Malm, what makes this a 'class' project is the position that 'steam already held over the bourgeois mind',[84] and the fact that steam fetishism represented an articulation of the *ideas* of the bourgeoisie as a class. This, again, is problematic, as it reproduces a notion that the relationship between class and ideology is one anchored in the conscious deliberations of this class as a set of concrete individuals. As Malm writes:

> Just like any other human beings, capitalists are more – or less – than exclusively rational creatures, and ideology can arouse passions, orient actions, egg on its adherents in their practical life, including the sphere of commodity production. It cannot be ruled out that the masters fell under the spell.[85]

It was the fact that the individual capitalists 'fell under the spell' of steam fetishism that explains the shift from water to steam in this formulation. This again privileges an interpretation of social relations as an act of conscious entering-into by the agents implicated in those relations. The problem with this idea is that it undermines the materialism of the analysis undertaken here, where the materiality of social relations is subservient to the actions of concrete individuals: 'Steam fetishism did not just grow spontaneously out of the material (and semiotic) fabric of society: it came into being by bourgeois intellectuals *articulating it openly* as others did liberalism or socialism'.[86]

Given this insistence on the notion that social relations are essentially relations between human beings, Malm relies on the same theory of alienated labour that is reproduced within the Anthropocene discourse, in order to explain the emergence and development of fossil capital. For Malm, the 'fun-

---

83   Ibid.
84   Ibid.
85   Malm 2016, p.211.
86   Malm 2016, p.222.

damental intra-species fracture'[87] introduced by private property set in motion an alienation between the human species and nature, which facilitated the important shift from water power to steam power at the centre of this history of fossil capital. As Malm writes, with fossil capital:

> A primordial rift in the relation between humans and the rest of nature is propagated in space and time, severing human beings from the qualitative properties of both as labour is relocated to places and moments set aside strictly for the purpose [of accumulating capital].[88]

The fact that unlike the flow of natural energies such as water, the stock of fossil fuels does not abide by the natural rhythms of the earth, this meant that it uprooted human labour itself from those very rhythms with disastrous consequences: 'Prior to capital, production was rooted in home and weather; with capital, it must be uprooted from both, since its purpose is no longer use- but exchange-value'.[89] Much as it is within the Anthropocene discourse, this alienated condition is then reflected in the conscious decision-making of individual agents. Malm suggests, for example, that 'the original act of the capitalists is to insert themselves in the metabolism between human beings and the rest of nature *as it is*, like a spider taking over another one's web',[90] relying once more on the humanist idea that social relations are things freely entered into by individual agents. According to Malm, the shift to steam power '*had to be chosen*'[91] by capitalists as concrete agents, endowed with a 'peculiar human capacity for energetic division', 'exceptional purchasing power' and the *possession* of a 'renewed, expanded power to purchase and command human life'.[92] Thus, by positioning the history of fossil capital through the lens of the concept of labour, Malm here does not adequately break with the assumptions and ideology of the Anthropocene discourse, to the detriment of his analysis of capitalist social relations, interpreted here as the machinations of conscious and concrete agents as opposed to material realities encompassing much more than human beings.

The analysis presented by Jason W. Moore, particularly in his text *Capitalism in the Web of Life*, offers an alternative approach to this history from that

---

87   Malm 2016, p.286.
88   Malm 2016, p.307.
89   Ibid.
90   Malm 2016, p.309.
91   Ibid.
92   Malm 2016, p.315.

of Malm. The argument forwarded here is that whereas Malm's history begins from a perspective of production (which permits the concept of labour and its humanist ideological weight), Moore begins, as per Romé's Althusser, from the perspective of *reproduction*. What this section argues is that it is Moore's theoretical anti-humanism that permits this perspective and that this perspective simultaneously allows for the continued critique and evacuation of the human subject from theory.

Whilst Malm focuses on the notion of fossil capital, Moore turns his attention to what he describes as the capitalist *world-ecology*. For Moore, the capitalist world-ecology cannot be reduced down to the simple interaction between humans and nature within the labour-process, but rather describes the ways in which society and nature are immanently co-reproduced within particular historical circumstances, which, in turn, reproduces a set of historical social relations. Moore describes this world-ecology as 'an ongoing movement between bodies and environment, production and reproduction, on the "ground floor" of everyday life and the dynamics of world accumulation, world power, and world knowledge'.[93] At this initial stage, the capitalist world-ecology evacuates the human subject as the motor of its development, instead centralising the very reproduction of social relations observed in the dialectic between nature and society: 'From here, it follows that *all* relations between humans are always – already – relations at once "*of*" nature" and "*to* the rest of nature"'.[94]

In order to produce this concept of world-ecology and privilege the perspective of reproduction in this way, Moore argues that it is necessary to establish a theoretically anti-humanist position. Moore achieves this position through a critique of existing Marxist approaches to this problem, which observe this problem as one of a 'metabolic rift' between humanity and nature. Moore argues that this perspective – popularised by John Bellamy Foster and Paul Burkett, and indeed echoed by Malm – emphasises a separation between humans and nature in order to pronounce its critique of capitalism. The problem with this approach is, as has been demonstrated above, that it produces an interpretation of social relations that requires the intervention of a conscious and deliberate human subject, which acts upon nature in some way (for example, the mill owners who *choose* to move from water power to steam power). As Moore argues:

> In this logic, relations between humans are regarded as ontologically prior to the relations of nature, a meta-theoretical procedure that allows one to

[93] Moore 2015, p.26.
[94] Ibid.

speak of modernity as a set of social relations that act upon, rather than develop through, the web of life.[95]

The dualism of this approach, according to Moore, has 'reduced nature to flows and stocks within and between pre-formed units',[96] where capitalism describes the disruption of these flows and stocks by the intervention of human labour in the act of production. Such a view closes off the perspective of reproduction, of appreciating 'value as a logic of re/producing the flow of life',[97] and of understanding the ways in which both society and nature are co-reproduced by, and reproductive of, capitalist social relations. Therefore, Moore argues that it is necessary to collapse this dualism between humans and nature, and thereby remove the human subject from the centre of enquiry: 'The historical task is not one of explaining the separation of humanity and nature. The priority is to specify the historical forms of humanity-in-nature, and therefore nature-in-humanity'.[98]

In order to collapse this dualism, Moore finds it necessary to begin from the point of view of reproduction. Moore admits that, whilst 'the exploitation of commodified labor-power is central to capital accumulation, and to the survival of individual capitalists ... this cannot be the end of the story'.[99] Rather, as well as the productive consumption of labour-power as a commodity, Moore explains that capital 'must ceaselessly search for, and find new ways to produce, Cheap Natures: a rising stream of low-cost food, labor-power, energy, and raw materials to the factory gates (or office doors, or ...)'.[100] In short, capitalism cannot survive simply on the basis of production alone, but must secure its reproduction in various ways: ways that implicate both human and non-human beings. As Moore continues:

> The movements creating the necessary relations and conditions of Cheap Nature cannot be reduced to the immediate processes of production, or even commodity production and exchange as a whole. These are crucial and indispensable. But they are not sufficient. For capitalism depends on a repertoire of strategies for *appropriating* the unpaid work/energy of humans and the rest of nature outside the commodity system.[101]

---

95 Moore 2015, p.77.
96 Moore 2015, p.81.
97 Ibid.
98 Moore 2015, p.82.
99 Moore 2015, p.53.
100 Ibid.
101 Moore 2015, p.54.

It is for this reason that Moore can offer a very Althusserian justification for this shift in perspective: 'While Marxist political economy has taken value to be an *economic* phenomenon with systemic implications, the inverse formulation may be more plausible: value-relations are a *systemic* phenomenon with a pivotal economic moment'.[102] In short, what the perspective of reproduction allows for is the demonstration that capitalist social relations are only determined by the economy in the last instance, are overdetermined by economic relations, but never reducible to them.

Moore operationalises this perspective through the development of a critique of the concept of 'labour'. Using Marx's theory of value, Moore argues that labour cannot be reduced simply to a productive activity in the humanist sense, nor simply as those acts which are deemed only productive of value. 'On the one hand,' Moore explains, 'capitalism lives and dies on the expanded reproduction of capital: value-in-motion. The substance of value is abstract social labor, or socially necessary labor-time'.[103] But on the other, value cannot exist without those labours which may not contribute to its direct production, but are nonetheless crucial for its creation: 'this production of value is particular – it does not value everything, only labor-power in the circuit of capital – and therefore rests upon a series of devaluations'.[104] Therefore, just as important as labour-power is the existence of labours that escape valuation and therefore this definition as such: 'Plenty of work – the majority of work in the orbit of capitalism – does not register as valuable. Work by humans, especially women; but also 'work' performed by extra-human natures'.[105] This critique of labour, as it did for the Marxist-feminists who developed it, opens up the perspective of reproduction: 'Capital and value relations cannot be reduced to a relation between the owners of capital and the possessors of labor-power. *The historical condition of socially necessary labor-time is socially necessary unpaid work*'.[106]

Whilst Malm's analysis turns on the ways in which the stock and the flow were incorporated into productive activity, Moore's innovation is to demonstrate the role that nature has played in the reproduction of capitalism, emphasising the relationship between the production of 'Cheap Natures' (labour-power, food, energy and raw materials) and the 'expanded reproduction of the capital-*un*paid work relation'.[107] Moore operationalises the concept

---

102 Moore 2015, pp.54–5.
103 Moore 2015, p.65.
104 Ibid.
105 Ibid.
106 Moore 2015, p.69.
107 Moore 2015, p.62.

of 'appropriation' in order to demonstrate this relation between capital and unpaid work. As Moore explains:

> Capitalism depends upon a repertoire of strategies for *appropriating* the unpaid work/energy of humans and the rest of nature outside the commodity system ... Absent massive streams of unpaid work/energy from the rest of nature – including that delivered by women – the costs of production would rise, and accumulation would slow. Every act of exploitation (of commodified labour-power) therefore depends on an even greater act of appropriation (of unpaid work/energy).[108]

It is this view of appropriation, developed from the perspective of reproduction, which allows Moore to analyse what he calls the 'capitalocene' in contrast to Malm's fossil capital: an era which long predates the Industrial Revolution, which fetishizes the development of productive forces alone. Focusing on the Industrial Revolution 'is to prioritize shutting down the steam engines and the coal pits (and their twenty-first-century incarnations)',[109] that is, to focus only on the forces of production. By shifting to the point of view of reproduction, early capitalism, beginning after 1450, opens up as a more suitable time period from which to view the origins of climate change, and prioritise the 'strategies of global conquest, endless commodification, and relentless rationalization ... the relations of power, capital, and nature that rendered fossil capital so deadly in the first place'.[110] Rather than the steam engine, Moore dates the origins of the capitalocene in the mass deforestation in Brazil of the long seventeenth century. This initiated a complex set of relations which opened up global sugar markets but also set in motion new techniques for the colonial appropriation of cheap labour-power, reproductive labours and cheap natures vital for the reproduction of these markets.

It is not simply the shift in historical dates which is the important outcome of this move to the perspective of reproduction. It is the evacuation of the human subject from the centre of theory which is the most important innovation here. Whilst Malm's analysis prioritises the position of the human subject from the point of production, the perspective of reproduction here forwarded by Moore aims to 'transcend the man/woman, nature/society boundaries upon which the whole edifice of modernist thought depends'.[111] The per-

---

108 Moore 2015, p.54.
109 Moore 2015, p.172.
110 Ibid.
111 Moore 2015, p.69.

spective of reproduction opens up a view of 'capitalism as a contradictory unity of production and reproduction that crosses the Cartesian boundary',[112] as relations of appropriation cannot be reduced down to the level of concrete human individuals alone. Just as Romé emphasises the importance of the concept of reproduction in considering the complexity of a given historical situation as a process without a subject, Moore demonstrates how the concept of appropriation 'allows us to connect the production and accumulation of surplus value with its necessary conditions of reproduction' in a way that 'transcends the Cartesian divide, encompassing both human and extra-human work outside, but necessary to, the circuit of capital and the production of value'.[113]

4 Conclusion

This chapter has demonstrated how the persistence of the concept of labour throughout the Anthropocene discourse is responsible for the reproduction of a theoretical humanism throughout its formulations. From the theoretically humanist perspective of the Anthropocene discourse, labour is configured as the distinct and geo-historical activity of the human subject, through which this subject is able to *make* and *re-make* history. The conditions of the Anthropocene, in this formulation, confront the sociologist as the alienated product of this labour: an alienation that is codified in the reinforcement of a false separation between human and natural histories within modern discourse. The ability of the human subject to transcend these geo-historically unfavourable conditions depends upon this subject's consciousness as to its geo-historical power in this way: a consciousness that first sees humanity confronted with the discontents of its historical action and thereafter compelled to transcend the historical conditions reflective of these discontents. However, this theoretically humanist approach to the Anthropocene has been shown to reproduce ideological effects, mystifying the relationship between the social relations of capitalist production and appropriation and these conditions of planetary crisis. What modern ideology hides is not the geo-historical alienation of the human subject, but the world-ecological character of capitalism, the class-struggle of which is reflected not only in historically specific orientations of human society, but also historically specific configurations of nature.

---

112 Ibid.
113 Moore 2015, p.55.

Where Marxist theory has been able to displace the concept of labour, it has been more successful in overcoming the limitations established by theoretical humanism in thinking about climate change and ecological crisis. In moving from a perspective of production grounded in the concept of labour towards a perspective of reproduction grounded in the concept of appropriation, Jason W. Moore opens up the space, theoretically, to displace the human subject from the centre of this narrative and produce an explanation of this crisis that does not depend upon the conscious deliberations of a concrete human subject. Malm's history of fossil capital, in maintaining the concept of labour at its centre, is plagued by the persistent necessity of a concrete human subject at the core of its narrative in order to explain the relationship between capitalist social relations and the burning of fossil fuels.

The development of a sociology of work in the context of 'the Anthropocene' is still forthcoming. The discourse is relatively new, inaugurating a proliferation of exploratory theoretical texts within the social sciences. But what has been made clear in this chapter is that, theoretically, this discourse seems to leave humanist ideology unthought in relation to the consideration of work and labour: an oversight that could prove particularly problematic for the development of any future sociology of work. Moving into the concluding chapter of this book, the considerations of theory in the Anthropocene here completed, stress the necessity of the critique of ideology as a central theoretical task for the construction of the sociology of work.

CONCLUSION

Marxism in Sociology

Across the chapters of this book, it has been argued that theoretical humanism and humanist ideological concepts underwrite a significant and persistent weakness throughout the sociology of work. In various ways and through various theoretical interactions with the concepts of labour and work, humanism has been shown to repeatedly emerge to the detriment of sociological analysis, mystifying key social relations of work, prioritising certain social perspectives over others and reinforcing the precise ideologies with which contemporary social inequalities are justified. Analyses of the social relations of work – the commodification of labour-power, the inequalities that dictate its mobilisation and exploitation, the social relations that underpin the reproduction of this labour-power and the unique class struggles that are reflected in these relations – have all been mystified, obscured and rendered-invisible by repeated appeals to humanist ideology as an explanation for contemporary social phenomena. Ideological concerns regarding human subjectivity, human alienation and human self-affirmation have, in various ways, been substituted for sociological analysis in relation to work, signifying human experience but offering a limited understanding of its concrete implications. The book has therefore shown that both humanism and ideology are by no means problems of the past: they have been shown to pose a persistent danger to the sociology of work today. Despite the influences of Althusser and his contemporaries upon philosophy and upon social science more broadly, humanism has here been shown to persist as an ideological problem for contemporary sociology. What has been made clear in this book is that if the sociology of work is to emerge as an adequate and effective explanatory framework in the face of contemporary transformations of work, it must necessarily include a theoretical critique of humanism and humanist ideology as a central task.

Althusser was clear in his argument that the only force capable of dismantling ideologies strewn along the path towards knowledge, is *science*. Marxism, or historical materialism, has a scientific quality for Althusser, to the extent that the dismantling of ideology is central to its theoretical operation. As William Lewis writes:

> Unlike ideological practice, which tends to the reproduction of existing socio-economic relations, one of the most important things about historical materialism for Althusser is that, once inaugurated, its practice tends

to replace existing ideas about our social and natural relations and to generate new and politically reliable knowledge about the world.[1]

In the context of the political sociologies discussed throughout this book, this scientific character to historical materialism is even more important. Given that ideologies are only ever the reflection of given material realities, the theoretical dismantling of ideology is simultaneously a revelation of the conditions that give rise to it, with this revelation a necessary precondition for the alteration of those conditions. As Lewis continues, 'this new awareness and this new knowledge of social relations is practical knowledge or knowledge for practice. Insofar as it is correct, it allows us to change ourselves and to change our world'.[2] It's from here, from this production of a scientific knowledge of the material conditions of existence, that the space opens for philosophy to intervene into politics:

> With this knowledge, philosophy can then argue in politics. It can demonstrate what ideas about the social world are ideological (including philosophical ones), explain why they exist, and it can suggest the correct actions to be taken if we want to change not only these ideas but also the social forces that produce and sustain them.[3]

For Althusser, it is impossible to be a 'Marxist philosopher': the non-scientific character of philosophy makes such a position untenable. As Althusser writes, '*philosophy is not a science*, and that it therefore does not pose problems as the sciences do, nor, as the sciences do, discover their solutions, which constitute concrete knowledge'.[4] It was only possible, as the title of Althusser's text alludes to, to be a Marxist *in* philosophy. What is evident from the investigations carried out in this book is that the same approach must be taken to sociology as a discipline: the struggle is not to create a 'Marxist sociology,' but to establish a position as Marxists *in* sociology. In the same text, Althusser describes sociology as one among many 'scientific discoveries and scientific impostures', which came forward claiming to be 'capable of unifying knowledge of the world under the aegis of their theories'.[5] Therefore, the development of any political sociology of work must correctly identify the motor of knowledge production:

---

1 Lewis 2022, p.30.
2 Ibid.
3 Lewis 2022, p.36.
4 Althusser 2017, p.23.
5 Althusser 2017, p.26.

not as sociology, but as *Marxism*, or *historical materialism* itself. A Marxist sociology cannot, by definition, exist. The best that can be hoped for is the existence of Marxism in sociology.

Though Althusser was sceptical of sociology, others such as Mario Tronti sought to defend sociology and advocated the existence of a Marxism *in* sociology: the value of this relationship for Tronti is evident, when he says that 'Marxism presents itself as the only true sociology, that is, as the only science of society'.[6] For Tronti, sociology is useful insofar as it facilitates the holding-together of theory and practice which is integral to the advancement of historical materialism. As Tronti writes, the Marxist scientist must hold together 'an equilibrium of the concrete bond between theory, on the one side, and practice – that is, with the class, with the party – on the other'.[7] Crucially, the scientific properties of historical materialism must mean the erasure of this distinction between theoretical and practical labour. As Althusser writes, echoing Tronti here, 'if you take Marxist theory, which you assume to be true, and, having decided to apply it to the concrete, wait for this "application" to generate the truth of the concrete itself, you're in for a long wait'.[8] The scientific quality of Marxism exists precisely in its ability to hold theory and practice together in an immanent relation with one another and change both simultaneously through interventions on either side. It is this quality which must guide the Marxist in sociology: 'Otherwise, we lapse into "vulgar sociology"'.[9]

The argument forwarded in this book is that the condition of any Marxism in sociology has to be *theoretical anti-humanism*. Frédéric Lordon has highlighted the ways in which there exists, within sociology itself, the space for the development of a theoretical anti-humanism. Lordon argues that sociology offers a defence against what he calls 'the paradigm of the association [that] haunts all of modern thought', a paradigm which says that 'people only bind together because they *want* to, perhaps at some initial and distant moment in the past'.[10] Lordon echoes Althusser's critique of those ideological notions of social relations as something into which humans *enter*, of their own free will. Repeating here a passage from Lordon cited towards the beginning of this book:

> Sociology, however, takes a very different view of 'society'. On the one hand, it asserts that the cohesive principle underpinning societies is to

---

6   Tronti 2020, p.48.
7   Tronti 2020, p.50.
8   Althusser 2020b, p.20.
9   Althusser 2020b, p.2.
10 Lordon 2022, p.33.

be understood independently of the external influence of the state, but, above all, it asserts that there is much more to human collectivities than the effects of voluntary associations and that bonds arise elsewhere than from carefully-thought-through 'engagements'.[11]

Sociology is capable of capturing the fact that, when talking about society, 'there is an *exceedence* of the whole in relation to the parts'.[12] This exceedance, as this book has argued, is what both Marx and Althusser have attempted to capture with the concept of the 'social relation'. For Lordon, such a sociological perspective is crucial for the consideration of any future politics:

> The group affects itself, and in a way that exceeds the actions of each of its members, giving rise *from* them but also *above* them to something that transcends all of them. To this production of the social, Spinoza gives a name: the power of the multitude.[13]

This is what Althusser meant when he said that his account was 'much more Spinozist than structuralist'.[14] It is not that subjects do not matter, but that their behaviour has to be placed in the context of something irreducible to their own intent or psychology. For Lordon, the study of this excess in society is the object of sociology and should be rescued for today.

The question remains as to whether the sociology of work, specifically, is to be a fruitful discourse for the development of any kind of Marxism in sociology. For sociologists like Luc Boltanski and Eve Chiapello, though sceptical of (Althusserian) Marxism's ability to make sense of the 'New Spirit of Capitalism' emerging within discourses on the management of work, it is necessary for sociological critique to be able to conceptualise this excess as it exists within the social relations of work and employment, without reducing it to the level of the concrete individual. As Boltanski and Chiapello write:

> It is at the very least hasty, and possibly even inappropriate, to characterize it as 'individual': its recognition by individuals in fact depends on the way in which they identify with groups by means of a labour of characterization and creation of equivalence that is collective and historical from start to finish.[15]

---

11 Lordon 2022, p.36.
12 Ibid.
13 Lordon 2022, p.40.
14 Althusser 1976, p.126.
15 Boltanski and Chiapello 2017, p.532.

Within the sociology of work, Boltanski and Chiapello warn that the reduction of its phenomena to the individual level in this way is bound to produce a limited sociological analysis. As they continue, 'this translates into seeking a single, totalizing cause for the changes that have affected capitalism and the societies it is embedded in over the last thirty years, be it the competition of "low-wage countries", globalization, or technological innovation'.[16] The book has demonstrated the extent to which these overarching sociological explanations of certain 'crises' or phenomena, are rooted in the reliance of the sociologist on a theoretically humanist ideological structure. The individualisation of social phenomena is, as Boltanski and Chiapello indicate here, linked to the production of vague and totalising sociological explanations for these phenomena, behind which their material and historical complexity remains hidden.

In closing, the goal ought not be the production of a 'Marxist sociology'. The goal must be the reconstruction of a Marxism *in* sociology. The marker of this reconstruction must be its theoretical anti-humanism. The only way to guarantee a materialism in sociology, achieved in the immanence of theory and practice, is through the evacuation of the human subject *from theory*. Sociology must, at all times, reconstruct its premises based on the total elimination of the human subject from the centre of its epistemological orientation. It is Marx that shows the way in this regard: 'By rejecting the essence of man as his theoretical basis, Marx rejected the whole of this organic system of postulates'.[17] This book has demonstrated how this rejection of the human subject in thought was the basis of Marx's understanding of work and labour under capitalism as social and historical phenomena. Therefore, the radicalism of any political sociology today cannot be located in a vulgar opposition to the 'alienating' or 'commodifying' nature of work under capitalism. The truly radical route is the rejection of a set of theoretical postulates to which political sociology has been wedded for too long: postulates that emerge from an ideological system grounded in the material reality of the very social formation these sociologies seek to critique and change. Marx and Althusser are the guides in this endeavour. But it will be for the Marxist in sociology to undertake this most important task, if sociology is to have any value at all in the achievement of a communist future.

16   Boltanski and Chiapello 2017, p.533.
17   Althusser 1996, p.228.

References

Alberti, Gabriella, Ioulia Bessa, Kate Hardy, Vera Trappman, and Charles Umney. 2018. 'In, against and beyond Precarity: Work in Insecure Times.' *Work, Employment and Society* 32 (3):447–57. https://doi.org/10.1177%2F0950017018762088.

Althusser, Louis. 1976. *Essays in Self-Criticism*. London, United Kingdom: New Left Books.

Althusser, Louis. 1979. 'The Crisis of Marxism.' In *Power and Opposition in Post-Revolutionary Societies*, by Rossana Rossanda, 225–37. London, United Kingdom: Ink Links.

Althusser, Louis. 1993. *The Future Lasts Forever: A Memoir*. New York, NY: The New Press.

Althusser, Louis. 1996. *For Marx*. London, United Kingdom: Verso.

Althusser, Louis. 2000. *Machiavelli and Us*. London, United Kingdom: Verso.

Althusser, Louis. 2003. *The Humanist Controversy and Other Writings*. London, United Kingdom: Verso.

Althusser, Louis. 2007. *Politics and History: Montesquieu, Rousseau, Marx*. London, United Kingdom: Verso.

Althusser, Louis. 2008. *On Ideology*. London, United Kingdom: Verso.

Althusser, Louis. 2014a. *On the Reproduction of Capitalism: Ideology and Ideological State Apparatuses*. London, United Kingdom: Verso.

Althusser, Louis. 2014b. 'The International of Decent Feelings.' In *The Spectre of Hegel: Early Writings.*, by Louis Althusser, 1–15. London, United Kingdom: Verso.

Althusser, Louis. 2015. 'The Object of Capital.' In *Reading Capital*, edited by Louis Althusser, Étienne Balibar, Jacques Ranciere, and Pierre Macherey, 217–355. London, United Kingdom: Verso.

Althusser, Louis. 2016. *Psychoanalysis and the Human Sciences*. New York, NY: Columbia University Press.

Althusser, Louis. 2017. *How to Be a Marxist in Philosophy*. London, United Kingdom: Bloomsbury.

Althusser, Louis. 2020a. *History and Imperialism*. Cambridge, United Kingdom: Polity.

Althusser, Louis. 2020b. *What Is to Be Done?* Cambridge, United Kingdom: Polity.

Anderson, Bridget. 2002. 'Just Another Job? The Commodification of Domestic Labor.' In *Global Woman: Nannies, Maids and Sex Workers in the New Economy.*, by Barbara Ehrenreich and Arlie R. Hochschild, 104–14. London, United Kingdom: Granta.

Badiou, Alain. 2018. 'The Neolithic, Capitalism and Communism.' *Verso Blog* (blog). 2018. https://www.versobooks.com/blogs/3948-the-neolithic-capitalism-and-communism.

Balibar, Étienne. 1994. *Masses, Classes, Ideas: Studies on Politics and Philosophy before and after Marx*. New York, USA.: Routledge.

Balibar, Étienne. 2008. *Spinoza and Politics*. London, United Kingdom: Verso.
Balibar, Étienne. 2017. *The Philosophy of Marx*. London, United Kingdom: Verso.
Balibar, Étienne. 2020. *Spinoza, the Transindividual*. Edinburgh, United Kingdom: Edinburgh University Press.
Banyard, Kat. 2016. *Pimp State: Sex, Money and the Future of Equality*. London, United Kingdom: Faber and Faber.
Beck, Ulrich. 2000. *The Brave New World of Work*. Cambridge, United Kingdom: Polity.
Benanav, Aaron. 2020. *Automation and the Future of Work*. London, United Kingdom: Verso.
Bennett, Jane. 2004. 'The Force of Things: Steps toward an Ecology of Matter.' *Political Theory* 32 (3):347–72. https://doi.org/10.1177/0090591703260853.
Bhattacharya, Tithi. 2017. 'Introduction: Mapping Social Reproduction Theory.' In *Social Reproduction Theory: Remapping Class, Recentering Oppression.*, by Tithi Bhattacharya, 1–20. London, United Kingdom: Pluto.
Boltanski, Luc, and Eve Chiapello. 2017. *The New Spirit of Capitalism*. London, United Kingdom: Verso.
Bonneuil, Christophe, and Jean-Baptise Fressoz. 2016. *The Shock of the Anthropocene: The Earth, History and Us*. London, United Kingdom: Verso.
Boris, Eileen, and Rhacel Parreñas S. 2010. *Intimate Labors: Cultures, Technologies, and the Politics of Care*. Stanford, CA: Stanford University Press.
Braverman, Harry. 1974. *Labor and Monopoly Capital: The Degradation of Work in the Twentieth Century*. New York, NY: Monthly Review Press.
Burawoy, Michael. 1985. *The Politics of Production: Factory Regimes under Capitalism and Socialism*. London, United Kingdom: Verso.
Caffentzis, George. 2013. 'A Critique of "Cognitive Capitalism".' In *In Letters of Blood and Fire: Work, Machines and the Crisis of Capitalism.*, by George Caffentzis, 95–123. Oakland, CA: PM Press.
Cederström, Carl, and Peter Fleming. 2012. *Dead Man Working*. Harts, United Kingdom: Zero Books.
Chakrabarty, Dipesh. 2009. 'The Climate of History: Four Theses.' *Critical Enquiry* 35 (2):197–222. https://doi.org/10.1086/596640.
Chakrabarty, Dipesh. 2015. 'The Anthropocene and the Convergence of Histories.' In *The Anthropocene and the Global Environmental Crisis.*, by Clive Hamilton, Christophe Bonneuil, and Francois Gemenne, 44–56. Oxon, United Kingdom: Routledge.
Chapin, F. Stuart, Stephen R. Carpenter, Gary Kofinas P., Carl Folke, Nick Abel, William Clark C., Per Olsson, et al. 2010. 'Ecosystem Stewardship: Sustainability Strategies for a Rapidly Changing Planet.' *Trends in Ecology & Evolution* 25:241–49.
Cole, Matthew. 2017. 'Automation.' Autonomy. https://autonomy.work/wp-content/uploads/2018/08/Automation-V6.pdf.

Cooper, Melinda, and Catherine Waldby. 2014. *Clinical Labor: Tissue Donors and Research Subjects in the Global Bioeconomy*. Durham, NC: Duke University Press.

Crist, Eileen. 2016. 'On the Poverty of Our Nomenclature.' In *Anthropocene or Capitalocene? Nature, History, and the Crisis of Capitalism.*, by Jason Moore W., 14–33. Oakland, CA: PM Press.

Crutzen, Paul J., and Eugene F. Stoermer. 2000. 'The "Anthropocene."' *Global Change Newsletter* 41:17–18.

Cruz, Katie, Kate Hardy, and Teela Sanders. 2017. 'False Self-Employment, Autonomy and Regulating Decent Work: Improving Working Conditions in the UK Stripping Industry.' *British Journal of Industrial Relations* 55 (2):274–94. https://doi.org/10.1111/bjir.12201.

Dalla Costa, Mariarosa, and Selma James. 1975. *The Power of Women and the Subversion of the Community*. Bristol, United Kingdom: Falling Wall Press.

D'Eramo, Marco. 2020. 'The Philosopher's Epidemic.' *New Left Review* 122:23–28.

Dickenson, Donna. 2007. *Property in the Body: Feminist Perspectives*. Cambridge, United Kingdom: Cambridge University Press.

Dines, Gail. 2010. *Pornland: How Porn Has Hijacked Our Sexuality*. Boston, MA: Beacon.

Eder, Klaus. 1996. *The Social Construction of Nature*. London, United Kingdom: SAGE.

Elliott, Gregory. 2009. *Althusser: The Detour of Theory*. Chicago, IL.: Haymarket.

Farruggia, Francesca, Phil Jones, and Julian Siravo. 2020. 'The New Normal: A Blueprint for Remote Working.' Autonomy. https://autonomy.work/wp-content/uploads/2020/10/2020_OCT26_RWB.pdf.

Federici, Silvia. 2004. *Caliban and the Witch: Women, the Body and Primitive Accumulation*. Brooklyn, NY: Autonomedia.

Federici, Silvia. 2012a. 'Wages against Housework.' In *Revolution at Point Zero: Housework, Reproduction, and Feminist Struggle.*, by Silvia Federici, 15–22. Oakland, CA: PM Press.

Federici, Silvia. 2012b. 'Why Sexuality Is Work.' In *Revolution at Point Zero: Housework, Reproduction, and Feminist Struggle.*, by Silvia Federici, 23–27. Oakland, CA: PM Press.

Ferguson, Susan. 2020. *Women and Work: Feminism, Labour and Social Reproduction*. London, United Kingdom: Pluto.

Firestone, Shulamith. 1979. *The Dialectic of Sex: The Case for Feminist Revolution*. London, United Kingdom: The Women's Press.

Fleming, Peter. 2017. *The Death of Homo Economicus: Work, Debt and the Myth of Endless Accumulation*. London, United Kingdom: Pluto.

Foucault, Michel. 1970. *The Order of Things: An Archaeology of the Human Sciences*. London, United Kingdom: Tavistock Publications.

Frayne, David. 2015. *The Refusal of Work: The Theory and Practice of Resistance to Work*. London, United Kingdom: Zed.

Gorz, André. 1968. *Strategy for Labour: A Radical Proposal*. Boston, MA: Beacon.

Gorz, André. 1983. *Farewell to the Working Class: An Essay on Post-Industrial Socialism*. London, United Kingdom: Pluto.

Gorz, André. 2012. *Capitalism, Socialism, Ecology*. London, United Kingdom: Verso.

Graeber, David. 2013. 'On the Phenomenon of Bullshit Jobs.' *Strike! Magazine* (blog). 2013. http://strikemag.org.

Hamilton, Clive, Christophe Bonneuil, and Francois Gemenne. 2015. 'Thinking the Anthropocene'. In *The Anthropocene and the Global Environmental Crisis: Rethinking Modernity in a New Epoch.*, by Clive Hamilton, Christophe Bonneuil, and Francois Gemenne, 1–13. Oxon, United Kingdom: Routledge.

Hamza, Agon. 2016. 'Christianity as a Condition.' In *Althuser and Theology: Religion, Politics and Philosophy.*, edited by Agon Hamza, 47–63. Illinois, USA: Haymarket.

Haraway, Donna. 2015. 'Anthropocene, Capitalocene, Plantationocene, Chthulucene: Making Kin.' *Environmental Humanities* 6 (1):159–65. https://doi.org/10.1215/22011919-3615934.

Haraway, Donna. 2016. *Staying with the Trouble: Making Kin in the Chthulucene*. Durham, NC: Duke University Press.

Hardt, Michael, and Antonio Negri. 2001. *Empire*. Cambridge, MA: Harvard University Press.

Hobsbawm, Eric, J. 2011. *How to Change the World: Tales of Marx and Marxism*. London, United Kingdom: Abacus.

Hochschild, Arlie R. 1983. *The Managed Heart: Commercialization of Human Feeling*. Los Angeles, CA: University of California Press.

International Labour Organization. 2021a. 'Rural and Urban Labour Markets: Different Challenges for Promoting Decent Work.' International Labour Organization. https://ilo.org/wcmsp5/groups/public/---dgreports/---stat/documents/publication/wcms_757960.pdf.

International Labour Organization. 2021b. 'World Employment and Social Outlook: Trends 2021.' International Labour Organization. https://www.ilo.org/wcmsp5/groups/public/---dgreports/---dcomm/---publ/documents/publication/wcms_795453.pdf.

Latour, Bruno. 1993. *We Have Never Been Modern*. Cambridge, MA: Harvard University Press.

Latour, Bruno. 2014. 'Agency in the Time of the Anthropocene.' *New Literary History* 45 (1):1–18. https://doi.org/10.1353/nlh.2014.0003.

Latour, Bruno. 2015. 'Telling Friends from Foes in the Time of the Anthropocene.' In *The Anthropocene and the Global Environment Crisis: Rethinking Modernity in a New Epoch.*, by Clive Hamilton, Christophe Bonneuil, and Francois Gemenne, 145–55. London, United Kingdom: Routledge.

REFERENCES

Latour, Bruno. 2017. *Facing Gaia: Eight Lectures on the New Climatic Regime.* Cambridge, United Kingdom: Polity.

LeCain, Timothy, J. 2016. 'Heralding a New Humanism: The Radical Implications of Chakrabarty's "Four Theses".' In *Whose Anthropocene? Revisiting Dipesh Chakrabarty's 'Four Theses'.*, by Robert Emmett and Thomas Lekan, 15–21.

Lee, Robyn, and Rhacel Parreñas S. 2016. 'Intimate Labour and Social Justice: Engaging with the Work of Rhacel Salazar Parreñas'. *Studies in Social Justice* 10 (2):284–88. https://doi.org/10.26522/ssj.v10i2.1427.

Lenin, Vladimir I. 1973. *What Is to Be Done?* Peking, China.: Foreign Languages Press.

Lewis, William, S. 2022. *Concrete Critical Theory: Althusser's Marxism.* Leiden, The Netherlands: Brill.

Lordon, Frédéric. 2014. *Willing Slaves of Capital: Spinoza and Marx on Desire.* London, United Kingdom: Verso.

Lordon, Frédéric. 2022. *Imperium: Structures and Affects of Political Bodies.* London, United Kingdom: Verso.

Macciocchi, Maria. 1973. *Letters from inside the Italian Communist Party to Louis Althusser.* London, United Kingdom: New Left Books.

Macherey, Pierre. 2011. *Hegel or Spinoza.* Minnesota, USA.: University of Minnesota Press.

Malm, Andreas. 2016. *Fossil Capital: The Rise of Steam Power and the Roots of Global Warming.* London, United Kingdom: Verso.

Marx, Karl. 1981. *Economic and Philosophic Manuscripts 1844.* London, United Kingdom: Lawrence and Wishart.

Marx, Karl. 1986. 'Economic Manuscripts of 1857–58'. In *Marx and Engels Collected Works,* Vol. 28. London, United Kingdom: Lawrence and Wishart.

Marx, Karl. 1989a. 'Critique of the Gotha Programme'. In *Marx and Engels Collected Works*, 24:75–99. London, United Kingdom: Lawrence and Wishart.

Marx, Karl. 1989b. 'Marginal Notes on Adolph Wagner's Lehrbuch Der Politischen Oekonomie.' In *Marx and Engels Collected Works*, 24:531–62. London, United Kingdom: Lawrence and Wishart.

Marx, Karl. 1991. *Capital: Volume 3.* London, United Kingdom: Penguin.

Marx, Karl. 2013. *Capital: Volume 1.* Hertfordshire, United Kingdom: Wordsworth Editions.

Marx, Karl, and Friedrich Engels. 1976. 'The German Ideology: Critique of Modern German Philosophy According to Its Representatives Feuerbach, B. Bauer and Stirner, and of German Socialism According to Its Various Prophets.' In *Collected Works of Marx and Engels*, 5:21–451. London, United Kingdom: Lawrence and Wishart.

Marx, Karl, and Friedrich Engels. 2002. *The Communist Manifesto.* London, United Kingdom: Penguin.

Mason, Paul. 2015. *Postcapitalism: A Guide to Our Future*. London, United Kingdom: Allen Lane.

Mies, Maria. 2014. *Patriarchy and Accumulation on a World Scale: Women in the International Division of Labour*. London, United Kingdom: Zed.

Moisander, Johanna, Claudia Groß, and Kirsi Eräranta. 2018. 'Mechanisms of Biopower and Neoliberal Governmentality in Precarious Work: Mobilizing the Dependent Self-Employed as Independent Business Owners.' *Human Relations* 71 (3):375–98. https://doi.org/10.1177/0018726717718918.

Montag, Warren. 1999. *Bodies, Masses, Power: Spinoza and His Contemporaries*. London, United Kingdom: Verso.

Moore, Jason, W. 2015. *Capitalism in the Web of Life: Ecology and the Accumulation of Capital*. London, United Kingdom: Verso.

Moore, Jason, W. 2016. 'The Rise of Cheap Nature.' In *Anthropocene or Capitalocene? Nature, History, and the Crisis of Capitalism*., by Jason Moore W., 78–115. Oakland, CA: PM Press.

Mueller, Gavin. 2021. *Breaking Things at Work: The Luddites Were Right about Why You Hate Your Job*. London, United Kingdom: Verso.

Murray, Nic. 2019. 'No Crying in the Breakroom.' In *The Work Cure: Critical Essays on Work and Wellness*., by David Frayne, 45–60. Monmouth, United Kingdom: PCCS Books.

Neilson, Brett, and Ned Rossiter. 2008. 'Precarity as a Political Concept, or, Fordism as Exception.' *Theory, Culture and Society* 25 (7–8):51–72.https://doi.org/10.1177%2F0263276408097796.

Nesbitt, Nick. 2017. 'Rereading Reading Capital.' In *The Concept in Crisis: Reading Capital Today*., by Nick Nesbitt, 1–18. Durham, NC: Duke University Press.

Palsson, Gisli, Bronislaw Szerszynski, Sverker Sörlin, John Marks, Bernard Avril, Carole Crumley, Heide Hackmann, et al. 2012. 'Reconceptualizing the "Anthropos" in the Anthropocene: Integrating Social Sciences and Humanities in Global Environmental Change Research.' *Environmental Science & Policy* 28:3–13. https://doi.org/10.1016/j.envsci.2012.11.004.

Pêcheux, Michel. 1982. *Language, Semantics and Ideology: Stating the Obvious*. London, United Kingdom: Macmillan.

Pfannebecker, Mareile, and James Smith A. 2020. *Work, Want, Work: Labour and Desire at the End of Capitalism*. London, United Kingdom: Zed.

Pitts, Frederick, H. 2017. 'Beyond the Fragment: Postoperaismo, Postcapitalism and Marx's "Notes on Machines", 45 Years On.' *Economy and Society* 46 (3–4):324–45. https://doi.org/10.1080/03085147.2017.1397360.

Pitts, Frederick, H., and Ana Dinerstein C. 2017. 'Postcapitalism, Basic Income and the End of Work: A Critique and Alternative.' *Bath Papers in International Development and Wellbeing* 55:1–28.

Power, Nina. 2017. 'Reading Social Reproduction into Reading Capital.' In *The Concept in Crisis: Reading Capital Today.*, edited by Nick Nesbitt, 219–28. Durham, NC: Duke University Press.

Read, Jason. 2016. *The Politics of Transindividuality*. Illinois, USA: Haymarket.

Romé, Natalia. 2021. *For Theory: Althusser and the Politics of Time*. London, United Kingdom: Rowman and Littlefield.

Satz, Debra. 2010. *Why Some Things Should Not Be for Sale: The Moral Limits of Markets*. Oxford, United Kingdom: Oxford University Press.

Schroeder, Amber, N., Traci Bricka M., and Julia Whitaker H. 2021. 'Work Design in a Digitized Gig Economy.' *Human Resource Management Review* 31 (1):1–16. https://doi.org/10.1016/j.hrmr.2019.100692.

Schwägerl, Christian. 2013. 'Neurogeology: The Anthropocene's Inspirational Power.' In *Anthropocene: Envisioning the Future of the Age of Humans.*, by Helmuth Trischler, 29–39. http://doi.org/10.5282/rcc/5603.

Sotiris, Panagiotis. 2021. *A Philosophy for Communism: Rethinking Althusser*. Chicago, IL.: Haymarket.

Spencer, David. 2017. 'Work in and beyond the Second Machine Age: The Politics of Production and Digital Technologies.' *Work, Employment and Society* 31 (1):142–52. https://doi.org/10.1177/0950017016645716.

Srnicek, Nick. 2016. *Platform Capitalism*. London, United Kingdom: Polity.

Srnicek, Nick, and Alex Williams. 2013. '#ACCELERATE MANIFESTO for an Accelerationist Politics.' *Critical Legal Thinking* (blog). 2013. http://www.criticallegalthinking.com.

Srnicek, Nick, and Alex Williams. 2015. *Inventing the Future: Postcapitalism and a World without Work*. London, United Kingdom: Verso.

Standing, Guy. 2016. *The Precariat: The New Dangerous Class*. London, United Kingdom: Bloomsbury.

Steffen, Will, Åsa Persson, Lisa Deutsch, Jan Zalasiwicz, Mark Williams, Katherine Richardson, Carole Crumley, et al. 2011. 'The Anthropocene: From Global Change to Planetary Stewardship.' *Ambio* 40 (7):739–61. https://doi.org/10.1007/s13280-011-0185-x.

Stronge, Will, and Kyle Lewis. 2021. *Overtime: Why We Need a Shorter Working Week*. London, United Kingdom: Verso.

Thompson, Edward, P. 1991. *The Making of the English Working Class*. London, United Kingdom: Penguin.

Tronti, Mario. 2020. 'On Marxism and Sociology'. In *The Weapon of Organization: Mario Tronti's Political Revolution in Marxism.*, 45–50. Brooklyn, NY: Common Notions.

Umney, Charles. 2018. *Class Matters: Inequality and Exploitation in 21st Century Britain*. London, United Kingdom: Pluto.

Vogel, Lise. 2013. *Marxism and the Oppression of Women: Toward a Unitary Theory*. Chicago, IL.: Haymarket.

Wark, Mackenzie. 2015. *Molecular Red: Theory for the Anthropocene*. London, United Kingdom: Verso.

Weeks, Kathi. 2011. *The Problem with Work: Feminism, Marxism, Antiwork Politics, and Postwork Imaginaries*. Durham, NC: Duke University Press.

Weeks, Kathi. 2016. 'Utopian Therapy: Work, Nonwork, and the Political Imagination.' In *An American Utopia: Dual Power and the Universal Army.*, by Slavoj Žižek, 243–65. London, United Kingdom: Verso.

Weeks, Kathi. 2018. *Constituting Feminist Subjects*. London, United Kingdom: Verso.

Woodcock, Jamie. 2019. 'Understanding Affective Labour: The Demand for Workers to Really Care.' In *The Work Cure: Critical Essays on Work and Wellness.*, by David Frayne, 61–74. Monmouth, United Kingdom: PCCS Books.

Woods, Imogen. 2022. 'Lessons from Italian Feminism: Wages for Housework and Maria Macciocchi.' *Prometheus*. https://prometheusjournal.org/2022/02/25/lessons-from-italian-feminism-wages-for-housework-and-maria-macciocchi/.

Wright, Erik, O. 1981. 'The Value Controversy and Social Research.' In *The Value Controversy.*, by Ian Steedman, Paul Sweezy, Simon Mohun, Anwar Shaikh, Sue Himmelweit, Geoff Hodgson, Erik Wright O., et al. London, United Kingdom: Verso.

Žižek, Slavoj. 2008. *The Sublime Object of Ideology*. London, United Kingdom: Verso.

Žižek, Slavoj. 2022. 'Hegel: The Spirit of Distrust.' In *Reading Hegel.*, edited by Slavoj Žižek, Frank Ruda, and Agon Hamza. Cambridge, United Kingdom: Polity.

Index

anthropocene 8, 159, 160–164, 166–184, 186–187, 192–193
anthropology 21, 23–25, 27, 39, 58, 100, 116, 125, 131, 151
alienation 2–4, 7–8, 11, 14–15, 23–24, 31, 40–42, 47–48, 50, 52, 56–57, 59–65, 75–78, 80, 84, 86, 89–90, 93–95, 100, 116–123, 126–127, 128, 135–140, 142–147, 157–159, 170–172, 175–183, 187, 192, 194
  See also Karl Marx; labour
Althusser, Louis
  Althusserianism 1, 5, 23, 26, 29–32, 35, 109, 129, 131, 157, 190, 197
  and Baruch Spinoza 23, 29, 32, 197
  crisis of Marxism 2–3, 5, 130
  critique of Stalinism 3, 17–18
  critique of 'social labour' 37, 76–78, 98
  epistemological break 13, 16
  Humanist Controversy, The 37, 76, 98, 183
  fetishism of technology 99, 126
  history 2, 11–13, 15–16, 35–37, 77, 156, 163–164, 180
  ideology 1, 13–14, 16, 24–25, 30, 32, 35, 39, 99–100
  'Ideology of Work' 1
  influence in the PCF 17
  interpellation 28–30, 39
  and Jacques Lacan 9
  labour 44–45, 74, 163
  and Maria Machiocchi 21, 130
  and Niccolò Machiavelli 21–22
  On the Reproduction of Capitalism 1, 38, 99, 129, 132
  overdetermination 132, 155
  philosophy 131, 195
  political economy 12, 14, 45, 65, 147
  reproduction 129, 132, 188
  Reading Capital 16, 129
  science 194–196
  social relations 183, 196–198
  sociology 195–196
  strikes in Italy 18–20
  symptomatic reading 147
  theoretical anti-humanism 1, 8, 9–23, 26, 34–39, 66, 77, 126, 132–133, 163–164, 194
  work 37–39, 111
  young and mature Marx 13–15
  See also Étienne Balibar; ideology; Marxism

Balibar, Étienne 5, 10, 33
  and Baruch Spinoza 23, 25, 27
  class struggle 65
  commodity fetishism 24–25
  and Karl Marx 23–24, 45, 58–60, 63, 65
  and Louis Althusser 23
  politics of labour 58–59
  reproduction 129
  social relations 58–60
  theoretical anti-humanism 23–24, 27, 58, 63
Bhattacharya, Tithi 129, 156–158
Braverman, Harry 6, 87–90, 94, 97

class struggle 1–4, 8, 13–19, 32, 38–39, 48, 54–60, 62, 64–65, 67, 75–76, 86–87, 97–98, 100, 111, 120, 123, 126, 135–136, 142, 145–146, 151, 155, 160, 181, 184, 192
  See also Étienne Balibar; Karl Marx

Deleuze, Gilles 23
Derrida, Jacques 23

Engels, Friedrich 44, 59, 130–131, 148, 150
  Condition of the Working Class in England 53
  See also Karl Marx

Federici, Silvia 151–153, 155, 158
Ferguson, Susan 7, 129, 133–134, 147
Feuerbach, Ludwig 14–15, 23–24, 77
Foucault, Michel 23, 44
Freud, Sigmund 29, 35, 43
  See also Karl Marx; Jacques Lacan

Gorz, André 4, 6, 76, 93–98, 117–119, 121–122
  A Strategy for Labour 4

Hamza, Agon 35–37
Hegel, G.W.F. 10, 23, 26–27, 32–33, 35–37, 43, 94, 164
Hobsbawm, Eric 53n

ideology
　Althusser's theory of　24–25, 29–33, 35, 157
　and commodity fetishism　33–34
　humanist　1–3, 5–8, 13–17, 31, 66–67, 73, 75–76, 93, 98, 100, 130–131, 148, 151–152, 155
　and idealism　16
　Marx's theory of　44–45, 65–68, 72–73, 153, 157
　and political economy　16, 112
　and science　193–194
　of work　38–39
　See also Louis Althusser; Karl Marx

Labour
　abstract　37, 51, 81, 190
　alienated　14, 46–48, 135–137, 140, 142–147, 158–159, 186–187
　concept of　5–6, 8, 37, 44–46, 49, 57–68, 70, 73, 78, 160, 166, 183–184, 188, 190, 192–193, 194
　concrete　57
　division between intellectual and manual　24, 196
　division of　6, 38, 44, 61–62, 101, 129, 145, 148, 150, 152, 154–155, 158
　emotional　7, 91, 119, 136–137, 139
　human　14, 46, 67, 75, 77–78, 81, 85, 87–89, 93–98, 106, 108, 111, 117, 119–120, 150, 160, 162–163, 166–170, 180, 187, 189
　immaterial　76, 90–93, 97
　intimate　136–137, 158
　necessary　52–53, 55, 57, 81, 149
　power　7, 20, 24, 37, 50–54, 57, 67–68, 76, 81, 99, 108, 111, 120, 135, 148–150, 156, 184, 189–191, 194
　politics of　45, 58–59
　process　37, 48–53, 56–57, 59, 70–72, 86–90, 97, 107–108, 129, 148, 150, 183, 185, 188
　reproductive　7, 127, 128–129, 134–137, 139–140, 142–143, 145–147, 154, 156–159, 191
　social　6, 37, 75–93, 95–98
　surplus　52–57, 69
　time　49–53, 57, 149
　waged　7–8, 70–71, 96–97, 99, 101, 104, 106, 119–120, 122–123, 136, 144–145, 150, 153, 185
　See also Louis Althusser; Étienne Balibar; Karl Marx; work
Lacan, Jacques　9–10, 23, 29, 31–33, 35, 37, 43
　See also Sigmund Freud
Latour, Bruno　162, 173–176
Lenin, Vladimir I.　17
Lordon, Frédéric　5, 10, 39–42, 196–197

Macherey, Pierre　26–27
Machiavelli, Niccolò　21–22
　The Prince　21
Malm, Andreas　8, 160, 182–188, 190–191, 193
Marx, Karl
　alienation　14, 23, 42, 46–48, 52, 61–62, 80–81, 137
　and Baruch Spinoza　23, 41–42
　Capital (Vol. I.)　3, 23, 45, 48, 53, 70, 81, 148, 153
　Capital (Vol. II.)　69
　Capital (Vol. III.)　6, 44–45, 68–69
　class consciousness　23
　communism　63–64, 68, 77, 122, 177
　Communist Manifesto, The　44–45, 64
　critique of political economy　5, 9, 13–16, 25, 37, 43, 44–48, 65, 68–69, 71–72, 74, 79
　Critique of the Gotha Programme　44–45, 66, 68
　Economic and Philosophic Manuscripts 1844　14, 45–46, 49, 52, 54, 57, 59, 61, 63
　fetishism　24–25, 33–35, 79
　German Ideology, The　6, 44, 60–63, 65, 78
　Grundrisse　6, 75, 78–79, 81, 98
　history　13, 15, 18, 55–56, 63, 78
　Holy Family, The　14
　human nature　14–15, 46, 64
　mode of production　55
　politics　58–60, 62–63, 65, 68, 73
　private property　47
　and Sigmund Freud　35
　species-being　46–47
　social relations　30, 34, 42–43, 53, 57–65, 67, 73, 78–79, 197
　surplus-value　49, 53
　subject　24–26

INDEX

theoretical anti-humanism   5, 9, 25, 37, 43, 51, 54–55, 57–58, 63–64, 66–67, 71–73, 78, 148, 150, 158, 198
the family   148–150
the state   62, 67
work   48, 53, 56, 68, 70, 73–74, 122, 198
working-day   52, 54–56
young and mature   13–15, 18, 23, 45–46, 59–60, 75, 77–78, 81, 117, 177
See also Louis Althusser; class struggle; Friedrich Engels; ideology; labour; Marxism

Marxism
crisis of   2–5, 130
and feminism   7, 128, 130, 157
and humanism   1, 16, 22–23, 43, 130
and Louis Althusser   1–2, 5, 11, 13, 16, 194–195, 197
and politics   82
and sociology   1, 8, 194, 196–198
and work   5–7, 74
See also Louis Althusser; Friedrich Engels; Karl Marx; sociology

Montag, Warren   26
Moore, Jason, W.   8, 160, 182–183, 187–193

Negri, Antonio
and Michael Hardt   6, 76, 90–93, 97
Nesbitt, Nick   3

Pêcheux, Michel   29–32, 35
proletariat   9, 14, 17, 36, 56, 62–63, 65, 67, 89–93, 95–96, 115, 118, 156

Read, Jason   27–29
revolution   17, 24, 29, 31, 36, 58–59, 65, 77, 84, 90, 92–93, 95, 97, 152, 163
Ricardo, David   16, 182
Romé, Natalia   4, 7, 31–32, 35, 100, 129, 131–134, 147, 155–158, 188, 192

Smith, Adam   16
social reproduction theory   7, 128–130, 132, 147–149, 151, 153, 155–159

sociology
and anti-humanism   19, 39–40, 42–43, 194
feminist   7, 128–129, 134–136, 157–159
historical   73, 83, 85–86
of immaterial labour   73, 90–91
Marxism in   1, 6, 8, 195–198
political   2, 8, 74, 76, 97–98, 100, 109, 195, 198
of post-work   6–7, 103, 116, 120
of work, (*See* work)
Sotiris, Panagiotis   3
Spinoza, Baruch   21, 23, 25–29, 32, 35–36, 39–43, 197
See also Louis Althusser; Étienne Balibar; Karl Marx
Srnicek, Nick
and Alex Williams   10, 105–107, 110–112, 121

Thompson, Edward P.   6, 76, 83–86, 97

Vogel, Lise   7, 81, 129–131, 134, 136, 147–150, 158

Weeks, Kathi   4–5, 7, 90, 109–113, 129, 132–134, 147, 151, 158
work
feminist critique of   7, 112–113, 127, 128, 133–135, 154–159
and anti-humanism   37–42
post-   6–7, 76, 95–98, 99–100, 103, 107–126
refusal of   90, 92–93, 97, 133, 151
sociology of   1–2, 6–8, 40, 42–43, 76, 83, 86, 90, 93, 97–98, 99–100, 102, 109, 115–116, 193, 194–195, 197–198
See also Louis Althusser; labour; Karl Marx; sociology

Žižek, Slavoj   5, 10, 32–35

www.ingramcontent.com/pod-product-compliance
Lightning Source LLC
Chambersburg PA
CBHW070621030426
42337CB00020B/3879